EVERYTHING YOU NEED TO KNOW

STREETBIKES

BILL STERMER

MOTORBOOKS

First published in 2006 by Motorbooks, an imprint of MBI Publishing Company, Galtier Plaza, Suite 200, 380 Jackson Street, St. Paul, MN 55101-3885 USA

MBI Publishing Company titles are also available at discounts in bulk quantity for industrial or sales-promotional use. For details write to Special Sales Manager at MBI Publishing Company, Galtier Plaza, Suite 200, 380 Jackson Street, St. Paul, MN 55101-3885 USA

ISBN-13: 978-0-7603-2362-5
ISBN-10: 0-7603-2362-3

Editor: James Michels
Designer: Brenda C. Canales

Printed in China

On the cover: A rider bends into a turn on a Suzuki SV650. *American Suzuki Motor Corp.*

On the frontispiece: As this shot shows, it doesn't matter what you ride when you head down to Knoxville, Tennessee, and hook into a nice curve at the Honda Hoot. *American Honda Motor Co.*

On the title pages: (1) Harley-Davidson's big dresser tourer, the Electra Glide Ultra Classic. *Harley-Davidson Motor Co.*

(2) KTM's 950 Supermoto, a street-going machine with the nimbleness of a dirt bike. *KTM*

(3) MV Agusta's F1 is a top-line sportbike with beautiful lines. *MV Agusta*

(4) Yamaha hit a home run with its Road Star, a big-inch V-twin cruiser. *Yamaha Motor Corp., USA*

On the back cover: (top right) Scenery from a saddle always looks better. *American Honda Motor Corp.*

(bottom left) BMW's linked brake system. *BMW of North America*

(bottom right) Two riders on Moto Guzzi Grisos going hard in a corner. *Moto Guzzi*

About the author: Bill Stermer started riding in the 1960s and became a moto-journalist when he joined *Cycle* magazine in 1978. Since then he has tested hundreds of motorcycles and has written more than two thousand articles. His first book, *Motorcycle Touring*, was published in 1982 as a how-to for the touring rider. *On the Perimeter*, published the following year, was the as-told-to autobiography of Hazel Kolb, "The Motorcycling Grandma," which he did for Harley-Davidson.

After three years as editor of the trade magazine *Motorcycle Industry*, Stermer's touring background led him to *Rider* magazine in 1990. That same year his third book, *Motorcycle Touring and Travel*, was published. A second edition appeared in 1998.

In 1994 Stermer again returned to freelance writing. Today, his work regularly appears in *Rider, American Rider, Cruising Rider, Powersports Business,* and *V-Twin* magazines. His fifth book, *BMW R100RS*, was published in 2002. This is his sixth book.

In addition to writing, Stermer is an accomplished photographer and public speaker. He has appeared many times at the Americade rally in New York and at local club events.

Stermer lives in Southern California with his wife, Margery, and their children, Paul and Julia.

CONTENTS

Preface 6

Chapter 1
CHOOSING YOUR STREET MOTORCYCLE 8
Types of Street Motorcycles 10

Chapter 2
ENGINE FACTORS 18
Displacement, Number of Cylinders,
   and Engine Configuration 18
Engine Displacement 19
Number of Cylinders 21
Engine Configuration 23

Chapter 3
CHASSIS STUFF 32
Frames 32
Types of Frames 32
Other Bits of Frame Info 33
Brakes 39
FInal Drive 40

Chapter 4
BRANDS OF STREET MOTORCYCLES 44
Established Brands 44
Alternative V-Twin Manufacturers 50
Custom Motorcycles 54

Chapter 5
FEATURES AND OPTIONS 56
Adjustable Ergonomics 56
Braking Options 58
Cruise Control 60
Hard Luggage 60
Sound Systems 62
Other Niceities 64

Chapter 6
MOTORCYCLE ACCESSORIES 66
Electrical Accessories 66
Seats, Pegs, and Bars 70
Touring Accessories 75
Wind Proctection 79
Fairings 81
Bike Protection 81
Wheels 83

Chapter 7
SIDECARS, TRAILERS, AND TRIKES 86
Sidecars 86
Trailers 86
Trailers for Hauling Motorcycles 91
Trikes 93

Chapter 8
APPAREL 94
Helmets 94
Types of Helmets 96
Other Helmet Conderations 98
Motorcycle Clothing 102
What Makes a Good Riding Jacket 104
Women's Apparel 107
The Lower Half 108
Full Riding Suits 109
Rain Suits 110
Electric Clothing 112
Boots 114
Gloves 114

Chapter 9
PERFORMANCE CONSIDERATIONS 116
Adding Power 116
Suspension Upgrades 118
Lowering a Motorcycle 122
Brakes 125

Chapter 10
MAINTENANCE 126
Oil and Lubricants 126
Tires 130
Batteries 135
Picking up a Fallen Bike 137
Pre-ride Inspection 137

Chapter 11
LET'S RIDE! 138
Where to Ride 138
Road Strategies 138
Mechanical 141
Passengers 142
Women Who Ride 143
Commuting 144
Motorcycle Events, Rides, and Rallies 147
Camping by Motorcycle 148
Organized Tours 149
The Tourer's Packing List 149
Track Days 151
Racing 152

Appendix: Motorcycle Terms 154
Index 158

WHY I WROTE THIS BOOK....AND, POSSIBLY, WHY YOU NEED THIS BOOK

I was just reminiscing with a friend, a new rider, about how I had been riding motorcycles for more than 40 years, 28 of them as a motorcycle journalist. He leaned back and said, "Man, I wish I could have 40 years of riding knowledge downloaded to my head."

That got me to thinking. I started riding in the 1960s, and started writing about motorcycles professionally at *Cycle* magazine in 1978, the year Honda introduced its CBX six-cylinder. Since then I've written more than 2,000 articles and five books about street motorcycles. My friend suggested, "Why don't you write a book that covers all those things people need to know about streetbikes, a compendium of facts and tips and insights about them?" Distilling more than 40 years of street riding experience sounded like a good idea at the time, and many months later, you're holding that book in your hands.

Here is another reason I wrote this book: The most recent figures from the Motorcycle Industry Council (MIC) show that motorcycling has increased tremendously in popularity in recent years. In 1992 U.S. motorcycle retail sales were 278,000. By 1999 they had nearly doubled to 546,000. By 2005 they were estimated to have doubled again, to more than 1.1 million! That figure includes a whole lot of new riders and returning riders, and they have all sorts of questions:

- How do I choose a motorcycle?
- What's the best type of helmet to wear?
- Should I buy a leather or textile jacket?
- If a bike is available with anti-lock brakes, should I get them?
- Should I run that expensive motorcycle oil in my bike, or can I run car oil?
- What should I know about tires?

And on and on and on . . .

With that many people asking those kinds of questions, it seemed like a natural fit. Those, and many more, are answered within these pages.

WHAT THIS BOOK IS NOT

The hard part of writing any book of this sort is knowing when to stop. Entire books have been written about many aspects of motorcycling, so the hard part was judging how much information to give about a certain subject . . . and then leave it at that. The book is intentionally broad rather than deep, a compendium of information. The idea is to give new riders and returning riders an overview of street riding, a base from which to learn about motorcycling, from which they can further pursue in depth the aspects that most interest them. How does one do that? By hanging out with other riders, by reading more books, and by reading magazines. As a person who has written for various motorcycle magazines for nearly 30 years, I highly recommend subscribing to several of them, and reading them thoroughly. There is a lot of information contained in them.

Keep in mind this is not a skills book. This is not a book on how to ride. There are many sources of information about riding. I strongly suggest every new and returning motorcycle rider take a Motorcycle Safety Foundation RiderCourse (a class in how to ride), or if you're an experienced rider take an Experienced RiderCourse. Details on both are in here.

Also, there are many books on basic riding skills (including those by David Hough and Pat Hahn, to name a couple) and performance riding (by Reg Pridmore, Nick Ienatsch, and Lee Parks). Any or several of these should be on your shelf, as well. Those gentlemen can tell you how to ride better on the street; I'll tell you about many other aspects of street riding.

KEEP IT FUN

The final thing to keep in mind—or rather, the first thing as you begin this book—is that motorcycling is fun. Lots of fun. The most fun you can have with your clothes on! Enjoy it. Don't get bogged down in the details, just do it. If it turns out you don't yet have the specific kind of jacket you

Author Bill Stermer

ultimately want, plan to get that jacket and, in the meantime, go riding with the jacket you have. If you want a better set of saddlebags, fine; price them out and save for them, but for now go riding with the saddlebags you have. If you want to take a one-week tour across four states, but don't really have that ultimate touring bike yet, fine; outfit the bike you have for touring and go take that tour. Next year you can do it on your dream bike.

Don't put things off. Do it now. Enjoy it now. It just gets better. Nobody ever had fun riding by sitting at home wishing they could have fun riding . . . when they already have the equipment at hand. Don't get bogged down in the details. Just do it!

All the best,
Bill Stermer

CHOOSING YOUR STREET MOTORCYCLE

A cruiser is a bike that's high in style, low in seat height, and usually designed for laid-back riding. Most, like the Harley-Davidson Dyna and Softail Springer (both pictured), are powered by V-twin engines. *Harley-Davidson Motor Co.*

WHAT YOU WILL LEARN

- **The factors that go into choosing a motorcycle**

- **The six types of street motorcycles and their variations**

- **Pros and cons of each type of street bike**

The best way to choose your bike is to consider that a motorcycle is a tool for a job.

In my more than 25 years as a motorcycle journalist, the question I most frequently hear is "How do I choose the right motorcycle?" The best way to choose your bike is to consider that a motorcycle is a tool for a job; define the job you wish it to do, and that will point toward the type of motorcycle you will need to perform that job. Once you have specified the type of bike needed, you can shop among the models available in that category.

There are six general types of street motorcycle, with several subtypes among them. As an example of how the selection process goes, here are six typical rider responses to the question, "What job do you want your motorcycle to perform?"

Rider 1: "I'm not an aggressive rider; I just want to cruise around. I want a bike I can ride to work, and then maybe ride on Friday night when I take my girlfriend to dinner. We can go on weekend rides, and maybe do a few overnight trips. A lazy,

laid-back bike with good style and comfort are my priorities; I'm not into performance or handling."

Rider 2: "I want to be able to load a week's worth of luggage—or more—onto my bike and motor on down the highway with my wife for several thousand miles. My priorities are good wind protection, luggage capacity, and long-distance comfort for two. I'd like to be able to listen to the radio and CDs as we ride, and would also need good fuel capacity and range. Low priorities would be high-speed handling and performance."

Rider 3: "While I love to travel and need to carry luggage, I want something light and sporty enough to handle well in the curves. For weekend and longer rides, I want a comfortable bike with hard, locking saddlebags and the protection of a fairing (aerodynamic shell with windshield)—but not a big one—that will allow me to ride easily at speed. When I arrive at my destination, I want to be able to easily pop off those bags and go riding unencumbered."

Rider 4: "My joy is to go out on the twisty roads and really hook into the turns, ride aggressively. I want uncompromising power and top-notch suspension, state-of-the-art brakes, and speed capabilities up into the triple digits. Comfort and two-up riding are not an issue, as I want what is essentially a street-legal racer that I can take on back roads and to track days."

Rider 5: "I like performance, but I also want to keep it simple. I don't want all that plastic bodywork, crouching racer-type seating position, and aggressive styling that attracts cops and makes other riders want to race me. I just want a good, honest motorcycle that's reasonably comfortable and fast and competent, has good brakes and suspension, and that I can do anything with. I could put a pipe and upgraded shocks on it and go to track days, or throw on some soft luggage and a windshield and go touring. Or just ride it to work and on weekends the way it is

without a lot of excess weight or complication. I want reasonable power and comfort with lots of versatility."

Rider 6: "As an adventurous sort, I like to ride the back roads and, if I spot an intriguing dirt or gravel road heading up into the hills, I'd like to be able to take it. My bike has to be light, have only one or two cylinders, and offer good ground

How do you choose the best tool for a job? By defining the job. Once you understand if you need to turn a screw, tighten a bolt, or drive a nail, the tool becomes obvious. Likewise, a motorcycle is a tool for a job, and defining that job is the first step.

These motorcycles perform different jobs, yet they're able to travel together comfortably. The Honda VFR800 (left) is designed for sportier riding with comfort, and may be fitted with hard luggage. The Honda VTX cruiser (right) is made for a more laid-back riding style. The Honda ST1300 (rear) will pack two riders and their luggage in great comfort, while still offering some sporting fun. *American Honda Motor Co.*

The power cruiser is a derivative of the cruiser, but offers more power, increased cornering clearance, and better brakes, making it more fun to ride in a sporting manner. Shown is the Yamaha Road Star Midnight Warrior. *Yamaha Motor Corp., USA*

There are six general types of street motorcycles, with several subtypes among them.

clearance and adequate suspension for the rough stuff. If I want to go off to Alaska or Mexico, it should be able to accommodate a pair of soft saddlebags, or maybe even hard bags. It's got to be extremely versatile."

TYPES OF STREET MOTORCYCLES

If you know motorcycling, you've likely recognized that these riders have defined the six major types of street bikes. Here's a quick look at each type in detail, along with its subgroup.

Cruisers

Our Rider Number 1 defines the job he wants done as offering him satisfaction through styling, comfort, and relaxation, while he needs little in terms of performance or handling. He wants to smell the flowers along the way, and will likely be happiest with a cruiser, a highly styled motorcycle with the accent on comfort and an easy-going riding pace.

A cruiser is usually a long, low, stylish bike that is often (but not always) powered by a V-twin engine (see Engine Configurations, p. 23) that's tuned for low-rpm torque (twisting power) rather than for high-end horsepower. This makes it easier to ride and more controllable for most riders. Besides, most riding gets done at lower speeds and rpm.

Cruisers have been the dominant-selling type of motorcycle since the 1980s, and are often the choice of newcomers or re-entry riders because they offer high style

POWER CRUISERS

A subgroup of cruisers is the power cruiser, which offers greater power than the standard cruiser and often has better brakes and suspension to match. While a standard cruiser may produce 50 to 70 horsepower stock, a power cruiser may offer from 80 to more than 100. As a premium machine, a power cruiser will usually offer upgraded styling and fit and finish.

with an unintimidating power. They tend to have a lower seat height (26 to 29 inches), so shorter and inexperienced riders have an easier time reaching the ground from their saddles. The compromise here is that, because they're low, cruisers don't usually offer much cornering clearance. Start riding them at sportier speeds on a winding road, and their footpegs, footboards, stands, or exhaust systems may begin to scrape the pavement when leaned way over.

Because they're often sold to new or re-entry riders who aren't looking for performance, most cruisers tend to put out a rather low amount of horsepower relative to their displacement, and are equipped with very basic suspension systems that offer few adjustments. With their accent on style, cruiser manufacturers and the after-market offer a huge range of bolt-on custom parts, so riders can personalize their machines. These include such items as mirrors, seats, handlebars, forward foot controls and footboards, chromed engine covers, backrests, wheels, performance parts, and much more. If you wish to personalize your motorcycle so there's not another one like it, a cruiser definitely offers the most options.

SCOOTERS

Another form of powered two-wheeler is the motor scooter, which has been around for many years and was quite popular in the 1960s. Scooters are now enjoying a popularity resurgence because of high gasoline prices, their friendly appearance, and because they're so easy to ride.

With their smaller wheels and all-enclosing bodywork, scooters look clean and docile. Almost cute. Automatic clutches and constantly-variable transmissions (CVT) mean there's no need to learn to use a clutch or shift gears—simply twist the throttle and go. Some have linked brakes, so using either brake control applies both the front and rear brakes. With their enclosed bodywork, scooters tend to be cleaner and quieter than motorcycles, and many offer a storage area under the seat for carrying small items.

Scooters tend to range from 50cc to 650cc in engine size, and I would suggest at least a 250cc engine if you intend to use the freeway. They're small and maneuverable, but keep in mind that the smaller the wheels the more problematic it is if the wheel enters a pothole or hits a rock. Dirt bikes tend to have 21-inch front wheels so they can step over rocks and logs, and out of potholes. A smaller wheel may drop into a pothole that a larger wheel would bounce over, which could cause a serious accident.

Despite their friendly appearance, keep in mind that scooters can do many of the same things motorcycles can do. Depending upon engine size, they can reach highway speeds; some can do 80 miles per hour. Don't think that, because of their docile appearance, you can go without a helmet or other safety gear. I have it on good authority that falling off a scooter at 50 miles per hour is much like falling off a motorcycle at 50 miles per hour.

Note that some manufacturers, which are usually based in the Far East, have been selling scooters, ATVs and small motorcycles at very low prices through nontraditional outlets such as hardware and mega stores. While the initial price may be low, keep in mind that service after the sale, spare parts, tune-ups, oil, and accessories for such machines may not be available at all. That's why I suggest that—because you're purchasing a vehicle upon which your safety depends and which could potentially leave you stranded somewhere—you're really better off purchasing from a legitimate dealer who will be there with spare parts, service, and accessories.

For more information on scooters, see the Motorbooks Workshop title *Scooters: Everything You Need to Know* by Eric Dregni.

Because they're low, cruisers don't usually offer much cornering clearance.

Want to spend some luxury time on the road hauling lots of gear, while enjoying a top-line sound system and great wind protection? Then you'll want a bike like this Honda GL1800 Gold Wing. *American Honda Motor Co.*

It's lighter than a dresser and has fewer amenities, but the sport tourer offers better handling. Luggage is removable for unfettered riding once you reach your destination. This BMW R1200RT offers an adjustable windshield, anti-lock brakes, and heated handgrips. *BMW of North America*

Gobs of torque allow dresser tourers to carry the largest loads in motorcycling.

Dresser Tourers

Large-displacement bikes with fairings, hard-sided saddlebags, and sometimes trunks are often referred to as "dressers" because they are "dressed" with all that equipment. They are designed for touring and have big, slow-turning engines for easy power at low revs. Their gobs of torque allow them to carry the largest loads in motorcycling, and they're designed for comfort on the highway. Their engines run very smoothly, are counterbalanced, or are rubber isolated so the rider does not feel their vibration. Big, cushy seats pamper the rider and passenger, and a fairing with lowers (a lower extension designed to keep the wind off the legs) and windshield will protect the riders.

These bikes are often also dressed with sound systems and air-assisted suspension systems for entertainment and comfort on the road. However, in order to offer all this, the bikes are very heavy (around 850 to 900 pounds "wet"—fully fueled), and with rider, passenger, and luggage aboard, the whole package can weigh in at 1,300 to 1,400 pounds! A dresser can be a handful at low speeds, especially for an inexperienced or older rider.

Sport Tourers

If you like to travel, but don't want your bike encumbered with a lot of extra equipment and weight, sport tourers offer fairings and hard saddlebags, but are smaller and lighter than dressers. Though their engines offer less displacement, they tend to develop more horsepower than dressers, and they can get down the road much more quickly. Their luggage is carried in hard-sided, lockable saddlebags (and sometimes a trunk) that are easily removable with the turn of a key. Their fairings do not offer quite as much coverage as a dresser's fairing, but some have electrically adjustable wind-

shields. The suspension system on most sport tourers is relatively adjustable, and they offer a slightly more aggressive seating position. Wet weight will be in the range of about 550 to 720 pounds.

Sport tourers are positioned between dresser tourer and sportbikes. Though not as big and heavy as dressers, they still offer decent weather protection, luggage capacity, and comfort. And while much bigger, heavier, and more comfort-able than sportbikes, they make a decent amount of power and handle well for their size and weight. Pull off the saddle-bags and adjust the suspension, and a skilled rider can whip a sport tourer down a winding road with surprising speed and precision.

Sportbikes

Rider Number 4 places a high priority on performance and handling, and very little

Aggressive style, excellent brakes, racetrack handling, and true performance make a sportbike a joy on a winding road or track. Though the Japanese fours are more associated with the sportbike genre, here's a V-twin-powered Buell XB12S Lightning rider having fun on a back road. *Buell American Motorcycles*

SO YOU WANT THE LATEST, GREATEST SPORTBIKE

With all this performance comes a warning. Since the largest of these bikes will corner and accelerate harder than any street-legal vehicle (except perhaps some exotic sports cars costing hundreds of thousands of dollars), using them to their full capabilities on the street is stupid at best. Some of the bigger bikes have top speeds approaching 200 miles per hour (yes, 200!), and even the most skilled rider cannot hope to respond to all the variables on the street, which may include gravel, unpredictable traffic, and stray dogs. Whatever you ride, always wear full protection, ride within your abilities, and only explore the bike's—and your—limits at racetracks.

Sport tourers are positioned

between dresser tourers

and sportbikes.

Though it has a sporty fairing, Suzuki's Bandit 1200 is now considered a standard. It's a big, air/oil-cooled four-cylinder with an upright seating position. *American Suzuki Motor, USA*

ALL IN THE FAMILY

The choice between dual-sport and adventure tourer is clearly defined by usage. If you want a lightweight, uncomplicated bike for taking on the back roads and trails and for short trips, a single-cylinder dual-sport would be ideal. However, if you plan to expand your riding to include long-distance travel for days at a time and don't plan to go off-road, an adventure tourer will be more suitable and comfortable, whether you choose an adventure tourer or dual sport. With their great suspensions, nimbleness, versatility, ground clearance, and cornering clearance, either makes a great all-around street bike.

on comfort. He enjoys his fun in quick bursts of adrenaline rather than over the long haul. Obviously, he wants a sportbike. These machines are characterized by fully enclosed bodywork for streamlining, and by a crouching, leaned-forward, aggressive seating position that places the rider's weight low and forward over the front wheel for better aerodynamics, mass centralization, and grip.

Depending on displacement, a sportbike may develop 160 horsepower, yet weigh only 400 pounds.

Where'd the fairing go? A naked or "hooligan" bike is a sporty machine that seems to have been stripped of its fairing and thus has a purposeful, no-nonsense look, like this Triumph Speed Triple. *Triumph Motorcycles America*

Depending on displacement, a sportbike may develop from 100 to 160 horsepower or more, yet weigh only around 400 to 500 pounds—or less—wet. Power often is provided by a liquid-cooled four-cylinder engine, a triple, or a sporty V-twin. They run on radial tires, offer state-of-the-art suspensions and brakes, and are often raced in Superbike, Supersport, and Superstock classes. Riders interested in even more serious performance will add aftermarket exhaust and intake systems, and may upgrade their brakes and suspension to make their bikes ready for track days or racing.

While their performance capabilities are unquestioned, please note their crouching seating positions are not designed for long-distance comfort. For traveling they'll hold little more than a tank bag and tail bag. While it's possible to drape soft saddlebags over their flanks, these might scuff the paint or possibly interfere with the rear wheel. Passengers are usually forced into an extreme seating position, and some models don't even offer a rear seat.

Standard and Naked Bikes

For those who remember bikes as they used to be, before the age of specialization really took off in the 1980s, "standard" and "naked" bikes will seem familiar. A standard is the way most bikes used to be, like an old 650 Triumph Bonneville or an early Honda CB750. They were just barebones motorcycles without fairings or windshields, sporty bodywork, or luggage. Back in the 1970s, one bought a basic bike and added a fairing and bags for touring; an aftermarket exhaust system and upgraded shocks for sporty riding; or a stepped seat, shorty exhaust system, longer fork tubes, and a peanut tank to customize them.

The term "naked bike" came about when some riders crashed their sportbikes, found the replacement bodywork too expensive, and chose to leave off the damaged parts and just ride with the

> ## STRANDED BY TECHNOLOGY
>
> While there is no argument that high-tech features make newer bikes more competent, should any of those niceties be damaged out in the desert, the rider would be unlikely to be able to fix them himself.

A dual-sport allows you to ride the street, and go off on trails as you wish. With a dual-sport, a rider does not need the tow vehicle an off-road bike requires. Of course, a dual-sport comes with lights and other street-legal gear, so it's going to be heavier than a dirt bike, and its tires will be compromised both in the street and in the dirt. *Kawasaki Motors Corp., USA*

Since BMW started the adventure tourer genre with its original R80GS, it's fitting that we show its latest version, the R1200GS Adventurer. *BMW of North America*

The term "naked bike" came about when some riders crashed their sportbikes, found the replacement bodywork too expensive, and chose to leave off the damaged parts.

engines showing. They are referred to as "hooligan bikes" in Britain. When the manufacturers began offering naked bikes from the factory, they were sportier standard-style bikes with exposed engines, and they came with good power and quality suspension units.

The difference between standard and naked bikes is that the former are designed as simple, budget machines with decent power, basic suspension systems, and few frills. A naked bike, however, is much sportier and generally has more horsepower per displacement and higher quality brakes and suspension. Both, however, lend themselves well to a multitude of uses, including commuting, sporting, and touring.

Dual-Sports and Adventure Tourers

As the age of specialization has progressed, what used to be called simply "dual-sport" motorcycles have now split into two categories. Generally, a dual-sport is a lightweight machine powered by a single-cylinder engine displacing up to about 650cc, with a long-travel suspension system for traveling dirt roads and trails. These are usually simple, inexpensive bikes that are little more than dirt bikes with lights—great for taking on the back roads and trails, but rather limited in terms of carrying a passenger or luggage or for going serious distances. This is not to say they're totally unsuitable for travel; I once knew a couple from the Netherlands who traveled much of the world two-up on a Honda XL650.

With the advent of BMW's R80GS in 1980, adventuresome riders now had a large-displacement (797cc) bike with long-travel suspension, a small wind-deflector fairing, and the ability to carry hard-sided, lockable luggage and much more. With these new capabilities, riders happily rode these machines through the high, rough dirt passes of the Alps and the desert sands of the Sahara, and also took them to Alaska and down to Central and South America. This was truly adventure touring!

While both types of bikes had similar purposes, the adventure tourer was in essence an overgrown dual-sport, bigger and heavier and with greater fuel and luggage capacity, and often with two cylinders. As a result, it gained road manners at the expense of off-road capabilities. It was fine on paved and gravel roads, but because of its increased weight and wheelbase, it

The adventure tourer was in essence an overgrown dual-sport.

was no longer as suitable for trail riding except at very careful speeds. By 2005, BMW's R80GS had grown to the R1200GS, with a 1,170cc engine and such technical innovations as fuel injection, high-tech Telelever front suspension, Paralever driveshaft, and anti-lock brakes. However, from the R80 GS's wet weight of 440 pounds, the R1150GS was up to 578 pounds. BMW put the R1200GS on a diet; it weighed in at only 526 pounds. Besides BMW, true adventure tourers are also offered in the United States by Aprilia, Buell, KTM, Triumph, and others.

This R1200GS is outfitted for serious backroad and rough-country travel, and includes an adjustable windshield and aluminum luggage cases. *BMW of North America*

ENGINE FACTORS

Chapter 2

Inline four-cylinder engines have been a staple in motorcycling since the 1970s. Though they tend to be wide, fours also tend to be smooth and compact, and they offer a lot of high-end power. This cutaway of the BMW K1200 four-cylinder engine shows the valvetrain, transmission, and bevel gears necessary to turn the direction of rotation 90 degrees to link it with the driveshaft. *BMW of North America*

While bikes have grown in terms of displacement, weight, and power, it's important that you not feel obligated to join in and buy something beyond your means or comfort level.

WHAT YOU WILL LEARN

- **How torque and horsepower relate to engine displacement**

- **Why certain types of engines work better in certain types of bikes**

- **Liquid vs. air cooling**

- **The siren song of horsepower**

DISPLACEMENT, NUMBER OF CYLINDERS, AND ENGINE CONFIGURATION

Once you have defined which type of motorcycle you want, you will need to narrow your choice among other considerations, including engine displacement, number of cylinders, and configuration. The single most noticeable development in motorcycling since the 1980s has been the relentless increase in engine displacement, and with it complication and weight. In the 1960s, riders started on a 50, 90, or 125cc bike, then graduated to a 250 or 350cc, then eventually (if it suited them) up to a big bike like a Triumph 650, the new, breathtaking Honda CB750 four-cylinder (which debuted in 1969), or even a 74-cubic-inch Harley-Davidson.

In 1972 I took a memorable weeklong ride on my Honda CL350 from Michigan to Virginia, accompanied by my friend, Gil, on his Honda CB160. At 240 pounds, Gil weighed about the same as his motorcycle!

We had a wonderful trip, and didn't think we were doing anything particularly unusual or difficult at the time. Granted, the 160 would not be legal on some highways today, and we certainly could have used a bit more room. But now, more than 30 years later, our greatest difficulty in attempting to duplicate such a ride would be in finding a pair of street-worthy motorcycles with such small displacement. Today, many new riders start their riding careers on bikes that Gil and I would have considered way too big and powerful for anyone but the tough guys who hung out at the gas station.

My point is, while bikes have grown in terms of displacement, weight, and power, it's important that you not feel obligated to join in and buy something beyond your means or comfort level. Technology has moved on, but the laws of physics are the same. If two hardy guys could ride a 160 and a 350cc bike on an 800-mile trip 35 or 40 years ago, you could certainly do such a trip today on a 500 or 650cc bike and not

While big-inch V-twin engines are narrow and tend to be torquey, they don't necessarily generate a lot of power for their displacement and can be subject to vibration. Harley-Davidson has been associated with the V-twin since 1909, and its current standard engine is this air-cooled, 45-degree, 1,450cc Big Twin that puts out about 65 horsepower in stock trim. It solves the vibration problem with either counter-balancing or rubber mounting. *Harley-Davidson Motor Co.*

TIP

For the most part, if there's a number in the model's name, it refers to its engine's displacement.

$$\frac{\Pi}{4} \times \frac{\text{bore}^2 \times \text{stroke}}{\times \text{number}} = \text{displacement}$$
$$\text{of cylinders}$$

Notice those cylinder heads protruding from either side of this BMW R1200ST? An opposed engine can be quite smooth because its pistons move in and out together, theoretically canceling out each other's vibration. If it must be set high in the frame to allow for cornering clearance. *BMW of North America*

have to worry that perhaps it was under-powered or inadequate. You needn't trouble yourself that perhaps you should delay your trip till some future day when you could obtain a more appropriate 1,300cc or 1,800cc or larger bike. The fact is motorcycles today, even the 500s, are so good and so capable that they're adequate to handle the ride.

I also suggest riders consider moving up through the ranks as they did in the past. While the entry-level bikes of yesterday were 50, 80 and 125cc, today you might consider starting on a bike in the range of 250 to 500 or 650cc until you're comfortable with the size and power, and then move up.

ENGINE DISPLACEMENT

Different bikes come with differently sized engines. By size, we are referring to the volume of air/fuel mixture an engine can draw into its cylinders during one complete engine cycle. Engines made in the United States are measured in cubic inches (ci); all others are measured in cubic centimeters (cc). There is a caveat: since Japanese cruisers are basically imitations of Harleys, and since Harley engines are measured in cubic inches, some Japanese manufacturers are starting to express their cruiser engine sizes in cubic inches. For your edification, one cubic inch equals 16.4cc; one cubic centimeter equals 0.061 cubic inches; 61 cubic inches equals one liter (1000cc); 100 cubic inches equals 1.64 liters (1640cc).

So, how do you know how much bike is enough? By recognizing your needs and physical limitations. Also, understand what you gain and lose with displacement. First, engine displacement does not exist in a vacuum, but is part of a system. Any rider who has ever tried to shoehorn a large-displacement engine into a frame and

Wheelbase is the base on which the motorcycle rides. In general, all else being equal, bikes with longer wheelbases tend to steer more slowly but be more stable at speed, while those with shorter wheelbases steer more quickly. The Suzuki SV650S is a sporty V-twin with a wheelbase of 56.3 inches. *American Suzuki Motor Corp.*

SIZE MATTERS

Wheelbase is the distance from one axle center to the other, and is literally the "base" on which the bike rides. For example, here are the wheelbases of four Suzuki models of various displacements: RT125—53.4 inches; GS500F—55.3 inches; GSX-R750—55.1 inches; DL1000 V-Strom—60.4 inches; and Boulevard C90 (1,462cc) 66.9 inches.

Wheelbase is also a function of motorcycle type. Sportbikes tend to have shorter wheelbases because they need to steer quickly, while cruisers will have longer wheelbases. Examples? Honda's 583cc Shadow VLX cruiser has a 63-inch wheelbase, while its 599cc CBR600RR sportbike measures just 54.5 inches. Want a bigger example? Honda's VTX1300 cruiser measures 65.5 inches in wheelbase, but its ST1300 sport tourer is a much more compact 58.7 inches. All else being equal, a longer wheelbase indicates greater straight-line stability at speed, while a shorter wheelbase will lead to a more responsive, quicker steering chassis. Of course, many other factors play a part in how a motorcycle handles. We'll get into frame geometry later.

other running gear designed for a much smaller bike has learned this sad truth. A 750cc cruiser, for example, is an integral system in which the brakes, frame, suspension, and other parts are all designed to work in concert at a certain level. Stuff a more massive, more powerful engine into the existing frame, and ride it up to the capabilities of that engine, and you will soon overtax the system. The frame will get the wobbles, the tires may wear excessively and slide, the suspension may begin to wallow and bottom over bumps, and the brakes may prove inadequate to control the weight and speed of the new powerplant. Larger displacement bikes offer not only more in terms of size and wheelbase, but also all components mentioned

Do not be seduced by the siren song of horsepower.

The 600cc class has always been a hotbed of technical innovation and performance, including dual overhead cams (DOHC) and four-valve-per-cylinder heads. These hot little DOHC transverse fours deliver a lot of performance and handling for the money. *Yamaha Motor Corp., USA*

TORQUE AND HORSEPOWER

Let's start with some actual figures of various types of bikes.

V-Twin Cruisers	Max Horsepower	Max Torque
Kawasaki Vulcan 1500 Mean Streak	63.1 @ 5,700 rpm	74.3 @ 2,800 rpm
Yamaha Road Star Warrior (1,670cc)	74.5 @ 4,500 rpm	95.5 @ 3,500 rpm
Honda VTX1800	87.4 @ 5,200 rpm	97.4 @ 3,200 rpm
Harley-Davidson V-Rod (1,130cc)	105.6 @ 8,200 rpm	71.9 @ 6,500 rpm
Harley-Davidson Road King (1,450cc)	64.6 @ 5,200 rpm	75.3 @ 3,000 rpm
Sport Tourers		
BMW R1200ST ABS (2 cyl.)	95.3 @ 7,500 rpm	74.2 @ 6,250 rpm
BMW K1200GT ABS (4 cyl.)	113.9 @ 9,000 rpm	79.5 @ 8,000 rpm
Honda ST1300 ABS (4 cyl.)	111.4 @ 7,650 rpm	83.1 @ 6,000 rpm
Yamaha FJR1300 ABS (4 cyl.)	124.5 @ 7,800 rpm	90.2 @ 6,800 rpm

Here's something unexpected—the cruiser with the smallest displacement, the Harley V-Rod, offers by far the most horsepower in its class. However, it also offers the least amount of torque. And those with the most torque, the Honda and Yamaha, offer middling horsepower figures. Why?

Horsepower, according to my Webster's, is "1: the power that a horse exerts in pulling," and "2: a unit of power equal in the U.S. to 746 watts." Torque is, "a turning or twisting force."

To understand an engine, think in bicycle terms. Torque is that low-rpm pulling power when you're pedaling away from a stop. Your legs are pumping hard, your thigh muscles are working, then as you gain speed your legs are soon whirling so fast they're putting out very little force. That's when you shift up a gear and start pushing again. For our purposes, think of torque as low-end, pushing/twisting power and horsepower as the high-end, spinning power.

On our dyno chart, note that the V-Twin cruisers with bigger engines pump out prodigious torque that peaks from between 2,800 to 3,500 rpm. In order for the V-Rod to produce greater power from less displacement, it has to spin much faster—and likewise has to generate its peak torque at much higher rpm. All this has to do with

the V-Rod's four valves per cylinder, dual overhead cams, cam timing, fuel injection, exhaust tuning, and its overall breathing.

And it has very different riding characteristics. Traditional cruisers are all about that lovely rumble as you pull away from a stop at low rpm and shift lazily. The V-Rod engine feels much more like a sportbike's, with smooth, high-revving power.

Now take a look at the sport-tourer charts. These are different types of bikes designed for sportier riding, and despite the fact that most of them have less displacement than the cruisers, three of the four generate more horsepower than the Harley V-Rod, and those three all have four-cylinder engines. Generally, engines with more cylinders tend to rev higher and make more power, while those of comparable displacement with fewer cylinders tend to be lower revving and to make more torque.

Now look at the torque figures. While the peak figures are comparable between the two groups, most of the cruisers make their peak torque at a much lower rpm than the sport tourers. Why? Again, it's because of the number of cylinders and because of how their engines are designed and tuned.

above will be sized appropriately for the power of a given engine and the bike's weight.

Larger displacement often (but not always) means more power. Of course, power is also a factor of the kind of bikes being discussed. A 600-class sportbike may well generate more horsepower than a 1,500cc cruiser—but the big-inch cruiser would surely generate much more torque, or low-end power. Warning: Do not be seduced by the siren song of horsepower. While more of some things are better, horsepower is not necessarily one of them.

Torque, the low-rpm power that cruisers usually generate by the bushel, is much easier to control and makes for a more relaxing ride. High horsepower numbers are usually generated high up in the rpm range, which means you have to wind the engine out and ride aggressively to take advantage of them. Torque is generated at relatively low rpm.

NUMBER OF CYLINDERS

A given displacement will be divided among a certain number of cylinders. In the

A 750cc cruiser, for example, is an integral system in which the brakes, frame, and suspension are designed to work in concert.

Suzuki's C90T displaces 1,462cc, which is about 90 cubic inches. Despite this huge displacement advantage, it generates less horsepower than some 600cc sportbikes. That's okay, because cruisers thrive on torque, or low-end power, while sportbikes are designed for high-end power. *American Suzuki Motor Corp.*

650cc class, for example, over the years you could buy a single-cylinder model, a V-twin cruiser, a parallel twin, or a four-cylinder bike. Within the world of street motorcycling today you'll find singles, twins, triples, fours, and sixes; at this writing the only five-cylinder bikes are exotic racing machines. Let's look at some of the tradeoffs in cylinder number.

Generally, for a given displacement, the more cylinders an engine offers the smoother it will run and the higher it will rev. A single-cylinder 650 would likely be a

dual-sport with a slow-revving, high-torque engine. Conversely, a four-cylinder 650 would likely rev higher than the single and be smoother running, while offering greater horsepower but less torque.

As an example, below are the horsepower and torque figures for some representative sporty V-twins, triples, and fours in the 900–1,000cc displacement classes:

While these differently configured models are not directly comparable, they're all sporty machines. The fours (by dint of

Generally, for a given displacement, the more cylinders an engine offers the smoother it will run and the higher it will rev.

	Horsepower	Torque
Sporty V-twins		
Aprilia RSV1000 Tuono	114.0 @ 9,250 rpm	66.8 @ 8,500 rpm
Ducati 999R	139.0 @ 9,750 rpm	79.6 @ 8,000 rpm
Honda RC51	118.5 @ 9,000 rpm	72.1 @ 7,500 rpm
Triples		
Triumph Speed Triple	119.8 @ 9,250 rpm	73.4 @ 7,750 rpm
Triumph Daytona 955i	130.0 @ 10,500 rpm	68.0 @ 8,500 rpm
Fours		
Honda CBR1000RR	148.6 @ 10,750 rpm	76.4 @ 8,500 rpm
Kawasaki ZX-10R	163.4 @ 12,000 rpm	80.4 @ 9,750 rpm
Suzuki GSX-R1000	150.0 @ 11,000 rpm	77.2 @ 8,250 rpm
Yamaha YZF-R1	158.3 @ 12,500 rpm	74.0 @ 10,000 rpm

Single-cylinder streetable motorcycles tend to be either dual-sports or low-displacement entry-level bikes. Singles work great in the dirt because of their low weight and high torque, and their throbbing vibration largely goes unnoticed. On the street they're light, simple, and inexpensive. Shown is the Buell Blast. *Buell American Motorcycles*

their ability to rev so high) develop much more power and at higher rpm than the twins. Their torque figures, however, are comparable. When we compare them to V-twin cruisers (see sidebar on page 21), you find cruisers offer higher torque and lower horsepower figures.

ENGINE CONFIGURATION

How the engine is laid out, or configured, has a major effect on how the bike looks,

acts, and performs. Some common engine configurations include V, inline, and opposed, each available in various numbers of cylinders.

V

V-configuration engines may have their cylinders arranged front to back (like Harley-Davidson V-twins or the Honda VFR800 four-cylinder), or protruding to the sides like a Moto Guzzi V-twin or a

Some common engine configurations include V, inline, and opposed, each available in various numbers of cylinders.

Two-cylinder engines have been powering motorcycles for a hundred years, as twins offer greater smoothness than singles and the potential to rev higher. Triumph offers a full line of twin-cylinder models styled after their traditional bikes from the 1960s; here's the sporty Thruxton model. *Triumph Motorcycles America*

A three-cylinder engine can offer a nice compromise between the twin's thumping torque and the four's high-revving nature. Triumph offers a full line of high-performance triples, including this Daytona 955i. *Triumph Motorcycles America*

Why do most V-twin cruiser manufacturers go with shared-crankpin designs? Two words: Harley-Davidson.

SINGLE- VERSUS DUAL CRANKPIN V-TWINS

In an internal-combustion engine, the connecting rods join the crankshaft at the crankpin(s). On a V-twin engine, whether these two connecting rods share a single crankpin or separate (dual) crankpins is an important factor in engine performance.

How this works is most easily illustrated by using the bicycle analogy again. Okay, it's a crude example, but imagine pedaling a bicycle in the conventional manner—the two pedals represent a dual-crankpin engine. Now imagine if you were to place both feet on the same pedal and try to pedal—that's a single- (or shared) crankpin engine. The point is, a dual-crankpin engine is much smoother in operation and can be spun at much higher revolutions, while a shared-crankpin gets a much bigger push (torque) with each revolution, but is nowhere as smooth and will not generate as much high-end power.

With that said, why do most V-twin cruiser manufacturers go with shared-crankpin designs? Two words: Harley-Davidson. Since its first V-twin engine in 1909, H-D has utilized the shared-crankpin design, and who's to argue with their success? While they don't rev very high, and they shake a bit, the sound and feel of a Harley-Davidson

V-twin is iconic in motorcycling. The Motor Company would certainly gain power and smoothness by going to a dual-crankpin design, but by doing so would lose their unique firing order, sound, and power—and probably a large segment of their customers. They have successfully isolated their customers from vibration with rubber engine mounts and by counterbalancing the engines.

Honda introduced its dual-crankpin Shadow 1100 V-twin cruiser back in the 1980s, then in the middle 1990s introduced a shared-crankpin version of it, called the American Classic Edition (A.C.E.), while retaining the original version. The A.C.E. version produced sound and power characteristics very close to that of a Harley-Davidson V-twin–while also producing about 25 percent less power at a 25 percent lower redline than its own dual-pin sibling. Harley-Davidson protested that the A.C.E. intruded on its territory, and the company attempted to trademark its sound. Some years later H-D dropped its legal action, and Honda quietly dropped this controversial model. The point is there's a lot more involved in marketing motorcycles than just engineering.

Four-cylinder engines offer excellent smoothness with high-end horsepower and acceptable torque. For this reason they have become very popular in sportbikes, such as the Suzuki GSX-R1000 (left) and Kawasaki ZX-14 (above). *American Suzuki Motor Corp.; Kawasaki Motors Corp., USA*

Honda ST1300 V-4. A V-engine in which the cylinders are arranged at a 90-degree angle to each other offers perfect primary balance, and can be quite smooth. This is common on some sportbikes, but most cruisers offer a much steeper V-angle, closer to 45 or 50 degrees. The greater the V-angle, the longer the wheelbase may have to be to accommodate it, which is why some manufacturers tilt their longitudinal V-twin engines forward for better

cooling and a shorter wheelbase. Arranging the cylinders transversely, into the airstream, enhances cooling.

The great majority of cruisers are powered by V-twin engines, and V-twins are heavily identified with these usually big, slow-turning engines. However, this configuration is also utilized by Ducati, Honda, Buell, and others in sportbikes, so they're not necessarily for slow going. There are practical reasons for V-twins.

ONCE AND FUTURE BRITISH BIKES

While the Honda CB750 was great for motorcyclists, it spelled the end of the British motorcycle industry. Well, temporarily, at least. Triumph has come back successfully, and is once again producing bikes powered by parallel twins and inline triples. The Norton name, as of this writing, has been resurrected, although the bikes, while bearing a striking resemblance to Commandos of old, are now built in Oregon.

Though several manufacturers have flirted with six-cylinder engines, Honda's Gold Wing series has utilized them most successfully since 1988. Sixes are heavy and complex, but offer extremely smooth and tractable power. *American Honda Motor Co.*

V-twin engines have been around for a century, as they were the next logical step after the single-cylinder motorcycle. A longitudinally mounted (crankshaft runs front to back) V-twin is a natural. It keeps the bike narrow, which aids in moving through the air and in cornering clearance, and the crankshaft and transmission gears rotate on the same plane as the wheels, so it's easy to hook up a drive chain or belt. However, there can be cooling problems with the rear cylinder.

Riders who want to cruise tend to prefer a relaxed riding style that involves an unhurried, slow-turning engine putting out lots of low-end torque and that certain, loping sound. It's cooler, more relaxing, and less demanding. Cruisers are often classically styled, and many early bikes were V-twins.

Inline

By placing cylinders side by side, a lot of power can be generated in a relatively small space. Many British bikes of yesteryear, such as Triumph, Norton, BSA, and others, were parallel, or inline, twins. In 1969, Honda set the motorcycle industry ablaze when they introduced their CB750, powered by an inline, transversely-mounted, four-cylinder engine that produced a lot more power in a smoother-running package than similar displacement British and other twins. As you divide a given displacement by more cylinders, all else being equal, you gain smoothness and power.

The problem with inline, transversely-mounted engines is that they become wider as they gain cylinders, and cornering clearance suffers. Honda's six-

This single-cylinder Honda XR650L actually has more engine displacement than a typical four-cylinder 600cc sportbike and makes a lot more torque. However, the sportbike makes significantly more horsepower. *American Honda Motor Co.*

Why does this four-cylinder 600-class sporty bike make a lot more horsepower than a 650 single? Part of the reason is because those four little pistons, with their much smaller bores and shorter strokes, can rev much higher. *American Suzuki Motor Corp.*

As you divide a given displacement by more cylinders, all else being equal, you gain smoothness and power.

V-twins are not just for cruisers; their narrowness and torque also make them ideal for sportbikes. Here's a high-tech, liquid-cooled Ducati V-twin with DOHC and four valves per cylinder. *Ducati North America Inc.*

Turn that V-twin from lengthwise (longitudinal, like a Harley-Davidson or Ducati) to transverse (across the frame), and you have the Moto Guzzi line with its 90-degree air-cooled V-twins. Shown is the Breva. *Moto Guzzi USA*

cylinder CBX, introduced for 1978, was quite wide, as was Kawasaki's KZ1300, which hit the market a year later. Though very smooth and powerful, these bikes showed the limits of adding cylinders. They were the last sixes of this configuration from the major manufacturers. Later, the Japanese often moved electrical components (which used to be placed at the end of the crankshaft) back behind the engine to increase cornering clearance on their fours.

With their original K-series engines, BMW countered this problem by laying the cylinders flat and mounting the engine longitudinally. Today's K-series engines are more traditional, being transversely mounted, inline fours, although, true to form, they're not exactly normal: the cylinders are canted forward 55 degrees.

Opposed

BMW twins and the various Honda Gold Wings are the best modern examples of opposed engines. By having its cylinders opposed, BMW was able to get them out into the airstream for better cooling. The engines could be relatively smooth as both pistons moved in and out simultaneously. Honda, by having four- and then six-cylinder engines on its Gold Wings, made them very smooth indeed. Opposed engines also place the weight low in the chassis, which makes for easier handling.

The problem with opposed engines is that they tend to be wide, which can limit cornering clearance. Back when BMW made its air-cooled twins (through 1995) it was common for aggressive BMW riders to touch their valve covers on the pavement. When the company introduced its R1100

series for 1994, the engines were raised in the chassis several inches in the interest of greater cornering clearance.

Liquid or Air Cooling?

In the early days of motorcycling, when things were simpler, virtually all bikes had air-cooled engines. The liquid-cooled Scott Flying Squirrel was a major exception. It wasn't until the 1970s that liquid cooling was tried again, and since then it has become commonplace.

Air cooling places limitations on engine configuration, as all cylinders must have relatively equal access to the airflow. This was a problem for longitudinal inline engines, like the Indian Fours, and the Ariel Square Fours. Even on the ubiquitous longitudinal air-cooled V-twin the rear cylinder tends to run hotter, and transverse,

inline engines will always face their hot side (the exhaust valve side) forward to take advantage of the cooling airflow. If you're looking for an ideal configuration for efficient air cooling, BMW's opposed twins are among the best.

The great increase in the use of fully enclosed bodywork, the desire to innovate and to make more power, and tightening emissions regulations have all conspired to increase the popularity of liquid cooling for motorcycles. It's significant when such a traditional company as Harley-Davidson introduced its first liquid-cooled machine, the 2002 V-Rod, 99 years into its history.

The problem with air cooling is the wide range of riding situations it has to handle. A bike may be ridden in the desert at 110 degrees one day, and then taken up

Another wrinkle on the four-cylinder concept is the V-4, which Yamaha has used in its Venture tourers for years. On the other site are two more cylinders just like these. *Yamaha Motor Corp., USA*

Air cooling places limitations on engine configuration, as all cylinders must have relatively equal access to the airflow.

The V-4 can be narrow and compact, yet generate good horsepower and torque. Here's an inside look at the Honda VFR800's powerplant. It's a chain-drive bike that's sporty, yet comfortable. *American Honda Motor Co.*

A liquid cooling system includes a bothersome, ugly radiator and hoses, but its beauty is on the inside. It allows for a much more controlled temperature range, and for the engine to be built to closer tolerances. *Kawasaki Motors Corp., USA*

onto a snowcapped mountain the next. One rider may ride alone, lightly loaded, and another on an identical bike may carry a passenger and a full load of luggage while towing a trailer. Metal expands when it gets hot and contracts when it cools, and air-cooled engines run hotter than water-cooled ones. To allow for this wide range of temperatures, an air-cooled engine has to be put together with looser tolerances. Enclose that engine in water jackets, however, with a radiator and thermostat, and because it's now in a temperature-controlled environment, it has to deal with a much narrower temperature range and can be built to closer tolerances. When ridden hard, an air-cooled engine will generally be noisier, wear more quickly, make less power, and put out more emissions than a similar liquid-cooled engine.

If a bike is going to be fully loaded and ridden long distances, it will likely last longer if it has a liquid-cooled engine. Here's Emilio Scotto, who has ridden around the world on his older Honda Gold Wing with recirculating liquid-cooling system. The camel, by contrast, has a total-loss liquid-cooling system and must be topped up frequently. *American Honda Motor Co.*

Chapter 3

CHASSIS STUFF

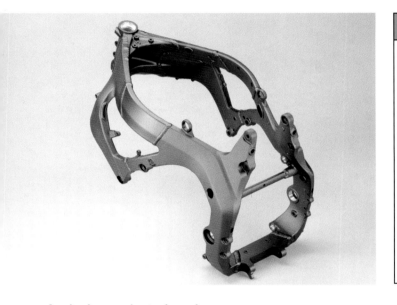

An aluminum perimeter frame is a favorite of sportbike manufacturers because it offers relative lightness and strength in one package. This frame handles the needs of Honda's CBR1000RR. *American Honda Motor Co.*

The frame is the

motorcycle's skeleton.

WHAT YOU WILL LEARN

- **The various types of frames**

- **Why rake and trail matter**

- **How wheelbase affects steering**

- **Shaft, chain, and belt final drive:**
  Which is best for you?

FRAMES

The frame is the motorcycle's skeleton. It supports, positions, and holds all the other parts in their proper places and relationships so they'll work well together. In addition, for good handling, it is absolutely essential that the frame always and consistently holds the two axles in constant relation to each other (allowing for suspension movement). While the axles are allowed to move up and down, they must not twist relative to one another.

The frame attaches to the fork with a pair of triple clamps at one end, and to the swingarm pivot points at the other (except on hardtail frames). These other components provide and support the suspension, steering, and braking functions.

Frames are usually made of steel or aluminum in an attempt to provide the most amount of support and rigidity (stiffness) with an acceptable amount of weight. It is ironic that, given these factors, a certain amount of elasticity is desirable. It is possible for a frame to be too stiff. This elasticity not only provides feedback the rider needs to sense what the bike is doing, but also helps the frame microadjust to cornering forces. I recall some years ago that one of the manufacturers developed a Grand Prix bike on which the frame was too stiff. The rider could push the bike really hard, but without the necessary elasticity and feedback, the tires would very suddenly let go without warning.

TYPES OF FRAMES
Single Backbone
This is the basic building block of frames. Some naked and small dirt bikes utilize a single backbone frame, which consists of a single, large tube connecting the headstock to the swingarm. The engine hangs from it, usually with mounts on the bottom at the crankcase and on the top at the cylinder head. It's relatively inexpensive to make and exposes the engine, but does not offer great rigidity.

Dual Spar Perimeter

As motorcycle engines became more powerful, designers found that frames with a single backbone were not sufficiently rigid to keep those axles in line. Racetrack experimentation revealed that rigidity could be gained by drawing as straight and short a line as possible from the steering head to the swingarm pivots. In order to do this, the backbone must be split to go around the engine. Dual-spar perimeter frames encircle the engine as seen from the top.

A dual-spar perimeter frame slopes steeply, is usually made of box-section aluminum for lightness and rigidity, and is routed around the perimeter of the engine. The resulting shape of the frame lends itself to a high degree of inherent rigidity, or stiffness, and it has become very popular on sportbikes.

Trellis

Basically, a subset of the dual spar, but using short, round tubes welded into a series of triangles instead of the traditional dual-spar box aluminum. Think of the sturdy structure of a trellis-type bridge with abundant use of triangulation, and you've got an idea of the trellis frame. Its steel or aluminum tubing triangles form a network of rigid members around the engine. Not only does it offer lightness, strength, and rigidity, but it also has strong visual appeal.

Single cradle

Think of a tubular-steel bicycle frame, then imagine it sized for a motorcycle. While this kind of single-tube, perimeter frame is fine for dealing with the forces generated by a bicycle rider, stick a heavy, powerful motor inside and torsional rigidity becomes a problem. Such frames are utilized mostly on older, steel-framed trail bikes.

Double Cradle

Bike builders found that by running a second set of lower frame tubes beside the first and tying them together, essentially doubling the frame, they could add a great deal of rigidity. Think of the difference in rigidity between a flat piece of cardboard and a cardboard box. The cradle halves usually join in a single frame member under the tank, and the engine sits in the cradle between the tube sections. With the engine and various braces tying the two cradle

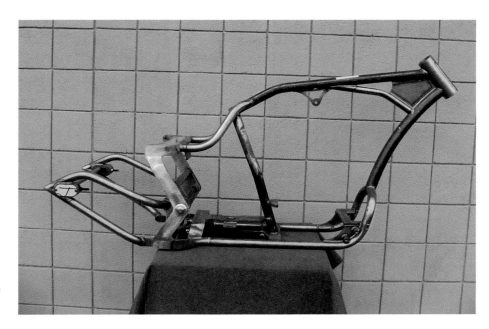

halves together, rigidity was greatly increased. Cruisers and other basic bikes often use double-cradle frames.

OTHER BITS OF FRAME INFO
Engine as Stressed Member

One day, I suspect, a clever engineer was looking at a motorcycle and wondered why they should not take advantage of the relative inflexibility of the engine cases and utilize the engine as part of the frame structure.

In a few extreme examples of stressed-member design, the bike is essentially frameless and the engine serves as the central piece, or the "stressed member"; subframes bolted to the engine support the fork, swingarm, seat, and the rest. Somewhat more common is for the swingarm to attach through the engine cases. For the most part, however, stressed-member design utilizes traditional frame theory and uses the engine, rather than cradles, to add rigidity.

This system saves the weight of the lower frame tubes, though much of that saving is given back because the engine casting has to be made sturdier. Still, rigidity can be top-notch. Many twin-spar frames utilize the engine cases as stressed or stabilizing members to bolster the frame and to transfer loads from one point on the frame to another.

Hardtail

Back in the early days, before rear suspensions became common, the frame on

The 2-Lo Magnum, a single-backbone frame by KC Creations/Big Inch Bikes Mfg. has a 40-degree rake. A hidden-shock swingarm frame, it's designed for big-inch customs with huge 260-series or larger rear tires. *KC Creations*

Cruisers and other basic bikes often use double-cradle frames.

Honda's GL1800 Gold Wing utilizes an aluminum-alloy dual-spar perimeter frame with the engine as a stressed member. *American Honda Motor Co.*

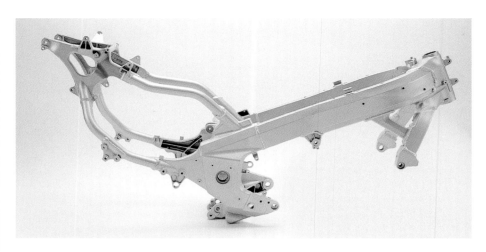

Rake and trail. Everyone kinda knows what they are, but aren't exactly sure what they mean.

most motorcycles stretched from the steering head to the rear axle. With no rear suspension, the term "hardtail" (they're also called "rigids") applied. A vintage bike will likely come with such a frame.

Today, many customs and bikes from the alternative builders offer rigid-frame models, but the mass-market manufacturers stay away from them. The appeal is that they're cool, they have a vintage/custom look, and they offer a very low seat height. Riders claim that with frame flex, they're more comfortable than one might think.

Hidden-Shock Swingarm

Among cruiser riders, a hardtail frame is cool—but it doesn't offer a very comfortable ride. That's why Harley-Davidson developed, in the early 1980s, a new motorcylce line it named the "Softail" for its unique frame. The

idea was that the Softail frame would provide the appearance of a hardtail, but with all the benefits of an actual suspension system.

With the Softail, the triangulated section that holds the rear axle appears to be a continuation of the frame, a solid piece, and no rear suspension is visible. In actuality, this rear frame section is part of a swingarm. The twin shocks are hidden, laid horizontally underneath the engine, and the ride feels much like that of any suspended motorcycle. While "Softail" is a Harley-Davidson trademark, other frames of this type are referred to as "hidden-shock."

Rake and Trail

Everyone kinda knows what they are, but aren't exactly sure what they mean.

Extend the line of the fork until it intersects the ground. Rake is the angle of the

KEEPING IT TRUE

Frames require very little maintenance except for checking and lubricating the swingarm and steering-head bearings. Eventually, worn or loose bearings can cause the bike to drift from a straight line, or give a little head shake upon deceleration. Periodically check that nuts and bolts are tight. If the bike has been crashed, its frame alignment should be checked by an expert.

Many Ducati models carry a trellis frame, which consists of a bridgework of triangulated tubular frame members. It's not only light and strong, but can also be quite attractive. *Ducati North America Inc.*

The Moto Guzzi Griso has a truly unique tube-steel dual-spur perimeter frame that bends around the outside of the fuel tank and supports the transverse air-cooled V-twin engine. *Moto Guzzi USA*

motorcycle's fork off vertical where that line meets the ground, measured in degrees—that's easy.

To measure trail, draw an imaginary vertical line down through the center of the motorcycle's steering head (not the fork legs) to a point where it intersects the ground. Now, drop a second vertical line straight down to the ground from the center of the front axle. The distance between the points where these two lines intersect the ground is called "trail."

As for what these figures signify, the steeper the rake, the more quickly the bike will steer. Because the tire contact patch is located *behind* the point at which the steering axis meets the ground, the tire is being *pulled* by the fork. This imposes a self-centering effect, or correcting torque, on the wheel. Bikes that need to react quickly, like dirt and sportbikes, have a steeper rake and short trail so there's less effect to overcome, but they can become twitchy at high speeds. Bikes with longer rake-and-trail figures tend to have greater stability at speed.

Because the tire contact patch is located behind the point at which the steering axis meets the ground, the tire is being pulled by the fork.

A BMW K1200S sporting an aluminum-alloy perimeter frame with a Duolever front end and the engine as a stressed member. *BMW of North America*

A rigid frame (also called a "hardtail," for obvious reasons) has no rear suspension, yet frame flex and tire flex make a rigid-framed bike somewhat livable. They're cool because they ride so low, and they identify the rider as a hard-nosed, avid biker. *Titan Motorcycle Company of America*

Here are some rake/trail figures for representative 2003 Yamahas:

Model/type	Rake/trail
YZF R6 sportbike	24 degrees/3.45 inches
YZ250 motocrosser	27 degrees/4.70 inches
Road Star cruiser	32 degrees/5.68 inches

Extreme rake, up around 40 degrees and beyond, is popular on custom choppers because it looks cool. While an extreme rake may make the bike very stable at the freeway speeds (although now you may run into fork flex), it not only makes it hard to steer, but also extends the wheelbase, which further complicates making it turn.

Wheelbase

Wheelbase is the distance measured from the center of the front axle to the center of

The Triumph Speed Triple's short 56.2-inch wheelbase with rake/trail figures of 23.5 degrees and 3.36 inches allow it to turn quickly for responsive handling. *Triumph Motorcycles America*

The 68.3-inch wheelbase of this Kawasaki Vulcan 2000 combined with its 32-inch rake and 7.2 inches of trail make it feel stable at speed. The tradeoff is that it turns much more deliberately than the Triumph Speed Triple. *Kawasaki Motors Corp., USA*

the rear axle, and is a related factor in steering. On a motorcycle, only the front wheel pivots, but it needs to steer the entire motorcycle. The rest of the bike hanging out behind the steering head represents a lever that wants to force the bike to continue in a straight line. It restrains the bike's ability to turn. All else being equal, the longer the wheelbase, the more straight-line force the steering must act against, and the less responsive the bike will be about turning.

Again, bikes that have to react quickly require shorter wheelbases. Here are some wheelbase figures for the same three Yamahas listed earlier:

YZF/R6 sportbike	54.3 inches
YZ250 motocrosser	58.3 inches
Road Star cruiser	66.3 inches

Gross Vehicle Weight Rating

Every motor vehicle sold in the United States is required to carry a plate that states several facts about it, including manufacturing data and gross vehicle weight rating (GVWR). On a motorcycle, this plate is usually attached to or near the steering stem. The GVWR figure tells the consumer the maximum weight the bike is designed to carry, including the bike's own weight. This figure is arrived at by considering the bike's tires, suspension, frame, brakes, and its performance and mileage characteristics.

It's not always easy for the consumer to weigh a motorcycle, or to figure actual vehicle weight. Many magazines weigh bikes during testing. Or, you can estimate your bike's wet (actual) weight from the dry weight figure often given in the owner's manual or in advertising materials. Dry weight does not include fluids (that's why it's called "dry") or the battery. To estimate wet weight, note the fuel and fluid capacities in the owner's manual, including engine oil and fork fluid, plus driveshaft and gearbox fluids and coolant (if any). Once you have listed the total capacity of onboard liquids, remember the old adage, "A pint's a pound the world around." Add about another 20 pounds for the battery. This figure, plus the weight of any accessories you have added, plus your bike's dry weight figure, should be a close approximation of its wet weight.

Depending upon usage, the GVWR should exceed the weight of the motorcycle

Remember the old adage, "A pint's a pound the world around."

by several hundred pounds. On a sportbike designed to only carry one person, and perhaps light luggage, the GVWR should exceed the wet weight of the bike by 250 to 300 pounds. On a dresser tourer expected to carry two persons and luggage, 400 to 500 pounds is a good margin.

To be certain you're within the bike's design parameters, first weigh yourself and your passenger (if any) in riding gear. Then, add in the weight of any gear you take with you, including luggage, tents, sleeping bags, etc. This total figure, added to your bike's wet weight, should not exceed the GVWR of your motorcycle. If it does by a small amount, don't despair that your tires may suddenly blow or your bike will break in half. It simply means you're

Things don't happen as fast on a cruiser. The rider on this Yamaha Roadliner is enjoying a spirited ride, but the 67.5-inch wheelbase and rake/tail figures of 31.3 degrees/5.98 inches advise a more relaxed pace than a quick-steering sportbike might. *Yamaha Motor Corp. USA*

A great deal of information is carried on the GVWR plate. It lists the motorcycle's model year, gross vehicle weight rating, recommended tire sizes and inflation, and more.

A drum brake is not nearly as effective as a disc, which is why drum brakes are usually relegated to the back end of low-performance bikes. This one's on a Yamaha Virago cruiser.

beyond the design capabilities of your motorcycle, which is not recommended. Try to pare your weight down to the GVWR figure. Also, if you're near the GVWR, keep your tires inflated to the higher range of recommended pressure.

BRAKES

Disc Versus Drum

You may remember from the old western movies that the original stagecoach brakes were a lever that the driver either pulled or stepped on to force a pad against the wagon's wheels. Things got a bit more technical early in the twentieth century with internal combustion engines and internal expanding drum brakes, which are still in use today. Nearly all modern motorcycles now have disc front brakes, many also have disc rears; drums have survived mostly on the rear of bikes designed to sell at a lower price.

Utilizing a drum brake actuates a cam that is attached to the brake shoes. As the cam rotates, it presses the shoes' pad material against the spinning brake drum, causing friction and slowing the bike. One problem with drum brakes is that under hard use they can become self-energizing. This means that when the shoes are pushed quite hard against the brake drum, it is possible that they will try to follow the drum around and jam against it, locking the wheel. Drums are also more prone to fading because they don't dissipate heat well. As for

High-quality brake calipers, like this four-piston by Nissin, are a major factor in making safe, controllable stops. Braking systems with a higher number of pistons (four or six rather than two) add "feel" and feedback, and require less effort. *Triumph Motorcycles America*

maintenance, drum brakes require only an occasional adjustment and inspection.

To understand a disc brake, imagine yourself descending a long stairway with one hand on the rail. If you get to motivatin' too fast, you may squeeze the rail with your hand to steady yourself. That's the concept of how a disc works—the caliper squeezes an endless "rail," the disc.

In a hydraulic disc brake system, when the rider squeezes the brake lever or pushes the pedal, fluid is forced through hoses, which pushes one or more pistons

Drum brakes have survived mostly on the rear ends of bikes designed to sell at a lower price.

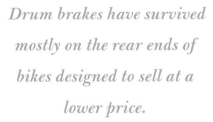

Chain final drive is very efficient and allows the rider to easily change overall gear ratios by changing sprockets. Sporting bikes, like this Kawasaki ZX1000, usually offer chain final drive for those reasons. Another tip-off that this is a sportbike is the very stout and well-braced swingarm. *Kawasaki Motors Corp., USA*

Belt drive involves a toothed Kevlar-reinforced belt that runs around pulleys rather than sprockets. Pulley wear is minimal, and belt drive is quieter than a chain. A belt requires no lubrication and much less adjustment, but it will not handle nearly as much power as a chain. Because they aren't as strong, drive belts must be much wider than drive chains to handle a given amount of power.

Some chain lube invariably is flung onto the rear wheel, where it picks up dirt and must be cleaned.

A driveshaft, like the one on this cruiser, is relatively heavy and expensive and eats up power, but it requires minimal maintenance and tends to be stone reliable.

LUBRICATING A DRIVE CHAIN

Lubricate the chain just after riding, while it is still warm. This allows the lubricant to penetrate deeper. Place the bike on its centerstand; if it doesn't have a stand, roll it several feet at a time and rest it on the sidestand as you lubricate sections of the chain. With the transmission in neutral and the engine off, rotate the rear wheel to bring a section of chain into view.

Most modern chain-drive bikes carry an O-ring chain on which a little rubber O-ring at each end of the rollers seals the factory-installed lubricant inside. With these, it is only necessary to lubricate between the sideplates and to keep the O-rings moistened so they don't dry out. Spray a thin amount of lubricant along the top surface of both edges of the lower race of chain. Many chain lubes utilize a thin solvent carrier that can penetrate between the plates; the solvent evaporates and leaves the lubricant behind. When the bike is ridden, centrifugal force will cause the lubricant to disperse outward between the plates. There should be sufficient overspray to lubricate the roller surfaces.

Drive chains wear out because of corrosion, hard use, and lack of maintenance. Maximize chain life with proper cleaning, lubrication, and by running O-ring chains with their self-lubricated bushings. Choose a high-quality chain lubricant that's made specifically for your type of chain.

within the caliper outward and presses the pad material against the brake disc. Commonly, a brake caliper will have from one to as many as six pistons. While it is often possible to lock a wheel with a single-piston caliper, the advantage of a greater number of pistons is usually finer control with less effort.

Brake Performance

Brake performance can usually be improved with a higher performance set of brake pads, a more sophisticated caliper, or larger disc rotor. Disc brakes are self-adjusting, but because hydraulic fluid can absorb moisture, the brake system should be flushed and replenished at the interval specified in your owner's manual. Inspect pads regularly for wear. When they need to be replaced, this can usually be done quite easily.

FINAL DRIVE
Chain Versus Belt Versus Shaft

Motorcycles use three basic means of transferring power from their engines to the rear wheel: a drive chain, drive belt, or driveshaft. And like anything in life, each method offers its advantages and disadvantages.

The chain and belt have been around since the dawn of motorcycling, and still have a lot to offer despite the rise in popularity of the driveshaft. These systems

connect the drive sprocket off the transmission to the driven sprocket on the rear wheel with a very simple and relatively inexpensive chain or belt. The system is light, and allows the rider to change overall gearing by selecting sprocket sizes. Most inexpensive bikes come with chain final drive, but don't let this fool you into thinking of chain as a poor second choice.

Chain Drive

If you follow racing, you'll notice that the great majority of sportbikes and racing machines utilize chain final drive. All else being equal, a chain drive is far lighter than a shaft, and eats up far less of the engine's power in friction losses. This means that more of the engine's power reaches the ground than on a bike equipped with a driveshaft. Also, a chain is stronger and narrower than a belt, and handles high horsepower easily.

The drawbacks to chain drive have to do with maintenance and longevity. Of the three types of power transfer systems, chains are by far the most maintenance intensive. Not only must the chain be adjusted as it wears (by loosening the rear axle and sliding the wheel rearward to compensate for the chain's elongation), but

it must also be lubricated periodically. Some of the lube invariably is flung onto the rear wheel, where it picks up dirt and must be cleaned. A chain is also noisier, and makes that familiar sizzling sound (or squeaking sound if not properly lubricated) in operation. And as the old saying goes, the chain is only as strong as its weakest link.

Among the chain drive system's advantages is that it can handle more power for a given width than a belt system. For example, while stock Harley-Davidsons have been equipped with belt final drives for many years, it's common for owners to replace belts with chain-drive systems once the engine has been built beyond a certain horsepower. After many miles, the chain and sprockets will need to be replaced, which can run into money. Don't try to save money by installing a new chain on questionable sprockets; worn sprockets will chew up a new chain and shorten its life.

Belt Drive

A belt final drive system is very similar to a chain final drive, except that in place of the steel chain and sprockets, the belt-drive system utilizes a flexible nylon toothed belt that's often Kevlar-reinforced and has toothed pulleys to match. Belt drive's

Before lubricating a drive chain, ride the bike to warm the chain so the lube will flow more freely. Spray the lubricant between the plates, where the pen is pointing. There will be sufficient overspray to lubricate the roller surfaces.

Don't try to save money by installing a new chain on questionable sprockets; worn sprockets will chew up a new chain and shorten its life.

Generally, drive sprockets are merely dull pieces made for getting the job done. Some manufacturers, however, offer sprockets that are chromed and styled to match wheels. *Performance Machine*

GEAR RATIOS

Gearing Basics

If your bike has chain or belt final drive, it's possible to easily change its sprockets or pulleys to enhance the overall gear ratio to achieve certain ends. If your bike has a driveshaft, however, you're welcome to skip this section, as quick-change driveshaft ratios are not generally available. While it's too complex to fully discuss the process here, let's cover gearing basics.

Gearing affects acceleration, top speed, fuel economy, engine wear, and even comfort. Changing sprocket or pulley sizes changes the relationship between the rpm the engine is spinning in any given gear, and the speed the bike is traveling.

Your bike's stock sprockets or pulleys were designed to deliver a good compromise among all these factors. However, you can set up your bike to meet specific needs. For example, you may hang out with a bunch of riders who are fond of stoplight-to-stoplight racing, or drag racing. If you want your bike to be able to accelerate harder in any given gear, or climb a big hill on the way to work, or to haul you, your significant other and a load of gear more easily on tour, you may wish to change gear ratios so that the engine spins a little higher rpm in any gear relative to its road speed (also called "shorter" or "lower" gearing). Just be aware that your engine will likely be a little noisier as a result, use a little more gas, and wear at a slightly faster rate.

On the other hand, if you have built your bike's engine for more power and already enjoy great acceleration, you may wish to gear it taller so your engine loafs along, yet still accelerates well. If your bike seems to have more than adequate power, there are several other reasons why you may wish for taller gearing. If you do most of your riding on the highway lightly loaded, and the bike seems to be straining at speed in top gear, taller gearing could help. It could also slightly improve fuel mileage, reduce the rate of engine wear, and quiet the engine for greater overall comfort. The tradeoff is lazier acceleration.

Gearing Considerations

Changing to a larger drive (front) sprocket with more teeth, or a smaller driven (rear) sprocket with fewer teeth, will raise overall gearing so your engine will turn fewer rpm at any given road speed. Conversely, going to a smaller drive or larger driven sprocket will do the opposite. To determine your current gear ratio, divide the number of teeth in your front sprocket into the number of teeth in your rear sprocket. For example, if your sprockets have 16 and 43 teeth, that's a ratio of 16/43 or 2.68. Remember, a little goes a long way. Don't change your overall gear ratio by more than a few percentage points. Going to a 16/41 will yield a ratio of 2.56 and will result in about a 4.6 percent decrease in engine rpm at any given road speed.

Generally, don't go to a smaller front (drive) sprocket, as that will increase the stress on the chain as it makes that sudden turn around the sprocket. When going up in size, be careful that the larger drive sprocket is not too big for its housing. Keep in mind that as you change sprocket or pulley size, you will have to adjust your chain or belt, and may even have to change chain or belt length.

As bikes have become more stylized, wheel manufacturers now offer belt pulleys to match. Here's a collection of stylized pulleys from Performance Machine. *Performance Machine*

advantages include quieter operation, no need for lubrication, and only the occasional need for adjustment. It will usually last much longer than a chain. Its disadvantages are that because it's not as strong as a chain, it must be wider to transmit a given amount of power.

Driveshaft

Sport-touring and dresser-touring motorcycles tend to transfer power to their rear wheels with an automotive-style driveshaft, because they tend to be high-mileage, heavy bikes. Within the rear hub the shaft ends in a worm gear that turns a ring gear on the hub. Because lubrication is sealed in rather than exposed to the elements (as on a chain), a driveshaft can go a lifetime without requiring adjustments, and its only maintenance is periodic fluid changes. Compared with a drive chain, a shaft is clean, extremely reliable, and relatively maintenance free.

The downside to a driveshaft is that it's heavy, complex, and expensive to manufacture. Changing the direction of rotation 90 degrees at the hub eats up power, and there are other friction losses down the line; I've heard estimates that utilizing a driveshaft will consume about 5 to 7 percent of the engine's power. And of course, there is usually no practical way to change gear ratios on a driveshaft.

I've heard estimates that a driveshaft consumes about 5 to 7 percent of the engine's power.

BMW's Paralever driveshaft has a universal joint at each end that is designed to cancel out the usual up/down jacking motion of the shaft. As a result, the rear of the bike stays fairly level, even during heavy throttle use. *BMW of North America*

The swingarm is part of the frame, as it supports the rear wheel. A single-sided swingarm is a recent innovation that can be made very rigid, and really simplifies rear wheel changing. *BMW of North America*

BRANDS OF STREET MOTORCYCLES

Well established in Gran Prix racing, Aprilia also produces several high-end street bikes such as the Tuono shown here. *Aprilia USA*

WHAT YOU WILL LEARN

- An overview of the various brands of street motorcycles

- The major considerations in buying a used bike

- Are alternative manufacturers worth considering?

- Should you buy a custom motorcycle?

Its biggest marketing coup occurred in the early 1990s, when Ducati brought the first naked production bike to the United States: the Monster.

Which brand of motorcycle should you consider? Here's a quick guide to the types of street bikes offered by the various motorcycle manufacturers in the United States as of this writing.

ESTABLISHED BRANDS
Aprilia
This Italian brand originally offered smaller bikes and scooters, and had great success in two-stroke grand prix racing. More recently, it has introduced its line of high-end, four-stroke sporty V-twins to the United States.

Benelli
Started in 1911, this Italian brand manufactured motorcycles for many years till the factory changed hands several times in the 1970s and 1980s. It has now made a comeback and is producing motorcycles again. These 900 and 1,130cc triples have exotic styling and are very sporting.

Bimota
This Italian company began production in 1970 by building exotic, lightweight chassis into which they installed high-performance engines from various established manufacturers. The result was exotic, expensive, and very functional performance. Unfortunately, when Bimota designed its own engine, the Vdue, it was a disaster on a number of levels, and put them out of business in 2000. The company came back in 2003 and is again offering its chassis adorned with sporty engines from other manufacturers.

BMW
BMW grew from a company that built aircraft engines for the Great War. In fact, the blue-and-white "roundel" logo of Bayerische Motoren Werke (Bavarian Motor Works) represents a spinning propeller blade. BMW's first real motorcycle, the R32 in 1923, was ahead of its time, as it had two horizontally opposed, air-cooled cylinders, a three-speed transmission with dry clutch, and driveshaft. Since then, BMW has built motorcycles of that same configuration, while it has also branched out into singles, triples, fours, and parallel twins.

BMW is known now for its standard and naked bikes, its tourers and sport tourers, and for inventing the adventure-touring market with its GS. Its engineering advances include anti-lock brakes and unique suspension components, such as the Telelever fork and Paralever driveshaft. Many BMW models offer heated grips and seats.

Buell

In the 1970s, Erik Buell was a Superbike racer who was determined to build a better sportbike. He decided to power it with a Harley-Davidson engine, an odd choice for a sportbike, but Buell knew that the engine's narrow profile and massive torque would more than make up for its lack of high-rpm power.

Today, Buell is a division of Harley-Davidson, but Erik Buell remains on staff. The company is known for its unique V-twin sport and naked bikes, and also for an adventure tourer. They also produce the Blast, a single-cylinder 492cc bike intended for beginners.

Ducati

The Italians are known for their emotional motor vehicles, and Ducati is no exception. Its motorcycles tend to be lightweight, sporting, big-inch 90-degree V-twins; the company has done well in Superbike racing. It also offers sport tourers with integral saddlebags in its ST line. Its biggest

Representing BMW's recent performance push, the K1200S is a sporty four-cylinder with such high-tech features as a Duolever front end, Paralever driveshaft, and anti-lock brakes. BMW of North America

marketing coup occurred in the early 1990s, when Ducati brought the first naked production bike to the United States, the Monster. It immediately became the best-selling bike in the lineup, and led to the introduction of naked bikes from almost every other manufacturer.

Harley-Davidson

What can one add about this cultural icon, which is the longest continual producer of motorcycles in the world? H-D celebrated its centennial in 2003, and to date its

Erik Buell is a former Superbike racer who wanted to build an American V-twin sportbike. His company is now a division of Harley-Davidson and manufactures a range of big-inch performance V-twins along with the entry-level single-cylinder Blast. Buell American Motorcycles

Ducati is an Italian company known for its sporting V-twins. The ST3S offers hard-sided, lockable saddlebags in a sporting package that provides long-distance touring capabilities. *Ducati North America Inc.*

Think of Harley-Davidson and one bike that comes to mind is its big dresser tourer, the Electra Glide Ultra Classic. The bike has a handlebar-mounted fairing with lowers to protect your legs, and lockable saddlebags and trunk. *Harley-Davidson Motor Co.*

machines are all big-inch V-twins. The great majority of its bikes are air-cooled cruisers and touring bikes, but it also offers the liquid-cooled V-Rod line, which includes high-tech, high-horsepower cruisers.

Honda
Since the late 1950s, Honda has produced some landmark machines that have included the popular CB350, the groundbreaking CB750 Four, the iconic six-cylinder CBX, CBR600 Hurricane, and many others. While most production today remains in Japan, Honda also has a plant in Marysville, Ohio. Today, Honda produces everything from dirtbikes and ATVs to

high-end sportbikes, the six-cylinder Gold Wing dresser, and high-tech cruisers.

Indian
This venerable American brand started business in 1901, then folded in the early 1950s after having built such classics as the Four and the Chief. It was revived for the 1999 model year by a group of investors, but suffered from the fact it utilized engines by aftermarket V-twin maker S&S. By the time it had developed its own 100-inch Powerplus engine in 2003, it was too late, and the company folded again. However, there is talk of resurrecting Indian again—stay tuned.

Kawasaki
Originally a builder of hot two-strokes, Kawasaki's gauntlet thrown in the face of the competition was the 1973 900 Z1. This fire-breathing four-stroke four trumped Honda's CB750 and established Kawasaki as having arrived in the serious motorcycle market. Today, Kawasaki manufactures dirt bikes, ATVs, and a full line of four-stroke cruisers, sportbikes, standards, and nakeds. While it still manufactures primarily in Japan, it has a plant in Lincoln, Nebraska.

KTM
Though this Austrian manufacturer is primarily known for its dirt bikes, it has offered some four-stroke street machines, including the hooligan Duke and the 950 Adventure, which is an adventure tourer that wrested away BMW's longstanding dominance of the Paris-Dakar rally's motorcycle class.

Kymco

This Taiwanese company entered the American market with a line of ATVs and scooters, and the 250 Venox motorcycle. Though only a 250cc, it sported a huge 63-inch wheelbase and in many ways felt like a much larger bike. Fit and finish are exceptional, and I expect good things from Kymco.

Moto Guzzi

This traditional Italian company specializes in building bikes powered by V-twin engines having transversely mounted cylinders and a driveshaft. Guzzi offers emotionally styled, futuristic looking sports in addition to old-line cruisers and tourers.

Moto Morini

Here's another legendary Italian marque that, like Bimota and Benelli, went out of business but returned because of the big motorcycle boom of the 1990s. As of this writing it offers an exotic 1,200cc V-twin in some markets, and will likely be available in the United States by around 2008.

MV Agusta

This spicy Italian company manufactures emotionally styled high-end sport and naked bikes that are highly desirable and full of character. They're powered by four-cylinder engines of 750cc and larger.

MZ

As of this time, this German company offers only its 999cc parallel twin sportbike, a 650 dual-sport, and some 125s in the United States.

Norton

If you recall the original Norton motorcycle that went out of business in the 1970s, you'll appreciate this modern classic. The 952 Commando is a new bike that takes design cues from the original British-made Commando and follows a similar architecture, but is a clean-sheet design. They're now built in Gladstone, Oregon.

Royal Enfield

Here's a good story. The British company Royal Enfield sold 500cc singles to the country of India for use by its military. By 1955 they were selling so many that Enfield opened a factory in India that still produces motorcycles to this day—even though Royal

Enfield went out of business in the early 1970s. The 500 singles have since been updated with a 12-volt electric system, electric starter, a five-speed transmission, and an optional disc front brake, but the bikes look and perform much like 1955 motorcycles.

USED BIKES

Like automobiles, motorcycles have become a whole lot more reliable and long-lived of late. It's not unusual for well-maintained bikes to record from 50,000 to 100,000 miles or more and still have a lot left in them. When shopping for a used bike, here are some basic considerations.

Will the bike fit your needs, now and for the near future? Remember, a used bike is a tool for a job, same as a new bike, so be mindful of the same considerations outlined in the first chapter when shopping.

Consider the overall condition of the bike. Does it appear to be well maintained? Is it washed and waxed? Does it show any rust or corrosion? Does the paint look cared for, and the chrome? Ask to see maintenance receipts, and the maintenance log that is in most owner's manuals. Does the seat show any obvious tears or cracks?

You want to note how well the bike was cared for, as the degree of care that shows on the outside is an indicator of its care on the inside. You would think that when it was placed for sale the owner (or shop) checked it over and brought everything up to optimal condition, but you could easily be wrong. Check the tires for use and wear. If the sides of the front tire show heavy scuffing, and there's more tread left in the center of the tread than at the sides, it's an indi-

cation that the bike was ridden hard in the turns. This is not necessarily a bad thing, but can be a tip-off that it's had hard use. Bring along a gauge and check tire pressure; low pressure indicates the bike may have been sitting a while, or has been neglected. If the tires are more than half used up, this factor can be used as a bargaining chip when it comes time to discuss price.

Check the engine oil level, which is very easy to do if it has a sight glass. Bring along a rag in case it has a dipstick. Low oil level and dirty oil are indicators the bike was not well cared for.

Check the battery. If fluid level is low, it's another indication of neglect. Likewise, if the bike has chain final drive, check the adjustment and lubrication. Take the bike off its stand and sit on it, then reach down with the rag and feel how much play there is in the lower race of chain midway between the sprockets. It should be around 1/2 to 3/4 of an inch.

How much is the chain worn? Replacing a drive chain and sprockets can run into several hundred dollars. Try to pull a roller out of the sprocket about halfway around; if much of it comes out easily, it's an indication of a worn chain. If the sprocket teeth are rounded excessively, the sprocket will need replacement.

A top-line sport tourer, Honda's ST1300 has removable saddlebags and is also available in an ABS model. It's powered by a smooth V-4 engine. *American Honda Motor Co.*

Suzuki

One of the Japanese "big four," Suzuki continues to offer a full line of streetbikes, dirt-bikes, scooters, and ATVs. Its street line consists of cruisers; standard-style bikes, including the Katanas; the V-Strom adventure/sports; and its top-line GSX-R sportbikes.

Triumph

This venerable British brand began in 1902, and in the 1960s was producing legendary machines like the air-cooled Bonneville and Thunderbird parallel twins. Although Triumph went out of business in the early 1980s, real estate magnate John Bloor soon resurrected the company. It began producing

After coming back from the dead in 1999, Indian Motorcycles were produced for several years in Gilroy, California, powered by S&S engines. They went out of business once again after the 2004 model year, just as they had introduced a new 100-inch engine called the Powerplus. At this writing, a group of investors is trying, once again, to resurrect this famous name, but you may still find a few used late-model Indians around. The Chief model was known for its heavily valanced fenders. *Indian Motorcycles*

An Austrian company, KTM is known both for its street and off-road motorcycles. Here's a shot of the 950 Supermoto, a street-going machine that has much of the nimbleness of a dirt bike. *KTM*

Kawasaki Motors has been known as a performance company since the introduction of its original 900cc four-cylinder Z1 in 1973. Today, it is well known for its line of Ninja sportbikes, such as this 1000cc four-cylinder ZX-10R model. *Kawasaki Motors Corp., USA*

new, modern liquid-cooled triples and fours for the 1991 model year. The company has since made a full comeback, and today has returned to its roots—the engines are all parallel twins and inline triples. In addition to its line of sport-bikes, Triumph also produces air-cooled, retrostyled bikes based on models from the company's storied past. At this writing, its 2,294cc Rocket III is the largest displacement mass-produced motorcycle available.

Victory

With cruisers doing so well, the Polaris snowmobile company in Minnesota began producing motorcycles in the late 1990s. Its Victory brand now offers retrostyled V-twin cruisers displacing 1,507 and 1,634cc, some of which are very dramatically styled.

MZ is a German company that has not yet established a full presence in the United States. In addition to a number of smaller off-road and street bikes, it also offers several artfully styled 1,000cc sportbikes. *MZ*

Today's Norton is built in Oregon, a modern interpretation of a classic British bike. Check that frame, Ohlins shock absorbers, and those modern brakes. *Norton Motorcycle*

Royal Enfield offers today what are essentially updates of 1955 British singles. They garner a lot of attention, and are great fun to ride—within their limitations. *Scott Hirko Photography*

Yamaha

Like the other members of the "Big Four" Japanese manufacturers, Yamaha also offers a full line of products for both street and dirt. Its FJR is the premiere sport-tourer, and its R1 and R6 are excellent sporting machines. Naked bikes include the FZ-1 and FZ-6, and it offers an extensive selection of cruisers in its Star line.

ALTERNATIVE V-TWIN MANUFACTURERS

An offshoot of cruisers today is the rise of the alternative V-twin manufacturers. Back in the early to middle 1990s, Harley-Davidsons were in short supply and dealers were selling them for well over suggested retail price.

Several entrepreneurs realized that if they purchased frames from various aftermarket manufacturers, engines from others, and additional components such as wheels and brakes and such, they could offer what were essentially custom bikes, but brand-new and complete with warranties and U.S. Department of Transportation (DOT) certification. Today, dozens of companies are currently manufacturing big-inch, air-cooled, custom-look V-twin-powered motorcycles in the United States. Most purchase powerplants from companies such as S&S, TP Engineering, RevTech, Harley-Davidson, and others, and a few build their own proprietary engines. And of course, most make considerably more power than a stock 88-inch Harley.

If a person can buy a new Harley for $16,000 to $20,000, why would they spend that much or more on some brand they'd never heard of? Well, consider what most people do with a new Harley: they install a set of pipes, a performance cam, an ignition system, and they revise the carburetor (or injectors) to enhance performance. Even more involved riders may install big-inch pistons and cylinders, and perhaps an after-market transmission. Some will buy new fenders, a tank, and more, have it custom painted, add aftermarket brakes, a seat, and a huge rear tire. In the end, if you're going to make the bike run better than stock and customize it to some extent, four things will happen: 1, you will spend a lot of money; 2, the process will take months; 3, you will void your factory warranty; and 4, all the parts you take off will be collecting dust in your garage.

The reason people buy V-twin bikes

from these smaller manufacturers is because they sidestep many of the problems cited above. According to the manufacturers, they meet all DOT and Environmental Protection Agency (EPA) mandates, and therefore you shouldn't be getting any tickets for excessive noise or too-high handlebars—so long as you leave them stock. They often have huge engines (100 cubic inches and more) and make huge power (100 horses and more is common). Rather than having a garage full of stock Harley parts gathering dust, you can choose the exact seat and fork you want, wheels and engine, brakes and ignition and pipes— right from the manufacturer. Custom paint is usually available.

When these smaller manufacturers first started up in the early 1990s, the bikes they made were originally dismissed as "Harley clones." Of course that wasn't true, as a clone is essentially a copy, and why would

Suzuki's strongest niche in the market since the 1980s has been its sportbikes, led by its line of GSX-Rs. These are essentially racebikes for the street and are often at the cutting edge of the sport. Although not a GSX-R, Suzuki's Hayabusa has been known to surpass 190 miles per hour in stock form. *American Suzuki Motor Corp.*

Back from the dead in the early 1990s, Triumph has re-established itself with a full line of sportbikes, naked bikes, and cruisers. Its Daytona 675 is a high-end sportbike with heritage that leads back to the Triumphs of long ago. *Triumph Motorcycles America*

Now that it has become an established rand in its own right, the American-built Victory has begun branching out with factory customs. This Vegas features a 100-cubic-inch engine with four-valve heads, six-speed transmission, 300mm disc rotors, and four-piston calipers. The company is part of the Polaris group, known for its ATVs and snowmobiles. *Victory Motorcycles*

Yamaha hit a huge home run with its Road Star, a big-inch V-twin cruiser. It has also backed it with an extensive line of chrome and other accessories. *Yamaha Motor Corp., USA*

Used bikes will save you a lot of money over buying new, so long as the machine is in good shape and has not been abused. All the bikes on this lot were cleaned and nicely prepped; I could not find a worn tire in the bunch.

A road test is important, especially for a used bike. Here, I put the newest superbike through my rigorous testing procedure.

anyone buy a copy of a Harley if it cost more yet didn't have that famous name? No, what these manufacturers offered was greater performance and a level of stock "customization" that H-D couldn't match.

If you've ever tried to mount an after-market accessory to a bike and had trouble making it fit, you can appreciate the problems a bike builder may have if it buys frames from one company, engines from another, forks from a third, wheels from a fourth, and so on as a customizer would. That's why it's always a plus when a manufacturer makes the majority of its parts in-house. Some of the major alternative manufacturers include Big Dog, American Ironhorse, Bourget's, Ultra, and Thunder Mountain.

Unlike custom builders, these guys manufacture from several dozen to several thousand machines a year, so you can be assured that they have some experience with raking a fork, mounting a wide tire, and much more. You can walk into a showroom, discuss what you want and perhaps take a test ride. Instead of waiting months, you may be able to ride off on your custom-look bike immediately. Because these machines are from actual manufacturers, there should be no problem financing, insuring, or licensing them. When you wish to sell, well, the NADA Blue Book should help legitimize your asking price.

How do these manufactured bikes vary from those made in Milwaukee? Let me count the ways: Harley won't sell you a rigid, a bike with a 250- or 300-series rear tire, or a stock engine thumping out 100 horsepower from well over 100 cubic inches. H-D doesn't do rake or stretch or

"overs." H-D doesn't do open primaries. The list goes on and on.

Get your Harley crankin' out 85 or 100 horsepower and you may well void the factory warranty—unless you have a Harley Screamin' Eagle kit installed by a dealer. Many of these alternative bikes crank out 100 horses or more while fully covered by factory warranty. In fact, it may actually cost *less* to have a bike done by a manufacturer than to build it up piecemeal yourself, and it will certainly be done in less time.

But you need to be cautious. Around the year 2000, many bike enthusiasts were excited that the renewed Indian and Excelsior-Henderson motorcycle companies were serious efforts cranking out new motorcycles. Each had the advantages of major financial backing and a famous name—yet each failed. Keep this in mind when dealing with small manufacturers. Investigate. Do your research. Talk to owners of the brand. Even the very best warranty won't do you much good if the company goes out of business.

Big Dog is acknowledged as the largest of the alternative V-twin manufacturers and has an extensive line of bikes. Shown is its Pit Bull, a hardtail with a big-inch motor. *Big Dog*

American IronHorse, one of the largest alternative V-twin manufacturers, offers a wide variety of motorcycles. Its Anniversary Texas Chopper is a hidden-shock model with a 38-degree frame rake, four more degrees in the trees, a 124-inch engine, and a 280-series rear tire. *American IronHorse*

Why buy an alternative V-twin rather than an established mainstream brand? Because the mainstream companies don't build radical machines like this Von Dutch Flying Dutchman hardtail chopper. If you really want to knock 'em dead, you'll need something like this. *Von Dutch Kustom Cycles*

CUSTOM MOTORCYCLES

Another possibility is to have a bike built for you by a custom shop. A true one-off involves an extraordinary amount of handwork, and that's going to be expensive. At an alternative V-Twin manufacturer, economies of scale can bring the price much lower than a custom builder can offer. Also, while we usually equate handwork with quality, that quality can vary from one customizer to another.

Order up your custom and prepare to sit back awhile—it will take some months to get it done exactly the way you want it. Once it's done, it may not comply with all the regulations of the U.S. Department of Transportation regarding lighting, brakes, mirrors, and the rest. And it may not comply with the Environmental Protection Agency's dictates regarding noise and exhaust emissions, either. These may not be an

Custom motorcycles can be works of art, like this beauty from Big Inch Bikes Mfg. It is the custom/production bike series from Kim Suter and KC Creations and offers a variety of models. *KC Creations*

IS WIDER BETTER?

The biggest trend in cruisers is fitting ever wider rear tires. At present, the widest tires being manufactured are the monster 330- and 350-series, and we hear that larger ones are coming!

No stock motorcycle can handle such a meaty tire, as they're too wide to fit within stock wheels and swingams. The biggest tires are being fitted to aftermarket wheels, frames, and swingarms. The 170- and 180-series rears are becoming common on metric cruisers. On any bike it is often possible to fit a tire one size larger than stock, but only if you check with the dealer and carefully evaluate that it will not rub on the swingarm or other parts.

Why are riders fitting ever larger rear tires to their cruisers? Now hear this: Primarily because they're cool! Other than somewhat longer wear and a little more rubber on the road for better grip, there is no practical reason for running rear tires larger than about a 250 series . . . other than possibly winning trophies at bike shows.

Fitting wider rear tires can lead to headaches. On a stock Harley, beyond a certain size, a larger rear tire will crowd the belt final drive and the bike must be converted to chain drive. Getting even wider moves the tire's center point farther left, and the bike becomes unbalanced; the center points of its front and rear tires no longer align. Now the transmission has to be offset to compensate. As a solution, some companies offer right-side-drive kits.

Single-track vehicles turn by leaning. Think of a bicycle with its skinny tires; they're so narrow that the radius (arc) of the tire is very steep. A tiny bit of bike movement corresponds to a great deal of lean. That, combined with the short wheelbase and steep fork rake, causes a bicycle to steer very quickly; it becomes twitchy at high speeds.

Now consider a custom motorcycle with a 9-inch-wide 250-series rear tire. The arc is very shallow, which means it takes a relatively great amount of bike movement to cause it to lean and turn. This, with the accompanying raked-out fork and long wheelbase, results in a bike that steers extremely slowly but is stable at speed.

Rear tires have gotten huge, especially on custom bikes. Now we're seeing 300-, 330-, and 350-series rear tires, and even larger ones may be on the way. *Avon Tyres*

One of the attractions of the alternative V-twin manufacturers is the big-inch engines that they buy from various suppliers. Here's an air-cooled 124-inch V-twin from TP Engineering, available from many alternative manufacturers, that puts out more than 100 horsepower. *TP Engineering*

issue to you, but tell it to the judge if you're ticketed for violations of any of these statutes. At least, however, it should be exactly what you want.

Finally, there's the matter of sympathy. When it comes to financing a one-off custom, is your banker going to be sympathetic when you tell him you want to borrow $25,000 to purchase what he only sees as an outrageously weird motorcycle? ("Hey, it doesn't even have a rear suspension!") Will the Department of Motor Vehicles (DMV) be sympathetic to licensing a "Special Construction" machine that does not seem to comply with many DOT and EPA dictates? Will your insurance agent be sympathetic to the idea that such a spare-looking motorcycle should be insured for $35,000? Finally, when you eventually want to sell it, will potential buyers be sympathetic to the idea that you were really into flaming skulls as a theme, while they actually would prefer teddy bears?

Chapter 5

FEATURES AND OPTIONS

WHAT YOU WILL LEARN

- **What to look for in adjustable motorcycle ergonomics**

- **How anti-lock brakes work and why they're worth having**

- **Motorcycle sound systems**

While you usually can adjust most tube-steel handlebars by rotating them in the handlebar clamp, BMW took a major step forward in 1994 with its R1100RS. This image shows the adjusters that allow the rider to set the angle of each bar separately.

It's an advantage when a motorcycle offers ergonomic adjustability in its handlebars, levers, seat, and more.

Let's take a look at features that are built into some motorcycle models, and may be optional on others. We'll consider what each does, and its potential benefits.

ADJUSTABLE ERGONOMICS
Motorcycles are generally designed and built for a universal Everyman, one who is of a certain range of height and weight, whose arms, legs, and fingers are of a certain length, and whose torso covers a predetermined span. Obviously, all of us are built differently, so it's an advantage when a motorcycle offers ergonomic adjustability in its handlebars, levers, seat, and more.

Handlebars
On motorcycles with tubular handlebars, the bars can be adjusted slightly by loosening the handlebar clamps and rotating the bars forward or back. When they feel like

they're in the right place, turn the fork from lock to lock and make sure the cables and hoses don't bind. Then tighten the clamps securely and ride on.

On a few bikes, the individual handlebars themselves are adjustable for height and/or angle. Again, be certain cables and hoses don't bind and bolts are properly torqued after adjustment.

Levers
If you've ever ridden a bike on which you could not reach the clutch and brake levers comfortably, you understand how important this seemingly minor consideration can be. If a lever is too far away, you must stretch your fingers to grasp it, reducing your grip strength and costing you reaction time. On the other hand, if it's too close, it can get in the way as you move your fingers from grip to lever. Also, if a lever is adjusted too close

to the grip, it could pinch whatever fingers you may have left on the grip.

Some bikes offer an adjustment wheel (about the size of a nickel) near the pivot point of one or both levers. The wheel will have several numbers (usually 1 through 4 or 5) around its circumference that correspond to its various settings. To adjust the lever, push it away from the grip, rotate the wheel to another setting, release the lever, and see if it feels right. Be certain the lever has seated in its adjustment slot. By cycling through the various settings, you will appreciate the full range of adjustment.

Shift Lever

If your toe barely fits under the shift lever, or if there's too much clearance and you have to lift your foot too high to shift, it's usually possible to adjust the shift lever. In most cases, the shift lever fits over a splined rod that projects from the transmission.

To mark the original position, use a pencil to draw a line across the end of the rod and onto the lever. Remove the bolt that secures the lever, and pull the lever outward (some wiggling may be necessary) till it comes free. Clean the lever and its splines, and reposition it on the rod by one or two teeth in the proper direction; use your pencil mark as a guide. Sit on the bike and compare the new position with the old. Adjust accordingly. When you're happy

with the new setting, replace the bolt that secures the rod and tighten accordingly.

Footpegs

A very few bikes come with adjustable footpegs; consult your owner's manual for specific instructions on adjusting them. Other bikes (but by no means all) have pegs that can be adjusted. Some of them utilize a serrated piece on each footpeg; the pegs can be loosened, pulled outward, and rotated to fit into a new tooth on the peg. In any case, if you adjust the pegs, it will then be necessary to reposition the shift lever and brake pedal accordingly.

Seats

One of the most daunting aspects of learning to ride a motorcycle is keeping it upright, especially when the bike is heavy and your legs are relatively short. Several manufacturers, including BMW, Honda, and a few others, offer models on which seat height is adjustable.

Adjusting seat height usually involves removing it by turning the ignition key in the seat lock and pulling the seat upward. Then, the adjusters on the seat base can be placed in any of two or three sets of receptors on the bike. The range of seat adjustment is usually about an inch or slightly more, depending on the model. For any such adjustments, always check your owner's manual.

For reasons of style and comfort, you may wish to order an aftermarket seat for your bike. This one can be added to Triumph's Rocket III. *Triumph Motorcycles America*

One of the most daunting aspects of learning to ride a motorcycle is keeping it upright

Some sport-touring bikes, such as this BMW K1200LT, offer an electrically-adjustable windshield. Push a button and the shield can be placed anywhere within the range of the low and high positions shown. At the lowest position the rider can get some breeze on a warm day; at the highest there is near total coverage for the upper body and helmet. *BMW of North America*

Locking the front brake will often put the bike down very quickly.

Here is some of the equipment involved in BMW's anti-lock braking system. When the brakes at either end approach lockup, the system releases hydraulic pressure to that brake then restores it immediately, pulsing in this manner many times per second until traction is restored. *BMW of North America*

Adjustable Windshields

Depending on your height and how much wind you want to feel, you may wish to change the height or angle of the windshield.

On a manually adjusted windshield, the rider pulls a pair of levers (while the motorcycle is stationary), moves the shield to the desired position, then locks the levers back down to secure the shield. On the BMW R1100/R1150 RS series, the rider pushes in a knob that then pops out when released; by rotating the knob, the rider sets the angle of the shield.

The real luxury of this class is the electrically adjustable windshield, which is available on some BMW, Honda ST1300, and Yamaha FJR1300 models. On them, the rider presses a button that activates a servomotor, which slowly raises and lowers the shield.

If your motorcycle doesn't have an adjustable windshield, you might look into whether different windshield sizes are available. If they are, you can tailor your wind protection qualities by replacing the windshield.

BRAKING OPTIONS
Anti-Lock Brake Systems

One of the most common accident situations in motorcycling is when the rider brakes too hard for traction conditions, locks one or both of the brakes, and loses control. While most of us have successfully ridden out a locked rear brake slide, locking the front brake will often put the bike down very quickly.

To neutralize this situation, some bike manufacturers have developed anti-lock braking systems (ABS) that prevent lockup. These systems are built into the bike and have been offered on certain models by BMW, Ducati, Honda, Kawasaki, Suzuki, and Yamaha. Here's a simplified explanation of how they work.

On most motorcycle systems, a device resembling a gear is mounted on or near the brake disc, and it rotates with the wheel. A sensor paired with this device "counts" the pulses as the "teeth" rotate past. If wheel rotation suddenly slows too quickly, signaling impending lockup, the sensor signals the computer and ABS immediately releases hydraulic pressure on that brake, then immediately restores it. This can happen more than 30 times per second as the system continues to monitor rotation and speed, and calculates the likelihood of lockup. In this way the system maintains braking force as long as the operator applies braking pressure, but does not allow the wheel to lock.

ABS is a major benefit when braking on wet, sandy, or otherwise uncertain surfaces. However, it is effective only when the bike is relatively straight up and down,

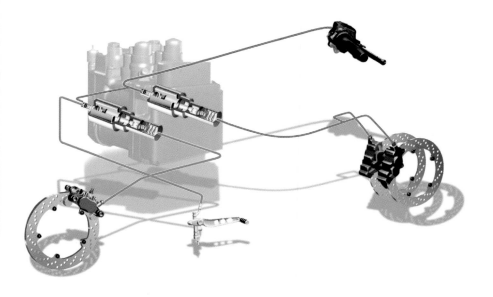

and will not necessarily save your bacon when the bike is leaned over. As the bike slows to around 2 miles per hour with the brakes still applied, ABS will shut off to prevent the bike from rolling endlessly on a really slippery surface.

On models on which ABS is optional, it will cost around $1,000 and add around 25 pounds to the motorcycle. That's about the weight of four gallons of gasoline. While $1,000 is a significant amount of money, one has to balance this against the fact that, if it saves the rider from a single fall in the bike's lifetime, it has probably paid for itself in terms of preventing cosmetic damage to the bike and riding gear. Add in the possibility of saving the rider from injury—or worse—and its benefits multiply rather quickly. Finally, some insurance companies offer lower rates for bikes with ABS.

Linked Braking Systems

Safety researchers learned long ago that one of the major factors in motorcycle accidents is a rider perceiving a hazardous situation, then overutilizing the rear brake and underutilizing the front. As a result, the rider locks the rear brake and throws the bike into a sideways skid. It's not hard to understand why, as the leg muscles that activate the rear brake are much more powerful than the hand muscles that activate the front.

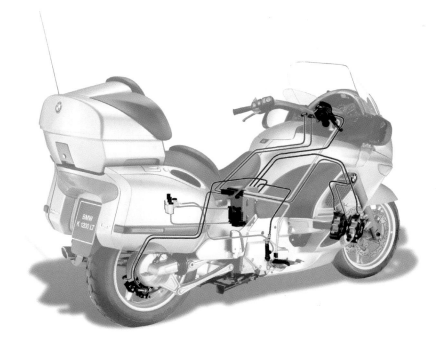

In an attempt to address this situation, some manufacturers (notably BMW, Honda, and Moto Guzzi) have offered a few models with linked braking systems (LBS), in which the brakes are linked together front and rear. In the system used on the Honda ST1300, each of its three disc brakes has a three-piston caliper. Pulling the front brake lever actuates the outer two pistons on each front brake caliper, and the middle piston of the rear caliper. Hitting the rear brake pedal actuates the two outer pistons on the rear disc,

On Honda's linked braking system, applying either the hand lever or foot pedal actuates the brakes at both ends of the bike. On the BMW system (shown), applying the hand lever actuates the front and rear brakes. However, applying the foot pedal only actuates the rear brake; it's not linked to the front. *BMW of North America*

IS BRAKING SAFELY WORTH IT?

One of the most common questions I'm asked by riders is if ABS is worth having. Some view it as a crutch, and say a skilled rider can probably stop in a shorter distance without ABS than with it. In my estimation, ABS is worth having. I consider myself to be a skilled rider, and have found myself in situations when I was glad I had it.

Once, in Pennsylvania, I was riding along a slippery bituminous-surfaced road when an ambulance decided to cross from a side road in a big hurry. I heard the siren late, was taken by surprise, and suddenly realized I would

have a difficult time stopping—until I remembered the bike had ABS. I simply nailed the brakes, and the result was a safe, secure stop.

Under controlled testing conditions, it may be possible for a skilled rider to out-brake an ABS system on a slippery surface. However, we don't normally ride under controlled testing conditions. I seriously doubt that, when the ambulance suddenly intrudes into his world, the skilled rider could stop in a shorter distance without ABS than with it. If ABS saves you from falling down one time in the life of the motorcycle, it has certainly paid for itself.

Safety researchers learned long ago that one of the major factors in motorcycle accidents is a rider perceiving a hazardous situation, then overutilizing the rear brake and underutilizing the front.

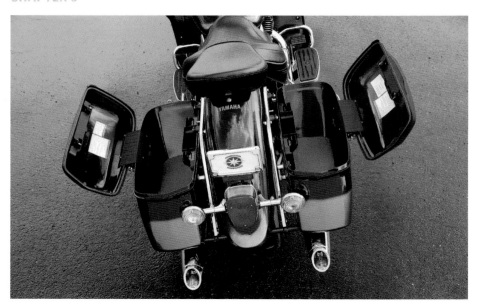

Fixed luggage gives a bike a more integrated look and often holds more than removable bags. These bags come with Yamaha's Venture touring cruiser. *Yamaha Motor Corp., USA*

THROTTLE LOCK

Don't confuse a true cruise control with a throttle lock, which is often incorrectly referred to as the former. A throttle lock is a mechanical device that screws into the end of the throttle or up from below the throttle grip. It introduces sufficient friction drag to overcome the return spring, so the throttle will no longer rotate closed when the rider removes his hand from the grip.

The throttle lock is basically a poor man's cruise control, as it will maintain the throttle setting, but will not compensate for hills or headwinds. Furthermore, it is essential that the rider dial in only enough friction to barely overcome the return spring. The rider should be able to easily override the throttle lock.

and the center piston on each of the front discs. The amount of braking pressure is regulated by a proportional control valve, which always sends more force to the brake that was actuated with the most force by the rider.

BMW, on the other hand, uses full and partial integration on various models. Their fully integrated systems work similarly to the Honda system, in which utilizing either control operates the brakes at both ends. With partial integration, however, the system is linked only front to rear. Actuating the front-brake lever also applies the rear brake. The rear-brake pedal actuates only the rear brake.

"Power" Brakes

At this time, only BMW offers servo-assisted brakes, which are to motorcycles what power brakes are to cars. Both front calipers feature an electric servo-assist mechanism. The early version, on the R1150-series bikes, was generally considered to be too powerful and to lack precise modulation; the later version, starting with the R1200 series, is more similar to conventional braking systems in feel. It is powerful and well controlled, but without the former system's grabbiness.

CRUISE CONTROL

The Cruise Control is an electro-mechanical device built into some bikes that allows

the motorcycle to maintain whatever speed the rider chooses. It allows the rider to relax on long stretches of road and move his hand away from the throttle. After the cruise control is turned on, it can be set by pushing a button when the desired speed is reached. Additional controls allow the rider to fine-tune the speed. The bike will maintain the set speed, regardless of hills or wind conditions. The cruise control can be overridden when the rider taps either brake, pulls in the clutch, or operates the throttle.

HARD LUGGAGE

If you do much traveling, or take overnight trips, hard luggage is a must—especially if you travel with a passenger. Hard luggage may be fixed (bolted to the bike), as on a dresser tourer, or the bags may be easily removable, as is common on a sport tourer. Always follow your bike manufacturer's loading recommendations; overloading your luggage can lead to handling irregularities.

Saddlebags are the basic luggage carriers. They fit along the sides of the bike and place the weight between the axles and down toward the center of gravity, where it belongs. Some bikes also carry a travel trunk, which sits on a horizontal rack behind the passenger portion of the seat.

Hard luggage is usually made of fiberglass or heavy plastic. Because they're lockable and not easily cut or broken into, hard bags are much more secure than soft bags. Provided they seal well, hard bags will also keep your luggage dry. They usually last as long as the bike, unlike soft luggage, and can be repaired if damaged. As they're usually color-matched to the bike, they provide an impressive, integrated appearance. Should your bike fall over, hard saddlebags will absorb some of the impact and may even prevent some cosmetic damage to the bike.

Fixed Saddlebags

Fixed luggage refers to bags that are permanently mounted to the motorcycle and are not designed to be removed easily. They're

Should your bike fall over, hard saddlebags will absorb some of the impact and may even prevent some cosmetic damage to the bike.

usually large and hold a great deal, and may have a framework of protective guards on the outside to prevent scrapes if the bike tips over. Sometimes the bags or guards incorporate additional lighting for added style and visibility. Keep in mind that hard bags are quite heavy, and will affect the bike's performance and fuel mileage, whether they're loaded or not.

One drawback of fixed bags is that, on some dressers, one or both of them must be removed (along with their bracketry) in order to change a rear tire. This can add several additional hours of shop labor to a tire change. If this is necessary on your bike, and you're handy with tools, you might consider removing your bags prior to taking in the bike. Of course, having fixed bags also means fixing a rear flat on the road is going to take some time and considerable effort.

Removable Saddlebags

On many sport-touring motorcycles, the hard saddlebags can be unlocked from the bike and removed with the turn of a key. They have handles for easy carrying, and some also offer liner bags for convenience. Removable hard saddlebags tend to be lighter than fixed bags, and can be left home when you don't need them. On some bikes, the brackets are unobtrusive or can also be removed, so they don't detract from the bike's looks. Finally, more attention is being paid to saddlebag styling, so most bikes look good whether the bags are on or off. Because they are designed to be removed, you should inspect their brackets,

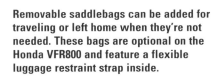

Removable saddlebags can be added for traveling or left home when they're not needed. These bags are optional on the Honda VFR800 and feature a flexible luggage restraint strap inside.

TIP

Imagine how inconvenient it would be to make endless trips from the house to the bike, carrying clothing, toiletries, and other small items out to your fixed hard luggage. Instead, most motorcycle companies offer saddlebag liners, which are lightweight nylon or cloth bags shaped to match the inner contours of the saddlebags and trunk. Pack your gear in these removable liners at home, and then stuff them into the saddlebags.

Here's a saddlebag liner at work. It was packed somewhere else, then carried to the bike and put into the saddlebag. Available for most fixed luggage, they're handy for removable bags, too. *Triumph Motorcycles America*

If a luggage rack can be mounted to a bike, a travel trunk can usually be mounted to the rack as an option. Here's a shot of a Ducati with optional travel trunk. *Ducati North America Inc.*

Harley-Davidson's newer Electra Glides can be ordered with a sophisticated sound system that can include an AM/FM radio, CB radio, satellite radio, and CD player. Tuning controls are near the grips, where the rider can operate them with his thumbs. *Harley-Davidson Motor Co.*

hardware, and locks regularly to be certain that everything is in secure working order.

Travel Trunks

Some big dresser tourers come with a travel trunk, which often has enough capacity to rival or exceed that of either saddlebag. With their large, lift-up lids, they're very convenient to use and are sometimes equipped with lights for greater visibility. Note that if the trunk opens from the side, the passenger may not have to dismount in order to access what's inside. If the trunk lid pivots forward, however, the passenger will

usually have to either lean way forward or dismount to get out of the way.

SOUND SYSTEMS

Many dressers are equipped with sound systems, but the problem is that motorcycles have notoriously lousy acoustics because of wind and other ambient noise. Sound systems are more practical when fairings and windshields block some of the wind.

Sun, wind, rain, and vibration all play havoc with sensitive sound systems, so it is imperative your components be well sealed from the elements. If your bike did not come with one from the factory, after-market sound systems are available. Be certain to use high-quality components specifically designed for motorcycle use. And, regardless of your sound system, for safety's sake be certain to always stay focused on the road.

Radio

AM/FM radio is the most basic type of sound system. It keeps you in touch with local weather and traffic conditions, but you're at the mercy of reception quality, which changes as you ride.

Satellite radio is now available for motorcycles. It not only offers a wealth of

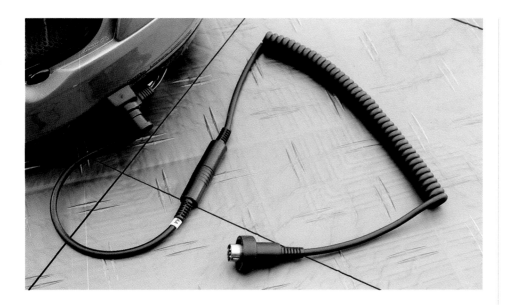

How obtrusive is a set of helmet speakers in a sound system? Not much at all. In fact, what you see in this shot is the only thing that shows outside the helmet: the attachment cord and helmet hookup.

specific channels, but also should not fade with distance because the signal comes from a satellite.

Cassette Tape Players

While stereo cassette tape players solve the problem of hearing what you want to hear when you want to hear it, they are now considered old technology, and are being replaced by compact disc (CD) players. Cassette tapes function best in a clean environment, and are susceptible to dirt and wear. Handle and store them with care, and keep your system as clean as possible.

Compact Disc Players

CDs are like tiny records played by a laser beam instead of a needle, and can skip when the bike hits a bump. Because only a beam of light touches the disc's surface under normal circumstances, it should not be harmed by a minimal amount of bouncing. However, severe bumps may cause the disc to contact something hard, which can damage it. The greater potential problem is that the delicate internal workings of the CD player itself may suffer in an environment that includes extreme temperature changes, dust, and vibration.

MP3 Players

MP3 players can also be plugged into some sound systems.

Citizens Band Radios

CB radios have a range of several miles, and allow the operator to both talk and listen. They're especially useful for learning about road, weather, and traffic conditions, fuel availability, the location of radar units (speed traps), and where to find the best food. CBs are now being used by guided motorcycle tour operators to provide a running commentary about the scenery and historic sights.

CB radios are offered both as standard and optional equipment on some dresser motorcycles, and as accessories through dealers. It's important to select a CB specifically designed for motorcycle use, as they provide better weather and vibration resistance than non-motorcycle units.

Helmet Speakers and Microphones

Helmet speakers are the best means of overcoming wind and other ambient noise to hear well while riding. They often mount under the helmet's comfort liner with hook-and-loop fasteners, and are quite light. Factory sound systems can usually be switched back and forth to put the sound through helmet or dashboard speakers.

Note: Check local laws regarding the legality of using speakers inside your helmet.

Microphones are available that attach either inside the chinbar of a full-face

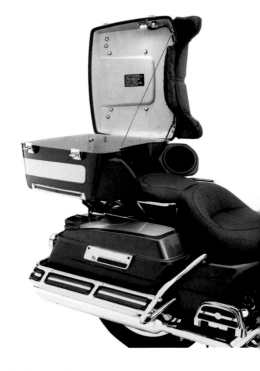

An integral travel trunk on a dresser helps give the bike a more complete look and usually holds more than an add-on trunk. *Harley-Davidson Motor Co.*

Heated grips and seats are a true luxury on a cool day, especially when they offer more than one setting. This is the Sun Ray Heated Seat, an option Harley-Davidson offers. *Harley-Davidson Motor Co.*

Regardless of your sound system, for safety's sake be certain to always stay focused on the road.

The oil-sight glass makes it easy to check engine oil level. Do so in the morning when the engine is cold, as the oil will have drained back down into the crankcase and will give a more accurate reading. Before checking, set the bike level on its centerstand or have a friend hold it level. This bike's oil level is right up to the maximum.

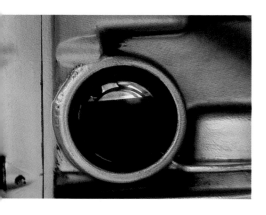

helmet, or on a stalk mounted on an open-face helmet. These can be used as part of an intercom system.

Intercoms

These systems allow the rider and passenger to speak directly to each other via microphones and helmet speakers. They are hard wired together, and are a major improvement over shouting in the wind.

Some dressers include them as part of their sound systems; they're also available as accessory units independent of the bike and powered by their own batteries. The better systems will have separate volume controls for rider and passenger, and they usually work well. Use independent systems judiciously, as leaving them on constantly will shorten battery life.

The drawback for any hard-wired system is that it must be unplugged each time riders dismount, so check that they have sturdy plugs and the wires are not susceptible to tangling while in use.

Cell Phones

It is now possible to plug a cell phone into a sound system so it can be used hands-free.

Radar Detectors

If you wish to run a radar detector, its audible warning signal can also be wired into a speaker system.

49 Megahertz

This bike-to-bike system is similar to the CB radio, but it operates on a 49-megahertz frequency and is powered by AA batteries. Effective range is only about 2/10 of a mile, in line of sight only. They're designed for two or more bikes traveling together and riding within a few hundred feet of each other. Depending upon bike, helmet, and wind conditions, the 49MHz systems tend to be overwhelmed by wind noise at higher speeds. They're also useful for keeping in touch with the rest of your group when you're not on the bikes, but, say, walking around a rally.

Family Radio

These sporty, hand-held, walkie-talkie-type radios are popular because of their broad range of use for hunting, fishing, hiking, skiing, etc., and have come to be known as "family" radios. In my experience they can be adapted quite successfully to motorcycle use when teamed with the proper helmet speakers and push-to-talk equipment. They offer a range of about 2 miles over varied terrain, including around corners. When the ride is over, the additional equipment can be unplugged and hand held for camping and other uses.

OTHER NICETIES
Heated Grips/Seats

Heated handgrips are one of the greatest luxuries in all of motorcycling.

Only a few bike manufacturers and aftermarket companies offer them, but I recommend them highly. Not only do heated grips keep your hands warm, but that warmed blood circulating through the rest of your body will keep you slightly warmer overall.

Lighter, thinner gloves are often more comfortable and offer a better feel for the controls than warmer, heavier gloves. Heated grips make it possible to wear lighter gloves comfortably in cooler temperatures. As for the question of whether I prefer heated grips or electrically heated gloves, I would go with the gloves. Not only are the gloves portable from bike to bike (once the battery lead is installed), but they also offer greater warmth, because they also heat the backs of your hands and insulate better.

At this writing, only BMW offers a heated seat, and only on select models. It's a nice luxury on a cold day. Some aftermarket seat manufacturers also offer optional heating.

Hydraulic Centerstand

As of this writing, only the late-model BMW K1200LT offers this innovation. When the rider is ready to park the bike, he has the option of deploying the side-stand conventionally, or using the hydraulic centerstand. After determining the bike is on a relatively solid, level surface, the rider pushes a button to deploy the stand.

There is a slight whirring, the bike momentarily rocks and stabilizes, then lifts (even with riders and luggage aboard) and settles into a parked position. The hydraulic centerstand is recommended for heavier or loaded bikes, and spares the rider the potential back pain of trying to raise it by hand.

Oil Sight Glass

One of the most critical maintenance factors is monitoring your bike's oil supply. It's easy to overlook this task if your bike only has a dipstick, as it can be a messy job and the bike should be level—which is more difficult when the bike has no centerstand. Many bikes have an oil sight glass built into the side of the crankcase, through which the oil supply can be viewed. Place the bike on both wheels or the centerstand as level and upright as possible, then make sure the oil supply is between the high and low marks beside the sight glass.

Electric Reverse

Anyone who has parked his bike in a forward-sloping spot, then found it difficult to walk the bike backward out of it, can appreciate the benefit of an electric reverse. It's easy to use, and standard on the Honda Gold Wing and some BMW K-LT models. To operate it, the rider shifts to neutral (with the engine running) and deploys a lever to engage reverse. Pushing the starter button now activates the starter motor in the reverse direction, which sends the bike backward at a very low speed. When the bike is positioned properly, the rider disengages the reverse lever and can ride away.

Not only do heated grips keep your hands warm, but that warmed blood circulating through the rest of your body will keep you slightly warmer overall.

If you've ever nosed a heavy bike into a parking space that slopes downhill, then tried to push it back out, you know why electric reverse is a good thing. It works by engaging the starter motor with the transmission and reversing the starter motor's rotation. This illustration shows the starter interfacing with the transmission on a BMW K1200LT. *BMW of North America*

MOTORCYCLE ACCESSORIES

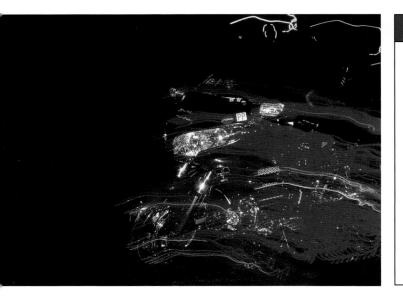

WHAT YOU WILL LEARN

- Things to add to your streetbike

- What electrical accessories are available

- How and why to change seats, pegs and bars

- Types of luggage and how to pack

Decorative auxiliary lighting (such as on this Honda Gold Wing) can really dress up a bike at night. I took this photo at the light show at the Americade rally in upstate New York by panning across a parked bike with the shutter open, then actuating the flash.

Once you buy a bike,

it's time to get serious

about making it yours.

Once you buy a bike, it's time to get serious about making it yours, personalizing it, making it do the job you want it to do more precisely. The aftermarket offers thousands of items for motorcycles, any of which can make the bike more functional or highly styled. Here's a quick rundown of some of the items you may wish to consider adding to your bike.

ELECTRICAL ACCESSORIES
Auxiliary Lighting
Lighting can be decorative, functional, or both. Decorative lighting includes such items as strip lights (low-wattage lights designed to make the motorcycle more visible or to decorate it, rather than to project illumination so the rider can see farther down the road) and neon. Decorative lighting tends to be so specialized it's beyond the scope of this book. However, let's delve a bit into functional lighting.

Motorcycles lean when they corner, which creates all sorts of illumination problems. Headlight bulbs come with shields over them that are designed as a cutoff to prevent the light from blinding oncoming motorists. The problem is, when motorcycles lean into left turns, they are essentially riding into the blind spot created by this cutoff.

Pencil beam driving lamps send a well-focused beam of light a long way ahead, and are best for use on relatively quiet, straight roads in the countryside. Wide beams, or "floods," pour light into the near area to supplement the low beam. They're useful for spotting gravel, potholes, and oil, and they help fill in that blind spot in turns. Other lights are for medium-range illumination.

Many cruising riders favor light bars for added functional lighting. The additional lights flanking the headlight can function as passing lamps and provide additional long-range illumination on lonely roads.

For many years, the typical headlight offered a parabolic reflector and fluted lens that spread the light to the sides. Though clear lenses with faceted reflectors are becoming popular, these more traditional headlights will likely remain on traditionally styled cruisers. *Triumph Motorcycles America*

Halogen and Xenon

Back in the late 1970s and early 1980s quartz-halogen lights became all the rage, and soon became standard equipment on cars and motorcycles. They offered a much brighter, whiter light when compared with the weak, yellowish sealed-beam headlights, as they burned at a higher temperature. They utilize sealed bulbs filled with an inert halogen gas that, when excited by electricity, allow the filament to glow brightly but not burn. The quartz glass lenses are designed to handle the additional heat they generate.

A generation later, the new technology is xenon HID (high-intensity discharge) lights. HID lamps utilize an arc of electricity passing between two anodes (rather than a filament) housed in a bulb filled with xenon gas. Xenon gas is used for its ability to promote ignition very quickly; without it, an HID light would not reach operating luminosity for several minutes. These lights can be quite expensive.

An HID light with xenon bulb may provide more than twice as much light as a modern H7 halogen bulb. The color temperature (often perceived in the blue scale) of the light emitted by the xenon bulb is more similar to daylight, which is why they appear blue to oncoming traffic. Because an HID light requires a lot of

voltage to initiate the arc, it has a ballast that must be located near the bulb. While it may put out 2 1/2 times as much light as a halogen, the xenon light will actually use a little less power (depending upon application) to maintain the arc.

Please note that optics are designed to fit a given light source, so do not attempt to place xenon HID lighting systems in housings and lenses designed for standard halogen bulbs, or to modify xenon bulbs to fit in these housings. Such conversions would change the photometrics. So long as the entire lighting unit is changed together (light source, reflector, and lens), all should be well.

Another major trend in headlights, for both autos and motorcycles, is to run clear lenses with faceted reflectors rather than the fluted, prismed lenses with parabolic reflectors of recent times. The fluting in a lens is designed to direct and disperse the light, but when light is bent in this manner, it loses some of its power and whiteness. A faceted reflector with clear lens can better direct and spread the light, which results in greater focus, power, and whiteness. More of the light energy reaches the road.

Most state laws require that driving lights be mounted no higher than the headlight, as lights mounted high tend to reflect back into the rider's eyes in foggy

TIP

Auxiliary functional lights not only illuminate the road, but also make your bike more visible to others. They can allow other motorists to get a better "read" on your speed and location, which helps with depth perception at night, making it less likely they'll pull out in front of you.

Xenon HID (high-intensity discharge) lights and fog lights are both available for motorcycles. They're easy to mount, look good, and add a degree of function and safety. *Triumph Motorcycles America*

When engineers learned that headlight fluting reduced illumination, they began offering clear lenses with faceted reflectors. Here is such a lens on a BMW K1200S. *BMW of North America*

SHEDDING LIGHT ON XENON

Now that xenon has become a buzzword equated with brighter headlights, beware of imitators. Some bargain basement companies offer xenon-filled halogen-style filament bulbs to which a blue film has been applied. They are marketed as xenon bulbs, and while this may be technically correct, it is misleading. These bulbs will produce no more light than a standard halogen, and often less because of the blue coating.

conditions. Mounting areas abound: fairings, light bars, crash bars, the fork, mirror stems, engine cases. Do not mount lights too far outboard, where they can be damaged in a tip-over.

Most companies that offer auxiliary lighting provide brackets for them, but often only for specific models. Honda Gold Wings, BMWs, and other sport tourers are popular, but for other models you may have to get creative.

GPS

Why should car drivers have all the fun with Global Positioning System (GPS) receivers? A network of satellites sends signals to the earth that are received by GPS units, and, through triangulation, the units can pinpoint their exact position to within a few feet. They're handy for directing a rider to an address and can help find gas stations, restaurants, motels, or pretty much anything else. Dirt riders and adventure tourers can rely on them for finding their way out of the boondocks.

Heated Grips and Seats

The first time I tried a bike with heated handgrips, I was sold. Not only are they a comfort on a cold day, but they're also a safety factor, as they allow the rider more precise control of the throttle, front brake, and clutch levers. Heated grips allow the rider to wear lighter gloves, which enhances feel for the controls. At this time, some manufacturers offer heated

POWER DRAW

Because a pair of auxiliary halogen lights will likely add maybe 70 to 100 watts of draw to your electrical system, they will not likely present a power problem for modern motorcycles. Try not to use them for long periods at low speeds, or in conjunction with heated garments. Xenon lights, however, often draw less power than the lights they replace. If in doubt, ask your dealer.

grips either stock, or as an option. They're also available from the aftermarket.

Look for heated grips that offer at least two (high and low) temperature settings to allow for changing weather conditions, and in which the heating elements are built into the grips themselves. Add-ons that install over the existing grips not only make the grips much larger, but also can potentially slide or rotate, lessening control.

Security

The characteristics that make motorcycles so desirable, their lightness and simplicity, work against them in terms of security. Motorcycles and their luggage are, by their very nature, vulnerable to theft. Because of their openness, there is little you can do to fully protect your bike from a determined thief. However, by doing enough, you can discourage a thief who is less than determined.

The two issues here are how to discourage the theft of items from the motorcycle, and also how to discourage the theft of the motorcycle itself. Anything that slows a thief and exposes him to detection is a discouragement to his slimy operation. Park in a well-lit area with lots of foot traffic.

In a city, a toll parking garage improves your chances. If there's a toll taker, ask permission to park your bike in his or her sight.

Soft luggage strapped to a bike is absurdly easy to steal, which is one reason I suggest using lockable hard cases, if available. If you must use soft luggage, try to conceal the buckles from the mounting system under the body of the bags. Use a tether on a magnetic tank bag. Better yet, if you're parking at a specific place where your bike will not be in view, remove the soft luggage and carry it with you. Your most

Where the heck are we? If you've ever wondered this, perhaps you need a GPS system. GPS systems will tell you where you are and even where to go if you program in your destination. *BMW of North America*

Why should car drivers have all the fun with GPS receivers?

Left: To discourage the theft of your bike, utilize the fork lock along with a second lock. If you can't lock the bike to a solid object, consider passing a case-hardened lock through the rear wheel. A Kryptonite U-lock keeps this Harley where it belongs.

Right: If you don't trust locks alone, consider an alarm. This photo shows an alarm that has been mounted under the motorcycle's seat. It's a rather bulky item, but installation isn't difficult. An alarm with pager is worth considering—so long as it isn't prone to giving false alarms.

This aftermarket Corbin seat is not only made of leather, but also offered with rider and passenger backrests

An alternative to a custom seat is a sheepskin or gel pad over the stock seat. A sheepskin provides increased comfort and allows air to circulate, virtually eliminating perspiration. The Comfort Max Gel Pad shown includes a Viscoelastic molded gel cushion that's been placed inside an Australian sheepskin cover. *American Motorcycle Specialties*

Your passenger deserves a backrest. Without it, he or she has to maintain constant muscle tension, which can be tiring. This Hondaline backrest for the VTX1800 includes an optional rack for carrying small items.

valuable items (passport, laptop, journal, itinerary) should come with you.

To discourage theft of the bike itself, utilize locks and alarms. Neither will protect your bike from a determined thief, but again may cause him to shuffle off, looking for easier prey. As a first line of defense, always use the fork lock. When possible, lock the bike to a solid object such as a lamppost, tree, or bench with a sturdy, case-hardened chain and lock. Most bike chains are available in a plastic sleeve that prevents them from scratching the bike. Try to mount the chain high and taut so it does not lie on the ground, as thieves who use bolt cutters will want to place the tool on the ground and stand on the handle for additional leverage.

A bike alarm should be mounted in whatever location will allow it to be heard, and protect it from tampering. Under the seat is the preferred location, where the alarm will be out of sight and out of mind till a thief learns it's there the hard way.

Some alarms have a "warn-off" signal, something like an electronic growl that is activated when the bike is jostled or moved slightly. If the warn-off is triggered several times within a certain time period, the full alarm will sound.

The characteristics that make motorcycles so desirable, their lightness and simplicity, work against them in terms of security.

Other desirable alarm features include an ignition disabler that automatically disables the ignition until a code is entered, and a pager that sends a signal to a hand-held device to alert the owner that the bike is being tampered with.

SEATS, PEGS, AND BARS
Aftermarket Seats

Each stock motorcycle seat is built within a budget to fit a universal rear end. There's a pretty good chance that your rear end is not universal. If that's the case, the stock seat probably won't fit you ideally. Also, it will look like everyone else's stock seat. If you wish to make your bike look like *your* bike, an aftermarket seat is also a styling touch.

In selecting an aftermarket seat, set your priorities. Define why you want a different seat. If it hurts to ride the stock seat, you definitely need to look toward comfort. Do you want just a solo seat, or will you carry a passenger? Do you want it thin and low-profile for a custom look, or wide, dished, and well padded for comfortable touring? If you're already having problems reaching the ground, you will definitely want to specify a thinner, lower seat. Often, a shorter rider will be better able to reach the ground if the seat tapers at the front. Seats range from the all-comfort, mega-mile touring seats to the knock-your-boots-off, high-styled customs you won't want to ride for more than five miles at a time . . . and everything in between.

Aftermarket Seats Versus Custom Seats

If you go to your dealer or shop through a catalog and buy a mass-produced, aftermarket seat, you may be treating yourself to exactly the same kinds of problems that caused you to want to replace your seat in the first place. Most seat manufacturers will happily build you a custom seat, but will need your input. Seats can be matched to your height, weight, inseam, and other needs, and can accommodate special prob-

---

TIP

The alarm is only as effective as its electrical supply. It may attach directly to the battery, or have its own independent power source. In either case, mount the alarm in such a way that it is difficult or impossible for its electrical connection to be severed.

---

lems. If you're short, for example, and have trouble getting your feet to the ground, the front of the seat can be narrowed. If your stock seat is too firm or too spongy, the manufacturer can custom blend the foam

Forward foot controls like these can add both style and comfort to a cruiser. These outrageous Flame controls are by Aeromach and designed for a Yamaha Road Star. *Aeromach*

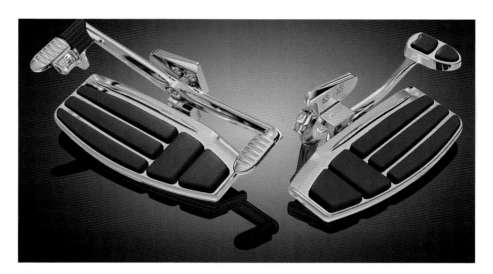

Forward controls don't necessarily have to be radically styled. These items by Kuryakyn offer a custom look, yet their style is subdued. *Kuryakyn*

HOW SEATS ARE MADE

Seats are based upon a pan, or baseplate, that may be made of steel, fiberglass, or plastic. A heavy rider who complains that his seat is squirmy should note the composition of the baseplate.

Seat foam starts as a two-part liquid polymer that is injected into a mold. The firmness can be regulated by varying the proportions of the two chemicals. This foam sets up in about 15 minutes to form the base, and then a layer of sheet foam is usually laid over the top. This dual-density approach allows the seat an initial softness when you sit down, yet it's underlaid with a firm base.

Stock seat covers are made of vinyl, a synthetic material that is durable and stretchy; it requires only soap and water for cleanup, and virtually no other maintenance. Many riders are interested in custom leather seats. Leather can be tooled, stitched, and colored to make a great-looking seat, but it's less stretchy and therefore can feel stiffer than a vinyl-covered seat. Leather absorbs moisture, does not weather well, and (like leather boots and jackets) requires conditioning and care. It's also a whole lot more expensive. Consider these drawbacks before you decide that you need a leather seat.

Another form of foot control is the heel-and-toe shifter. By extending the lever to the rear, the rider has the option of upshifting by either lifting the front lever conventionally with the toe or by pushing down the rear portion with the heel. *Triumph Motorcycles America*

Combining several aftermarket products can produce a dramatic effect. Here's an Aeromach Flame Mirror, Aeromach Knuckle Lever Set, and Pro-One Twisted Rubber Grip.

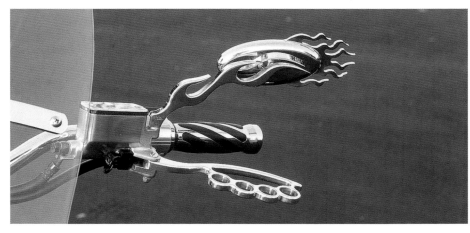

Changing the handlebar is relatively easy, but can have a dramatic effect on both style and comfort. Here's the T-Bar by Cruiser Performance. *Cruiser Performance*

for both you and your passenger. If you're tall and need legroom, your seat can be taller, or you can have the dish area set farther back. Some companies offer a "prostate divot" for men having that need.

One of the hottest items in seats is the so-called "gel" seat. The gel is a visco-elastic substance that feels something like a more solid form of Jell-O. It moves in a similar way and quivers slightly, but won't leak or melt. The idea is that a block of gel inset into a seat eliminates pressure points and conforms to the contour of your, well, you know.

The manufacturers who use gel tell me it allows a given amount of padding to offer greater comfort. Those who don't use it tell me it only works in high-pressure applications, like bicycle seats. They contend that it does not compress, and say that if it were so good you would see it in office, tractor, and other seats. I have ridden on gel seats, and find them a bit firm for my liking.

Seat Cushions

Rather than completely replacing your bike's seat in search of comfort, installing a seat cushion is an inexpensive and potentially more satisfying option. These items strap over the seat and are usually either inflatable or made of some type of gel or foam product. They can be more satisfying, because often there's some adjustment to them (in terms of air pressure), or they're available in various thicknesses or densities.

Drawbacks are that they won't likely be as attractive as your seat, and they'll add some height to what may already be a marginal perch for the rider. However, they are available separately for the rider and passenger, so each can enjoy individual comfort. They're usually black and may be hot in the sun, and inflatables will need some sort of porous covering so they'll breathe.

Backrests

The single most important piece of equipment for keeping a passenger happy is a backrest. Without it, he or she must maintain constant muscle tension, and can never fully relax on the back of your bike. Many bikes have small rear seats, some of which actually slope rearward. With a backrest, the passenger has something against which to lean and relax.

Be certain the backrest is the correct model for your bike, and that it comes with all appropriate hardware. Installation is usually simple and can be done by the home mechanic.

Rider backrests are available, but because the rider usually finds enough support and security by merely hanging onto the grips, they are not as much of a necessity. If your handlebar tilts you back-

Hard, fixed touring luggage integrates well into the bike, both mechanically and stylistically, and usually offers excellent capacity. The Honda GL1800 Gold Wing's bags hold a great deal. Here's the trunk; the bags are hidden below. *American Honda Motor Co.*

TIP

Before changing the handlebars, either remove the fuel tank or pad it with a cover so dropped tools will not damage it. If changing hydraulic lines, note that brake fluid will destroy paint. Cover the tank with a layer of plastic over the padding, and exercise extreme caution.

Triumph's Tiger Adventure model carries an example of removable hard luggage. It locks on and lifts off with the turn of a key. And it's color-matched to the bike. *Triumph Motorcycles America*

ward to the point you've got to struggle against the wind, you may be more comfortable with either a shorter bar or a backrest.

Forward Foot Controls

Forward foot controls have become very popular among cruiser riders. They take the place of stock brake and shift levers, and usually allow the rider to spread out more while adding a bit of chrome up front. Installation will require utilizing a different length of hydraulic line if the rear brake is hydraulically actuated (this will necessitate bleeding the brake), and the installation of different length linkage for the shift mechanism.

Grips and Levers

Most bikes come with perfectly adequate handgrips and clutch and brake levers, but some riders love to change them. Levers are usually changed for style reasons, while grips are also changed for comfort reasons.

Removable hard saddlebags are available for a number of bikes. These are available for the Buell Ulysses. Aftermarket bags that fit a variety of bikes are also available, but those available directly from the OEM (original equipment manufacturer) usually fit on the bike better and are color-matched. *Buell American Motorcycles*

TIP

Many of the aftermarket seat manufacturers offer backrests that are either permanently mounted, or that slip into brackets and are removable. Many of these rider backrests pivot flat so passengers can swing aboard more easily. I have ridden bikes with shorter handlebars and, because of the slight forward lean I found myself in, never actually utilized the rider backrest just behind me. Before you go to the trouble and expense of ordering a rider backrest, be sure it's actually going to do what you wish it to.

The single most important piece of equipment for keeping a passenger happy is a backrest.

As this shot from the Honda Hoot illustrates, riders will travel great distances on all types of motorcycles. The bikes will either have luggage or will need it. If hard luggage is not available, soft luggage certainly is. *American Honda Motor Co.*

Installation is usually quite easy, as only the pivot bolt must be removed to change the levers. Grips are usually held on with adhesive, and sometimes they must be cut to be removed. Another method is to pry an opening between the grip and the bar with a screwdriver, and shoot compressed air into the opening. Once the old grips are off, remove any adhesive residue by scraping or using acetone before applying a thin layer of rubber cement, or whatever the manufacturer specifies. Once the new grips have been pushed on, twist them a little to help spread the adhesive.

Handlebars

Another common change made to bikes is to replace the stock handlebars with an aftermarket unit. This can improve comfort, accommodate a new seat, or change the bike's style. So long as the new handlebars are of the same dimension as the stock unit, the bars should be able to utilize all existing brackets. You'll need to change the grips and reinstall clutch and brake lever housings, but the cables and wiring should not have to be removed or disturbed. If all wiring is external, this should be easy. If wires are routed inside the bars, it will take a little longer. Because the existing grips may have to be cut off, have a new set of grips handy for installation.

If the new handlebars are notably longer or higher than the ones they're replacing, it may be necessary to replace existing cables, wires, and hydraulic lines. This can run into

money and a lot of extra work. If you don't want to go through this, ask the handlebar manufacturer if it will be necessary. If so, you'll need to know how much longer these items will need to be, and order them in advance. Be very sure to tighten the handlebar clamps and other parts well and make certain cables and hoses don't bind, once the new bars are in their final position.

TOURING ACCESSORIES
Luggage (Hard)

For a full discussion of OEM hard luggage that's available with specific models, please see Chapter Five. In this chapter we'll consider aftermarket hard luggage.

Hard luggage offers the advantage of better protection, both in terms of keeping out the weather and in preventing theft. Hard, removable luggage is standard or optional on most BMW models and many Triumphs, and Honda offers such bags for its VFR800. Check with your dealer for availability of such bags for your bike. Aftermarket companies such as Givi also offer hard, removable saddlebags for many bikes. Many manufacturers offer hard bags for cruisers that have the appearance of leather.

If they're available, I suggest you first consider the hard luggage offered by the individual bike manufacturers for their own models. The bags may be styled more

appropriately, color-matched to the bike, and may be fit more tightly. Mounting hardware will likely be more specifically designed for that particular model, and adding factory-recommended bags should not lead to any warranty or handling problems—so long as the rider follows the loading recommendations provided by the manufacturer. Be aware that hard bags may limit access to your bike's rear suspension adjusters, tire valve stem, and helmet locks.

You can find soft luggage that fits virtually any bike. It is easy to mount, holds a lot, and can be quite stylish. When you don't need the luggage, remove it so it's not subject to wear and weather. Roadgear

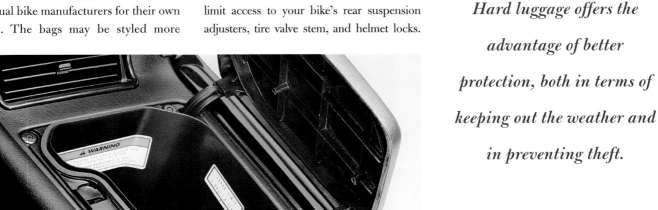

Hard luggage offers the advantage of better protection, both in terms of keeping out the weather and in preventing theft.

A fairing pocket is a great place to carry small items you'll need often such as a tire gauge, shield cleaner and rag, or neck scarf. American Honda Motor Co.

Nylon fabrics can be quite water resistant in themselves, but water can come through the stitch holes and zippers. For this reason get rain covers if they're available. They'll make it more difficult to access the luggage, but at least your stuff will be dry when you do so. Covers also keep filthy road spray off your attractive bags. The alternative is to pack your items in plastic liners inside the luggage, which also makes access difficult and doesn't protect the outside of the bags. *Roadgear*

A strap-on tank bag will fit any bike, but keep the straps tight and the tank waxed so the straps and pad do not scuff the tank. Pack only soft items in a tank bag in case of a frontal collision. While the map pouch is handy, don't let your eyes stray from the road. *Roadgear*

With the bags removed, their brackets may interfere with tire changing.

Luggage (Soft)

An alternative and a supplement to hard luggage is soft luggage bags made usually of pack cloth, Cordura nylon, or similar fabrics. Tank and tail (or "seat") bags can be used in conjunction with hard or soft saddlebags. Soft saddlebags are ideal for smaller bikes, those for which hard luggage is not available, and for riders who like to travel only occasionally. Stiffeners allow them to hold their shape even when empty, and they're often available in black with a variety of trim colors, including red, blue, gray, and others.

Installation is simple. Place them over the back portion of the seat, loop their front straps around the passenger footpegs and the rear around the turn signals, buckle and adjust them, and you're in business. Be very careful to keep them off the exhaust pipes, as the hot pipes can melt soft luggage. The high pipes on many sportbikes make it difficult for them to carry soft saddlebags.

The advantages of soft luggage include their decorative style, their lightness, and their ease of installation. Reach your destination, unbuckle these bags, and carry them off. They're also significantly less expensive than hard saddlebags.

Disadvantages include the fact that others can just as easily remove them, or steal from them. Because the stitches leave holes in the fabric, they'll need a rain cover to protect their contents in the rain—you may also wish to use seam sealer on them. Tank bags and soft saddlebags that rest on painted surfaces can scuff those surfaces over time. Be certain to keep the painted surfaces clean and free of dust, and wax them frequently. Attach the bags tightly so they don't wiggle and rub the bike.

The fabric will eventually fade, and it can tear. Because nylon is a petroleum product, it will melt if it comes in contact with a heat source such as the bike's exhaust system. Be very careful to mount soft saddlebags well away from the exhaust

system, and check them frequently, as their straps can slip or loosen over time.

Expandable soft luggage has an expansion panel of extra material sewn into the body. This panel is folded away behind a zipper when the bag is lightly loaded. When the rider needs extra room, he unzips the zipper and allows this panel (which usually adds about 3 or 4 inches) to come into play.

Tank Bags: A tank bag is a soft luggage bag that mounts to the bike's fuel tank by means of straps or magnets, and it's one of the most useful items you'll ever purchase for your motorcycle. A pad on the bottom protects the tank from being scuffed, and most come with a transparent map pouch on top. Because of the bag's location, you'll want to pack only soft items, as you could contact it with a very sensitive part of your anatomy in a frontal collision.

If you intend to utilize the map pouch, choose a bag with a pouch that's at least wide enough to display two folds of the map (about 8 inches), so you don't have to stop frequently to flip it over. Because maps can be hard to read while you're riding (and we do not recommend taking your eyes off the road), use a highlighter to mark your route so it's easy to find in a hurry. The safest way to utilize the map is to pull off the road and stop before you attempt to study it. And of course, never try to access the contents of the tank bag until you have pulled over and stopped.

What's really great about magnetic bags is the ease of installation. Simply place it on a steel fuel tank (test your bike's tank with a magnet if you're not sure of its composition), and it should stick like glue. Many come with a quick-detach tether cord that allows them to be directly connected to the handlebar should the wind blast overcome the magnets' ability to grip. Because magnetic bags will pick up any stray metal upon which they're set, inspect the pad periodically. If you work in a metal machining shop, you probably shouldn't use a magnetic tank bag.

Strap-on bags require a harness that may loop around the steering head, around a frame member at the rear of the tank under the seat, and/or join under the tank. They require some adjusting and must be tightened securely, or their loose straps and pad could scuff the tank. When mounting such a harness around the steering neck, be certain it doesn't pinch any wires or cables.

Think of a tank bag as your bike's purse. Carry in it items such as extra gloves, shield cleaning fluid and rags, a flashlight, maps, earplugs, first-aid kit, bungee cords, reading material, bottled water, etc.

Tail/Seat Bags: For the times you're not carrying a passenger, a tail bag that mounts to the rear portion of the seat can be very useful. Most are large enough to carry a full-face helmet, and they often have additional pockets for smaller, more solid items you may not wish to carry in a tank bag, such as a tire repair kit or tools.

Seat bags mount with straps and buckles or shock cords, and need to be attached firmly. While they won't likely scuff the seat, they can be disconcerting if they're wobbling around. On overnight or two-night trips when I've wanted to travel light, I have often been able to fit my gear into just a tank bag and seat bag. As with any soft luggage, I recommend a rain cover.

Duffels: In my early days of riding, back before quality hard and soft luggage was readily available, my standard luggage was an army-style duffel bag strapped to the back of the seat, the luggage rack, or both. Though sturdy and capacious, the duffel was an ungainly bit of luggage, long and limp if not fully stuffed. Trying to dig something out of it on the road was difficult if I had failed to pack with an eye toward which items would likely be needed first. The canvas duffel was not waterproof, and had to be covered or lined with plastic garbage bags.

Today, motorcycle-specific duffel bags are a huge improvement, with their strap mounting systems, rain covers, top opening, and extra pockets. Just as a motorcycle is a tool for a job, so is any piece of

luggage. What do you plan to carry in it? Do you need one large enough for tent poles and a camp chair, or something just a bit larger than a seat bag? Again, consider a rain cover. If the strap mounting system is too complex and time consuming, a pair of crossed bungee cords can be just as secure and less time consuming.

Several companies now offer for motorcycles a wheeled airline-type bag that comes with a hook-and-loop wrap designed to fasten around a backrest. They usually consist of a large main compartment with several smaller ones. When you reach your destination, lift it off the bike, set it on its wheels, deploy the retractable handle, and roll it away.

Day Packs: A day pack is much smaller than a backpack, and does not protrude to the sides or above the head. It usually comes with a pair of padded shoulder straps, and sometimes a waist strap. If you wish to use one, pack only soft objects and keep the weight reasonable.

Bungee Nets: For carrying a helmet or several loose objects on the back portion of the seat, a luggage net is a handy item. It is a loose-weave net made of several small shock cords that conform to the shape of the objects inside and attach under the seat or fender with a series of hooks. As with any piece of luggage, be certain it's firmly attached, and that the items being carried cannot slip out through the gaps.

While most soft luggage is textile, this Saddlemen Drifter Sissybag is an example of a leather bag. A seat bag is usually small, fits on the back portion of the seat, and holds little more than a helmet. Saddlemen

Duffel bags come in all sizes, usually sit on a luggage rack or the back portion of the seat, and attach either with bungee cords or their own shock cords and hooks. Because they're usually not waterproof, you'll want to get the optional rain covers. Roadgear

A day pack can hold a few useful items, and won't get in your way as long as you don't pack it too full. Do *not* carry anything in a day pack you'd rather not land on if you were thrown from the bike.

Don't let the trunk's great capacity and big lid fool you; this is the place only for light but bulky items

Luggage nets are useful for carrying larger loose items that can't fit through the net, such as a helmet, boots, or that jacket liner it's now too hot to wear.

MAKE A LIST

Before every trip I make a list of what I'm going to take, then bring it to the bedroom, where I pack things in my saddlebag liners. As I bring an item into the bedroom I place a single line \ beside it on the list. When it has actually been placed in the liner or bag I draw a second line / to complete the X. When I'm ready to go, I place the list in a file folder.

When I return home from the trip, I pull out the list and add anything to it I didn't take on the trip, but wished I had. Next time I travel, I make up my new list from the previous one from a similar trip. If you really want to get obsessive about it, you can make separate lists for riding trips, fly-and-ride trips, camping trips, family car vacations, and the rest.

Packing Basics

Mass Centralization: The concept of mass centralization has to do with the fact that dense items located farther out from the center of mass will have more of an effect on stability than those packed in tight to the center. For example, racers found that their bikes turned more quickly if heavier components, such as radiators, were kept in tight to the bike. For our purposes, it means to pack those denser, heavier items closer in to the bike, with lighter, less dense items to the outside. For example if you're traveling solo, the ideal location for your heaviest items would be either in the forward part of the saddlebags in toward the center of the bike, or on the seat behind you—*not* in the trunk!

Have you ever placed a heavy load in your trunk, and then noticed that your bike wanted to run wide in turns? Look at your bike from the side, and note the location of the rear axle relative to the trunk. It's likely that the greater part of the trunk is located *behind* the axle. The weight placed in it will press down *behind* the rear axle and use it as a fulcrum point to lever the weight off the front wheel. That's why the bike wants to run wide in turns!

The solution is simple—centralize mass by placing heavy items forward in the saddlebags, between the axles, where they will have less of an effect on handling. Use the trunk for lighter, less dense items such as rain suits and sleeping bags.

What Goes Where

Now that we've talked about a number of ways to carry luggage, here's a quick rundown of what sorts of items go where:

Jacket pockets: Smaller items needed quickly such as keys, change, earplugs, garage door remote, a small camera. Keep registration papers in your wallet, not on the bike. Should a thief steal your vehicle and be able to produce the registration papers, he may be able to convince a cop that you loaned him the bike.

Fairing pockets: Things that should be with the bike at all times, such as a tire gauge, tire repair kit, duct and electrical tape, multitool.

Day pack: Light, soft, transitory items, including lunch, a paperback book, spare sweater, computer discs.

Tank bag: Larger, less bulky items needed immediately such as maps, a flashlight, spare gloves, shield cleaner and rag, tire gauge, neck warmer, guidebook.

Underseat storage: Basic items that

TIP

If you expect to travel in rainy weather, buy the optional rain covers. These will also protect the bags from dirty road spray. Even so, you still may wish to pack the contents in sturdy plastic bags as added protection from the weather.

should be with the bike at all times, including a tool kit or tire repair kit.

Small seat bag: Larger or bulkier items that would be oversized or inappropriate for a tank bag, such as tools, a helmet, heavy books, or manuals.

Duffel bag on seat: Use it for those big items that stick out to the sides, such as camping gear or a camp chair.

Saddlebags: Because they're low and tucked into the bike, this is the place for heavy, bulky items, such as clothing and toiletries. In a pinch, light items such as sleeping bags can be strapped to the tops of the saddlebags if the proper anchors are added.

Trunk: Don't let the trunk's great capacity and big lid fool you; this is the place only for light but bulky items such as sleeping bags, rain suits, and helmets. See above for the explanation of why heavy items in the trunk will cause the bike to turn more slowly.

Luggage rack: If your luggage rack does not carry a trunk, you can still use it for a seat or duffel bag. Because it sits behind the rear axle, pack light, bulky items, such as sleeping bags and rain suits.

WIND PROTECTION

Windshields and fairings need to be considered separately, as they're two very different items with a common purpose.

Windshields

With the popularity of cruisers, and now touring cruisers with saddlebags, the traditional flat windshield has made a comeback. They're also available for standard-style motorcycles like Suzuki's Bandits, the Honda 750 Nighthawk, and others. A similar product is called the clear fairing, and both usually bolt to the handlebar and fork tubes. As for the difference between them, a windshield is generally flat and stops at about headlight level or slightly below. A clear fairing usually flares out around the hands and has "legs" that extend farther

down and provide some protection for the lower extremities.

Mounting: Most windshields mount with a pair of handlebar and fork-tube clamps. The rider should be able to look over the shield, as it can "white out" from oncoming headlights at night, and rain or dirt can diminish visibility at any time. The rake of the shield should be similar to that of the fork, though it can be pivoted slightly fore and aft. The rake figures of some cruisers exceed 35 degrees, and on these it's fine to angle the shield a little less. Even though the rider's eyes may be several inches above the shield, its angle will usually deflect the wind blast high enough to pass over the

A fanny pack is handy for carrying a pocket camera, notepad, tissues, lip balm, and other small items while you're walking around. However, as Dr. Gregory Frazier says in his book on motorcycle touring, a fanny pack announces to the world "Here's where I keep my valuables." I do not recommend carrying valuables here, as the fanny pack is too visible and vulnerable. *Roadgear*

TIP

A seat or duffel bag carried on the rear portion of the seat can complicate rider mounting and dismounting, as you'll have to lift your leg over or around it. I suggest you deploy the sidestand as an extra prop whenever attempting this maneuver. It gets tougher with age . . . trust me.

A luggage rack can be added to most bikes; here's one for Triumph's Rocket III cruiser. Like many others, it is available with a companion bolt-on backrest that your passenger will love. *Triumph Motorcycles America*

One of the more unique items available is this airbag Honda introduced for the 2006 model Gold Wing. An airbag can save a rider a lot of grief in a frontal collision. *American Honda Motor Co.*

A windshield adds not only weather protection but also a certain amount of style to a bike. This one is for a cruiser, but different sizes and types of new and replacement shields are also available for various bikes, including dressers, sport tourers, and sportbikes. *Triumph Motorcycles America*

rider's head and keep bugs from smacking the helmet shield. If the rider is unable to look over the shield, it should be trimmed to proper length.

Shield Height: To order a windshield of the proper height, sit on the bare bike out on the street and have a friend hold one end of a tape measure on the top of the headlight, where the shield will nearly rest. Look forward to a spot at which you can comfortably see the road . . . this will be about 15–20 feet ahead. Now have your friend pull out the tape measure till it reaches a height just below that of which you will look. Note that measurement.

Now subtract an inch from this measurement for the fact the shield will not actu-

ally rest on the headlight. Subtract another inch for the fact you don't want the edge of the shield in your sight line; if you're still not comfortable with it, subtract a third inch. The shield should be no taller above the headlight than this new figure.

While shield angle is the major adjustment, most windshields have enough adjustment built in that they can slide up an inch or two from the headlight. If you're ordering a shield that comes in length increments of two inches (as is common), and your "ideal" length splits the difference, choose the shorter unit. A slightly too-tall shield is much more aggravating than one that's an inch or two shorter than ideal. Besides, the shield should not rest flush on the headlight, but should have a slight gap. Fine-tune height by sliding the shield up or down.

Installation: Installation is simple and straightforward, and can usually be done in a half hour or less with simple hand tools. With the mounting hardware loosely in place, set the shield on the bike and attach the mounting hardware. The top brackets bolt to the handlebar, and the lower to the fork legs above the lower triple clamp. Adjust everything and snug it.

Go riding with the shield installed, and you'll notice much more sound being reflected back to you from the engine. In fact,

TRIMMING WINDSHIELDS

Whoa! Put down that saw and listen to me. Before doing anything drastic, determine if trimming is really necessary. Loosen the adjustments and try to slide the shield down farther, or angle it farther back. If this won't work, determine how much needs to be trimmed and apply enough masking tape to cover the top of the shield. Mark off the amount you expect to trim by drawing on the tape (use a ruler or make a template for the best results), and then check again. Remember the carpenter's adage: "Measure

twice, cut once." Once you're sure of the cut, remove the windshield and pad it so it won't be scratched by the saw table.

The safest tool for trimming is a band saw, as it makes a very even cut in one direction. I do not recommend reciprocating saber or jig saws, as these can produce a much less even cut and can promote cracking. Use a hacksaw if you must, but be very careful not to let it bind. Once the cut has been made, finish it off by sanding with 60- to 80-grit sandpaper or a coarse file.

it may seem as if someone has surreptitiously installed an aftermarket exhaust. You'll also notice that you'll feel wind gusts fed into the bike itself rather than buffeting you. With less wind reaching the rider, he or she will stay warmer, less frazzled, and more rested on longer trips. As with any newly installed product, check all fittings for tightness and adjustment after about 100 miles.

FAIRINGS

Once Craig Vetter had introduced his Windjammer and popularized the frame-mounted fairing back in the 1970s, a dozen or more manufacturers were soon offering handlebar- or frame-mounted motorcycle fairings. The introduction of the BMW R100RT for 1979 and the Honda GL1100 Gold Wing Interstate in 1981, each with its own frame-mounted fairing and integrated, color-matched luggage, was the death knell for what was at the time a huge aftermarket for fairings and saddlebags. Today, most riders either purchase a bike with fairing and bags from the manufacturer or go without.

Universal-fit fairings are no longer readily available through the aftermarket. However, many aftermarket suppliers offer fairings specifically designed for certain motorcycles, usually sportbikes, either as replacement parts for bikes that came with OE (original equipment) fairings or as lightweight alternatives for racing. While they're designed to be bike-specific, with a little research and ingenuity you might find something that will fit your nonfaired bike.

BIKE PROTECTION
Bras

Some manufacturers offer tank, fairing, and lower bras, usually made of a padded vinyl, to protect from stone chips and the rub marks caused by a tank bag. The bra itself requires only an occasional wipe-down or washing. Because they will tend to trap sand and dust, it's important that the painted area beneath them be cleaned periodically and kept waxed. The underside of the bra must also be kept clean.

Covers

If you keep your bike outside, I strongly recommend a bike cover to protect it. These covers are usually made of nylon or canvas, either lightweight or heavy, and will keep off the rain. However, the cover must be breathable or vented or it will hold moisture against the bike, which promotes corrosion.

Back in the 1970s, when bikes usually came bare, adding wind protection usually meant a big touring fairing. Now that most bikes come fully equipped, aftermarket fairings tend to be small sporty items like this one for the Harley V-Rod. *Harley-Davidson Motor Co.*

With the popularity of cruisers, and now touring cruisers with saddlebags, the traditional flat windshield has made a comeback.

The fairing not only provides wind protection, but also sometimes houses many features and adds a lot of convenience. The Harley-Davidson FLH Ultra Classic's fairing houses a lot of useful gauges and a full sound system. *Harley-Davidson Motor Co.*

TIP

Because a windshield can become obscured with dust, insect carcasses, rain, and fog, and can "white out" when struck with oncoming headlights at night, it's best for the rider to look over, rather than through, the shield. If you're looking through the windshield when seated on the bike, ask your dealer if he can get you a shorter shield. Or, you can cut the shield to proper height. To do this, find a place on the shield through which you need to look to see the minimal distance ahead of the bike. You want to cut the shield an inch or two lower than this, as it's very distracting to have the windshield edge right in your field of vision.

If you cannot park your bike in a garage, a cover will guard it against the rigors of weather and sunlight. It will also hide it from prying eyes that may be looking for just that sort of bike to steal. Lock your bike, and lock the cover so it doesn't disappear, either. *Triumph Motorcycles America*

TIP

While some riders expect that a windshield will be adversely affected by crosswinds, the reality is usually quite different. The gyroscopic action of the wheels, and the momentum pushing the front end, provide a great deal of force to keep a bike on the straight and narrow. Still, once a shield of this type is in place, a rider should take greater care with tire inflation pressures, suspension settings, and steering-head bearing adjustment.

Not all soft luggage is made of textile fabrics. Cruiser riders often prefer leather luggage, which is more in keeping with the classic style of their bikes. *Saddlemen*

Engine guards (also called case guards) bolt to the engine cases, and are intended to protect them in a fall. Some riders attach accessory footpegs to them. Be certain the case guards are not mounted so low as to limit cornering clearance turns, as that can lead to serious injury or worse. *Triumph Motorcycles America*

It's rather like wearing an impermeable rain suit on a humid day.

Be certain the cover fits tightly when stretched, as a loose-fitting cover can blow in the wind, creating rub marks on painted surfaces. Look for covers that have a soft lining material where they cover the windshield. Secure the cover so it will not blow off. Some covers have reinforced holes through which a cable lock may be passed to discourage theft. However, because they're made of cloth, covers can be cut or vandalized.

Because they conceal the bike, the cover may discourage thieves who are intending to steal a specific make or model. Some riders spraypaint their address on the cover to discourage theft. When removed, a damp cover must be stored loosely so it can dry thoroughly.

Engine Guards/Case Guards

Engine cases and covers can be damaged in a tip-over, so some riders bolt engine or case guards to their bikes. These are usually in the form of chromed tube-steel rails that can support the bike. Some riders bolt footpegs to them so they can spread out on the road, but this often places their feet far from the

controls. If you want to spread out, I suggest you install forward controls.

Frame and Bar Sliders

Sport, sport touring, naked, and standard bikes can use frame and bar sliders to add protection in a fall. These are cylindrical nylon bits that bolt to the bike or handlebars. Bar sliders are just that—they mount on the ends of the bars. Frame sliders are generally attached to the point where the cylinder head bolts to the frame, but lots of people get creative and find other spots, usually to keep the bike from sliding on the muffler in a crash.

WHEELS
Going Wider

The obvious trend in cruisers is toward ever wider wheels for ever wider rear tires. According to some riders and builders, they've now reached the point of near or absolute absurdity. With that said, front wheels are following suit, but to a lesser degree. As I write this, the widest rear tires available on stock cruisers from the major manufacturers are in the 200–240 series range, but anything goes in the alternative V-twin market. The aftermarket keeps

Motorcycle tires are going wider—especially rears. While a wider tire looks impressive and can offer better wear and handling characteristics, there is a limit beyond which steering and handling begin to suffer. Dunlop offers some functional wide tires, including this Elite 3 Radial. *Dunlop Tire*

> ## TIP
>
> Consider windshield models that are quickly detachable. You want the shield on the bike much of the time for touring, but once you reach Sturgis, Daytona, or the rally, you may wish to remove it for cruising around town. Once installed, most shields can be removed in one or two minutes with minimal tools, leaving the mounting hardware in place.
>
> A lightly tinted shield can cut down daytime glare by perhaps 10 percent, as with a car windshield. At night it can also cut headlight glare. As for how much tint you can have legally, check state and local laws.

Cast wheels are common on bikes, and are also available as accessories. This one is intended for the Harley V-Rod. Cast wheels usually carry tubeless tires, which is an advantage as they are less prone to going flat from a puncture. *Harley-Davidson Motor Co.*

Forged wheels are produced from a single billet forging, which makes them incredibly strong. Weld Wheels offers this one-piece forged billet wheel that was designed specifically for Avon's 330 tire series. *Weld Wheels*

TIP

Going to seriously wide rubber requires the use of a larger swingarm, and as the rear tire becomes wider beyond a certain point it adversely affects steering. I've heard some custom builders state that, in a practical sense, a 250-series is about the widest rear tire to consider if you really want the bike to function well.

offering ever wider hoops that are now in the 330-series range, and still wider tires are certainly coming.

Do these extremely wide tires and wheels work? After a fashion. Returning to our "tool for a job" guiding principle, if your desire is to gain attention with the old "mine is bigger than yours" school of thought, they certainly do work in that sense. However, keep in mind that these wider wheels and tires are heavy, which results in greater unsprung weight on suspended bikes, which will adversely affect the way the bike rides. The profile will affect how the bike leans into turns. It all becomes very complex.

Bringing these wide tire/wheel combinations to market is no easy proposition, and requires an orchestrated dance among several related companies. First,

the tire makers manufacture wider tires, then the aftermarket wheel makers have to come up with new tooling for wider wheels to fit them. Finally, the custom frame makers must develop the frames and swingarms to accommodate them. These enormous 300-series tires require wheels that are about 10 1/2 inches wide, and even wider 330-series tires are also now available.

As of this writing, 18 inches is the predominant wheel diameter, as it shows more wheel and less tire. Some manufacturers have told me that right-side-drive systems for custom bikes will become popular for use with 300-series and larger wheels, as they're necessary to keep the bike balanced.

Wheel Basics
Cast Wheels: Cast aluminum wheels are formed by pouring molten metal into a mold. Gas pockets can form during the molding

Wire wheels are not as strong as cast or forged wheels, and may require an occasional spoke tightening. However, many riders prefer them on a cruiser for their traditional style. *Harley-Davidson Motor Co.*

The Throttle Rocker is a device that clips to the twistgrip and allows the rider to operate the throttle with the palm. It negates the need to keep your hand wrapped around the throttle grip and is an alternative to a throttle lock for those long stretches of highway. *Roadgear*

process, which can cause weak spots. As a result, these wheels are sometimes made thicker and heavier to compensate. Over time, trapped gas can work its way to the surface and cause the chromed finish to separate and peel off. However, careful casting and chroming can minimize this.

Forged Wheels: Forged wheels are created from a solid piece of metal, often of 6061 aluminum billet, that has been cut to shape. It is heated till it's soft and malleable, then placed in forging dies and pressed under extreme pressure to finalize its shape. Forged wheels can be structurally sound and very strong, with no seams to potentially leak.

Wire Wheels: Wire spoke wheels are traditional on motorcycles, and were universal till the appearance of the cast hoops in the late 1970s. They're *de rigueur* on choppers and classic-styled bikes, and they look great. Manufacturers are doing a lot with different spoke numbers and shapes. While cast and forged wheels require no maintenance, the spokes in wire wheels can loosen over time and require tightening.

It's easy for small items to get lost in your tank bag or saddlebags, so utilize smaller luggage bags meant to separate those items for easy access. *Roadgear*

Because the spokes penetrate the rim, these wheels must usually be used with tubes. If a nail punctures a tube, the tube will deflate immediately. Tubeless tires, however, may capture the nail and the tire will continue to hold air, allowing the rider to get home safely. Some wire wheel manufacturers include a sealant material that they state will allow them to be used with tubeless tires.

> ### TIP
>
> For a bike that is parked outside, I recommend the larger, heavier, full cover for maximum coverage. For touring, or just to keep the dust off a bike stored in the garage, choose a thinner, lighter cover that may only protect the upper part of the bike. They fold up much smaller, and will at least prevent the seat from being wet in the morning.

> ### TIP
>
> One potential problem is that engine guards may protrude to the point that they can limit cornering clearance. Inspect them before mounting to be certain they won't restrict your bike's ability to lean in a turn, as such restrictions can cause you to run off the road or into oncoming traffic.

A small pouch may be mounted to a windshield, sissy bar, or frame member, and makes a handy place for carrying sunglasses, gloves, or whatnot on a cruiser. Also use such pouches for tools, a tire gauge, and a patch kit if you're short on room. *Saddlemen*

SIDECARS, TRAILERS, AND TRIKES

Chapter 7

Sidecars are real attention getters, especially a nice classic rig like this Indian.

Today, sidecars are coming back into fashion because they evoke nostalgia, and because they really are cool.

SIDECARS

Sidecars make a lot of sense in terms of practicality, hauling capacity, and style points. They became popular in Europe after World War II when times were rough and people needed to move their families around. Once things improved to the point that automobiles were affordable by most everyone, sidecars lost some of their practical appeal.

Today, they're coming back into fashion because they evoke some of that nostalgia, and because they really are cool. You can put mom on the back and the kids in the hack. Some folks stick the family dog in the sidecar, nose to the wind and wearing goggles. Hacks haul all your camping gear and more. And as the motorcycling population ages, well, a sidecar offers more stability when one wants to slow down.

And did I mention that sidecars garner a lot of attention everywhere they go? No matter if it's carrying dogs, kids, or lumber, pull up somewhere with a sidehack, and people are going to want to talk to you.

An excellent source of information is Doug Bingham, who owns Side Strider Inc., a sidecar shop in the Southern California area. Check out his website at www.sidestrider.com.

TRAILERS

There are two types of trailers, those that are used to haul motorcycles, and those that are hauled *by* motorcycles. Let's begin with the latter.

I was heading for a rally a few years ago when I came upon some other ralliers at a rest stop. It was a group of five bikes, two pulling cargo trailers, and my first reaction was a smirking, "Wouldn't you really rather have a Buick?"

What wiped that smirk off my face was when the group arrived at the rally that

afternoon, and started unpacking their magic boxes: tents, cots, mattresses, coolers, grilles, luggage, lawn chairs, sports equipment . . . as I was cramming my stuff into a little dome tent.

The second wave rolled in a little later with their camper trailers, and here came more of the above equipment. They had a good time playing catch and throwing the Frisbee, and spent the evening sitting around the fire in lawn chairs tinkling ice in their drinks from their coolers, with soft music playing in the background. I squatted in the dirt with a couple cans of warm beer.

When it rained that night I was mucking about trying to keep my gear dry and my air mattress afloat, while those guys were snoring away on cots or had real beds

If you're tired of sleeping on the ground, but still like to camp, use a small camping trailer. It's relatively light and easy to tow, yet can carry a good amount of luggage and fold out to a very comfortable home on the road. *Kompact Kamp*

A SIDECAR NAMED DESIRE

Sidecars have a different feel from riding a bare motorcycle, because they don't lean. Instead, the rider has to push and pull on the handlebar to turn them, and shifting his weight helps. With the sidecar mounted on the right side, turning left is very solid and stable with that "outrigger" wheel.

However, on right turns, the weight of the hack wants to push the motorcycle wide. In an extreme situation, the sidecar wheel could actually come off the pavement in a right turn and threaten to overturn the rig. But of course, you wouldn't do that, would you. . . .?

And did I mention sidecars garner a lot of attention everywhere they go?

Enclosed trailers for hauling motorcycles come in all sizes. Haulmark's Low Hauler can handle two bikes plus lots of luggage. Not only that, but at the race or other event it may suffice as a viewing platform. Finally, it can allow you to buy all sorts of gear from the vendors. *Haulmark*

TIP

When dealing with the manufacturer, be certain you understand exactly which equipment comes standard with your trailer, and which is optional. Trailers are often shown in very attractive colors that are extra-cost options.

If you're traveling solo, be certain you can set up your new camper trailer alone.

---

up off the ground. In the morning they could dress standing up while I was flat on my back struggling into wet jeans on a wet floor. And as I was stumbling off bleary eyed to wait in the rally chow line, they were passing around orange juice, bagels, and coffee and sizzling up a mess of bacon and eggs. Wouldn't you really rather have an enjoyable rally experience?

Hauling a trailer with a motorcycle isn't for everyone, but it sure as heck could have been for me that weekend. Trailers towed by motorcycles come in two flavors, cargo and camping. The former tend to be relatively inexpensive and will haul a lot, while the latter provide that coveted bed up off the ground while still offering a major amount of cargo space.

Cargo Trailers

Cargo trailers are basically big, enclosed boxes on wheels that will haul all manner of items, and generally carry from about 9 cubic feet on up to more than 20. The lid usually opens like a clam shell, and they offer options that include lid racks, coolers, larger wheels, light bars and bumpers, custom colors, and more. They'll carry a tent, but if you're camping you'll still probably wind up sleeping on the ground.

Camping Trailers

These are larger and fold out into full tents. On smaller versions the top lifts up to form a roof, while some larger ones have a fold-

---

out, stand-up vestibule that can be used for dressing and sitting. The underside is storage space.

If you're traveling solo, be certain you can set up your new camper trailer alone. Could you do it in a high wind? How long does it take to erect?

Motorcycle Size

Trailers vary greatly in size and weight, but for most I would recommend a motorcycle of at least 750cc. It would have the required power, tire size, and frame dimensions necessary to handle the extra weight. As a rule of thumb, a loaded trailer should weigh no more than half as much as the motorcycle towing it. Exceeding this can cause a "wag the dog" scenario, in which the trailer begins swaying side to side and can become difficult to control.

Both trailers and motorcycles have a gross vehicle weight rating (GVWR) plate, usually displayed inside the trailer in a prominent place, and on the motorcycle's steering stem. The figure lists the maximum allowable weight of vehicle *and* load, including luggage and rider(s). Exceeding this figure can affect the bike's handling. When hauling a trailer, remember to add the tongue weight to the total weight figure on the motorcycle.

Hitches

Motorcycle trailer hitch brackets usually attach to the top shock mounts, and to the

---

THE FUN FACTOR

Once you've assimilated all this information and have your trailer, be sure to have fun. And as you're sitting there in your lawn chair with your drink and your radio and your friends, don't forget those of us who are sleeping on the ground and who are less fortunate. Be sure to rub it in every chance you get.

TIP

Tongue weight should total about 10 percent of the total weight of the trailer and its load. For proper pulling with a single-axle trailer, load about 60 percent of the payload weight ahead of the axle, and about 40 percent behind it. This should result in a correct tongue weight, which is a significant factor in trailer stability. Consult your trailer owner's manual for the recommended tongue weight. If you carry a cooler, be aware that tongue weight will change as you consume its contents.

passenger footpeg mounts. When you talk with the trailer manufacturers, ask which brand of hitch they recommend. Installing the hitch will also involve tapping into your motorcycle's wiring so that the trailer's electrical system can be plugged into it.

Trailers tend to come with either ball-type or swivel hitches. While riders may have their personal opinions about which is better, I've turned up no research that indicates one to be superior to the other in all circumstances.

Safety Chains

I've heard several stories about state troopers who test the security of a trailer's safety chains by stepping up onto them. They regard chains as a serious safety issue, and so should you. The purpose of safety chains is to keep the trailer attached to the tow vehicle, should the hitch separate. Keeping things attached is the responsibility of the tow vehicle driver, and should things detach, he's the guy who should be at risk, not the family in the van approaching from the other direction.

When you attach the safety chains, allow them sufficient slack so that they will not bind when you turn the bike sharply at parking-lot speeds. Should the trailer tongue become detached while still attached

with safety chains, the worst possible scenario would be for the tongue to drop down, dig into the surface, and flip the trailer. This is why you want to **cross** the safety chains under the tongue like a cradle, so that the tongue can drop onto it.

Tongue Weight

No, I'm not talking about your mother-in-law's influence on your marriage, but whether the dog wags the tail or the tail wags the dog. Much of this will depend to a great extent upon the amount of tongue weight the tow vehicle carries. Tongue weight refers to the amount of downforce resting on the trailer tongue when it's being pulled. Loading too much weight behind the trailer axle will result in too little (negative) tongue weight, which will pull upward on the back of the tow vehicle and can induce the trailer to sway, and the two vehicles to wander and porpoise. On the other hand, excessive tongue weight (too much weight ahead of the trailer axle) could, depending upon hitch dynamics, overly weight the rear of the tow vehicle, causing the front to wander and understeer. This situation is also tough on the suspension and rear tire.

Here's an example of how to figure tongue weight on a large trailer. Let's say that your enclosed trailer carries a statement that it weighs 800 pounds empty, your motorcycle weighs 750 pounds, and you're carrying an additional 50 pounds of luggage in the trailer. The combined weight is 1,600 pounds, and 10 percent of that would be 160 pounds. To measure tongue weight, load the trailer as you would for the trip, then place milk crates or other suitable objects under

When hauling a trailer, remember to add the tongue weight to the total weight figure on the motorcycle.

To prevent the hitch from falling onto the pavement should it accidentally detach from the tow vehicle, cross the safety chains under it to form a cradle for it to drop into.

Trailers vary greatly in size and weight, but for most I would recommend a motorcycle of at least 750cc.

TIP

Keep the bike well tuned, and pay close attention to suspension settings and tire pressures. Maximum tire pressure is listed on the tire sidewall; do not exceed it. Note that a shorter or smaller trailer does not necessarily mean it's going to be easier to tow. See related information about tongue length.

I've heard several stories about state troopers who test the security of a trailer's safety chains by stepping up onto them. They regard chains as a serious safety issue, and so should you.

TIRE INFLATION

Be sure those little trailer tires are properly inflated to the pressure recommended in the owner's manual. Because a trailer will put additional weight and stress on your motorcycle's rear tire, correct inflation pressure is critical there, too. Consult your bike's owner's manual for a range of proper inflation, and inflate the rear tire accordingly. Keep a close eye on tire tread depth, as pulling a trailer will accelerate tire wear.

Cross the safety chains under the tongue like a cradle, so the tongue can drop onto it.

the tongue so you can position a bathroom scale on top of them at the same height as the hitch. Place the end of the trailer tongue on the scale. If tongue weight does not equal 10 percent of total weight, shift luggage in the trailer or reposition the motorcycle to achieve the desired figure.

Get it right. Too much tongue weight places too much weight on the rear of the tow vehicle, which unweights its front wheels, leading to braking and steering problems. Too little tongue weight, on the other hand, means that hard braking may allow the trailer to push upward on the rear of the tow vehicle, unweight the back end, and cause the vehicle and trailer to jackknife.

Wheel Size

Trailers designed for motorcycle use tend to be equipped with 8-, 10-, or 12-inch-diameter wheels. All else being equal, a larger wheel tends to provide a higher and smoother ride, as larger tires tend to step over holes that smaller wheels can drop into. An 8-inch wheel will rotate at a higher rpm at any given speed than a larger wheel, so tire wear could be more of a factor. With today's quality wheel bearings, rotational speeds should not pose a problem.

Electrical

The trailer manufacturer will provide the wiring and plug necessary to tie your trailer's lights into your bike's electrical system. As for providing the other end of the plug on your bike, it's usually a very simple deal to splice this colored wire into that colored wire. If you don't understand how it's done, take the bike and wiring harness to a dealer or service shop.

Rider Experience

Practice towing your trailer in a low-traffic area if you're new to trailering, or have a new trailer. The first rule is to never, ever forget that your trailer is back there. You're going to have to adjust to three tire tracks

SWAY

Ever see a towed vehicle sway from side to side? The amount of sway has to do with many factors, including the relation of axle width to length. A narrow-axle trailer with a short tongue will tend to wander side to side behind the tow vehicle, while a trailer with a longer tongue and wide axle will tend to pull straighter. A general rule of thumb is that the distance from the hitch ball to the axle should be about 1.5 times the length of the trailer axle.

when it comes to potholes and such, along with more leisurely acceleration and greater braking distances. You'll need much more distance to pass, as your vehicle is now considerably longer and heavier than it was previously. Always make sure that you can see the trailer in your mirrors; add flags or proximity indicators if you can't.

Slow down. Allow more time to get there, and don't try to keep up with others who have more experience or ability—or who aren't hauling a trailer.

Weather

When the weather turns nasty, you know what to do—slow down. Crosswinds can be a real handful with a tall trailer. On the other hand, some riders suggest that a trailer helps to stabilize their bike in crosswinds.

Fuel Mileage

When you're hauling a trailer, its additional weight, wind resistance, and rolling resistance will cause your bike to use more fuel to travel a given distance at a given speed. Expect to use about 20–25 percent more fuel, and plan your stops accordingly. High speeds or headwinds can increase fuel use even more.

Maintenance

Trailers are low-maintenance—but not no-maintenance—vehicles. Check wheel bearings periodically according to the instructions in your owner's manual. And keep the hitch ball or swivel lubricated.

TRAILERS FOR HAULING MOTORCYCLES

Riders who trailer their bikes to events take a lot of heat from the stalwarts who ride, but hauling your bike doesn't necessarily mean that you're less of a rider—or less of a . . . you know, less of a guy. Instead, it may mean very different things indeed.

Here are 10 good reasons why riders—real riders—will sometimes trailer their bikes instead of riding them.

1. There are 4-foot snowdrifts in your back yard when you leave for Daytona. Or, it's going to be around 100 degrees on the way to Sturgis.

2. You're hauling your show bike, and want it to be pristine when you get there.

3. You want to go with your buddies, and you'll have more fun partyin' in the truck for three days than grinding out the miles.

4. Why put all those miles on a couple of $25,000 customs when you can put them on a $10,000 used pickup instead?

5. You can carry a whole lot of tools, luggage, camping equipment, and riding gear.

6. You can load up at the swap meets, and from the vendors.

7. When you park at the event, it's possible to sit on top of a larger enclosed trailer for a better view of the festivities.

8. Bikes sometimes get stolen at these events, but there's less chance of that happening from a locked, enclosed trailer.

9. You aren't getting any younger. When you ride hundreds of miles for several days straight, your back hurts and your butt hurts. Things get stiff that shouldn't get stiff, and things that should—well, let's not go there.

10. Finally, if the bike breaks down—okay, let's not go there, either. Testing, 1-2-3, testing . . . is this thing on?

Open Trailers

The two basic types of trailers are open and enclosed. The open type, the flat or rail trailers, are much less expensive but they also expose the bikes and equipment to weather, theft, and rock damage. It's easier to tie your bikes down on an open trailer, as you can walk all around it and don't have to duck and bend much. Pull into a gas station or restaurant with your bike in full view, and people will often come up to admire it. Finally, when your trip is over, smaller open trailers may be stored upright against a wall, and some even fold.

To save potential damage, select an open trailer with a full floor (rather than open rails), full skirting up front and solid fenders. The floor will also allow the trailer to hold boxes of equipment in addition to bikes, especially when it's equipped with side skirting.

Enclosed Trailers

Enclosed trailers offer all the obvious advantages of full protection from the weather and from thieves. Provided you have the parking space at home, an enclosed

The first rule is to never, ever forget that your trailer is back there.

WHEN TRAILERS NEED BRAKES

Brakes are required by law on trailers with a load capacity of more than 3,000 pounds. Also, it's a good idea to have independent brakes if the loaded weight of the trailer exceeds 40 percent of the weight of the tow vehicle. An enclosed trailer set up to haul four motorcycles will likely have, and need, brakes.

Although this trailer has three rails, you'd be lucky to fit three mini-bikes on it. Two small road bikes might be able to go side by side, but tying them down in such a way as to get leverage on the outsides would be tricky at best. All things considered, the middle rail is likely to be used most. *Load Rite Trailers*

There are 4-foot snowdrifts in your back yard when you leave for Daytona. Or, it's going to be around 100 degrees on the way to Sturgis.

Since gasoline prices never seem to go down, trailer manufacturers are beginning to pay more attention to aerodynamics.

trailer can also come in handy for other hauling jobs—like moving the kids off to college. Negatives include the initial cost, weight, and attendant fuel costs, and storing the thing. You may wish to consider renting a trailer at first to see if it's what you want.

Trailer Trends

One of the major trends in trailers now is convertibility, or multipurpose usage. Some companies offer open trailers that can be adapted to haul motorcycles, watercraft, snowmobiles, lawn equipment, or whatever. And of course, enclosed trailers can haul darn near anything.

Storage

It's a pain having that trailer taking up parking space in your driveway. That's why open folding trailers have become popular. And again, renting a trailer solves the storage problem.

Aerodynamics

Since gasoline prices never seem to go down, trailer manufacturers are beginning to pay more attention to aerodynamics. Instead of the typical boxy shape, enclosed trailers are now sporting V-noses and aerodynamic rounded edges.

Living Quarters

If you've ever tried to get a room in Daytona for Bike Week, or Sturgis, or Myrtle Beach, you know all about limited availability and exorbitant rates. A large enclosed trailer with compact living quarters, however, parked in a campground, can save you a lot of money. Some such trailers have a drop-down ramp in the back, and a small area into which you can ride a couple bikes.

Brakes

The majority of trailer brakes are electric, which are usually less expensive, but they require a brake actuator. This black box allows the trailer's brakes to be applied independent of the tow vehicle's brakes. They're a plus in heavy traffic and in the wet. If a trailer begins to sway at speed, a touch on the trailer brakes will usually settle it down.

Should the trailer break away, it will disengage a plug from the tow vehicle that signals the trailer braking system to activate immediately. This system runs on its own battery power, so be sure to maintain this battery in a charged capacity.

Surge brakes are more expensive, noisier in operation, but fully independent of the tow vehicle. They have their own hydraulic system, which actuates by inertia. When the surge brakes sense the inertial change caused by the tow vehicle braking, they apply automatically.

Uni-servo surge brakes tend to actuate when the tow vehicle backs up. Free-backing surge brakes automatically lock out the brake shoes when the vehicle backs up, but they're more expensive. Surge brakes are also designed to apply

Trailers are low-maintenance—but not no-maintenance—vehicles.

There are some who believe that, as the Baby Boomers age and get too rickety for motorcycles, they'll begin riding trikes. I photographed this rig, which is based upon a Honda GL1200 Gold Wing, at Americade.

Towing laws vary by state. Visit your state Department of Motor Vehicles (DMV) for a booklet on your state's laws.

automatically should the trailer separate from the tow vehicle.

Towing Tips

Towing laws vary by state. Visit your state Department of Motor Vehicles (DMV) for a booklet on your state's laws. For information on proper tongue weight, see the above section on towing a trailer.

Be certain that the mirrors on the tow vehicle protrude far enough to show what's behind. Read the tow vehicle's owner's manual for towing recommendations. Likewise, read and understand the trailer's manual. Be sure the trailer is properly wired so that all lights work. Always use matching hitch and ball sizes. Be certain that the hitch is properly locked to the ball.

When it comes to loading the bike on the trailer, it's much easier to ride a bike up a full-width, drop-down ramp than to try to push one up a narrow, one-wheel ramp. On most enclosed (and some open) trailers, the rear end hinges down to form a full-width ramp. If you must push a bike up a one-wheel ramp, have one person push from behind as the other steadies the bike from the side and controls the front brake lever. I don't recommend riding up such ramps, as, if you were to stall the bike, you've got nowhere to step and could take a nasty fall.

Ratchet-type tie-downs are easier to use when working alone, and provide a more positive grip. Use soft straps rather than hooks for tying down, as there's less potential for damage. Check that handlebar clamps are tight before applying tie-downs. Tie to the handlebar, not the grips, as grips can loosen and rotate.

For security, remove the keys and lock the bikes to the trailer with case-hardened chains. Use a hitch lock—always.

Do not drive with the trailer in the fast lane of a multilane freeway, as vehicles towing trailers may only occupy the first two lanes. Allow more stopping and maneuvering distance. Be sure to follow a maintenance schedule for wheel bearings and other items.

Steel trailers are heavier, but stronger. Enclosed trailers with aluminum skins will ding easily. Aluminum walls should be protected on the inside with paneling. A half-inch-thick plywood floor may be adequate for handling a single machine or dirt bikes, but 3/4-inch plywood is recommended as a minimum for multiple street bikes.

Hitches are rated by the weight they can carry, so be certain to buy an appropriate hitch for the weight of your trailer, bike(s), and luggage. For ball hitches, the larger 2-inch ball has become the standard. Receiver hitches generally have higher ratings, and the smaller Class 2 is adequate for most two-bike trailers. For safety's sake, be certain the hitch is positioned so that the trailer can be towed level. A retractable wheel on the hitch is a desirable feature that makes it easy to move the trailer around when it's disconnected from the tow vehicle.

TRIKES

As riders age, it becomes harder to swing a leg over and hold up that big bike. One way to keep riding without the worries of falling over is to ride a trike. A trike is a three-wheeled vehicle that may have started as a standard motorcycle or as a purpose-built trike. Numerous companies offer trike conversion kits that turn a standard dresser into a three-wheeler, with the appropriate bodywork and differential. Because the rear wheels now take the place of the saddlebags, most trikes provide a trunk between the rear wheels.

THE LEGALITIES

By federal law, safety chains are required on every trailer, and are designed to keep the trailer connected to the tow vehicle should the hitch fail. Ask the manufacturer to specify that its safety chains meet or exceed the gross rating of the trailer.

Above all, a trailer must be safe! Be certain it meets or exceeds all applicable laws regarding such things as DOT lighting, safety chains, brakes, and tire tread depth. Other requirements vary by state. Hey, don't forget to check the tire pressure!

If you've ever tried to get a room in Daytona for Bike Week, or Sturgis, or Myrtle Beach, you know all about limited availability and exorbitant rates.

APPAREL

For noise control, the comfort liner of some helmets now protrudes quite a distance inward from the bottom of the shell. Its job is to seal around the base of the head, sealing out the wind and its ensuing noise. *Shoei Safety Helmet Corporation*

Over the years, helmets have become the politics and religion of motorcycling.

HELMETS

Over the years, helmets have become the politics and religion of motorcycling, the controversial subject one may not wish to mention in polite riding company. They have been passionately defended on one side by those who credit them with saving lives, and passionately derided on the other by those who see them as sinister governmental intrusion at best, and as a hazard at worst.

Whether you love helmets or hate them, you may wish to consider a statement from Harry Hurt, the researcher who studied motorcycle accidents back in the 1970s and whose "Hurt Report" was the definitive source of information on motorcycle accidents for 30 years. Mr. Hurt once told me that if a rider did not wear a helmet, he was easy to kill. All you had to do was knock him off his bike and have him hit his head. However, a helmeted rider had a much better chance of survival. Frankly, if football players, batters in baseball, jockeys, and construction workers accept the need to wear a helmet, and they all deal with much lower forces than those involved in motorcycle accidents, well, there must be something to it.

Noise Control

A less noisy ride is a more relaxing ride, and helmets are much quieter today than they were some years ago. The manufacturers have come to understand that noise control (or quietness) is a selling point, and that wind noise is principally generated from two areas.

One is the opening under the helmet; that's why the comfort liners of some helmets now protrude quite a distance inward from the bottom edge of the shell. You may have to push your head through it, as the fit is often quite snug along the bottom. Some helmets even have a chin curtain in the front to seal them better. All this is in the interest of preventing the wind blast from noisily stealing up from below.

The second source of noise is protrusions from the helmet, which is why many manufacturers have done away with the sideplates over the shield pivot area. They now utilize flat shields that place their pivoting mechanisms on the inside. Protruding vents can also generate noise, and helmet makers are now doing all kinds of interesting things with shell shapes in the interest of styling, aerodynamics, and noise control.

Earplugs

The wind that comes rattling around a windshield or helmet can vibrate your head. Some helmets are noisier than others, and an aftermarket exhaust can be loud and tiring. Earplugs give you the best of both worlds—a more relaxing ride and much better concentration. Plus, it won't sound like you're stressing your engine so much, which allows you to push it even harder! They're also darn handy when sharing a

It's important that any accident-involved helmet either be discarded, or disassembled and inspected by an expert

room with a buddy who snores like an unmuffled chain saw.

Foam earplugs are available in most bike, sport, and gun stores for about a dollar a pair, or free if you go to a bar with loud music. One size fits all, which has advantages and disadvantages. Another drawback is they work better on higher frequencies than lower ones. Some might find this kind of aggravating.

Custom-fit earplugs are also available—see an audiologist. They cost about a hundred times more than foam plugs, but fit and work about a hundred times better, too. Plus, you can get different filters for them. If you just want to use them for motorcycling, or jackhammering or cutting down forests, you can get completely closed filters. If you play in

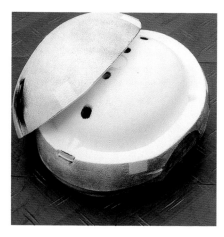

How do helmets protect the head? What's inside them? Here's the expanded polystyrene (EPS) foam liner from a full-face helmet. Under impact, the helmet shell spreads the impact over a wide area of foam, which crushes at a controlled rate and absorbs the impact. Because the foam crushes, the helmet should be inspected after impact and discarded if the foam has been used up. The holes in the liner are for ventilation.

HOW HELMETS WORK

A helmet consists of an interior comfort liner, a layer of closed-cell expanded polystyrene (EPS) foam and an outer shell. The shell is made of layers of plastic, fiberglass, or various composite fibers that are designed to spread the impact over a wide area, to resist penetration, and to prevent the EPS from shredding. The shell is also a major component in styling.

The EPS foam liner, which is about an inch thick and made to precise specifications, resides between the shell and comfort liner. It's a more high-tech version of the foam that's used in drink cups. The EPS foam is designed to crush at a controlled rate upon impact, absorbing and dispersing the energy that otherwise would have been fed directly into the rider's cranium.

Because the liner is designed to crush, it is very possible that even when an accident-involved helmet exhibits no outward sign of damage, the EPS inside may be crushed flat—used up. That's why it's important that any accident-involved helmet either be discarded, or disassembled and inspected by an expert before it is worn again.

A helmet also requires a good retention system. Be certain your helmet is fully and snugly strapped on every time you ride, whether it utilizes the conventional D-rings or some buckle arrangement. Try this: Buckle your helmet securely, and then shake your head as if you were emphatically saying "NO!" If the helmet moves independently of your head, it's not the helmet for you.

Some helmets now utilize flat shields that place their pivoting mechanisms on the inside. This eliminates protruding side plates that can generate wind noise. Helmet makers are now doing all kinds of interesting things with shell shapes in the interest of styling, aerodynamics, and noise control. *Shoei Safety Helmet Corporation*

Arai's Profile is a top-line full-face helmet that is not only light in weight but also features great venting and graphics. Shown is the Aoyama Replica model. *Arai America*

Modular helmets are those on which the front piece pivots open so the rider can eat or talk or get a little air—when stopped. They're also handy for eyeglass wearers who want the convenience of getting into them without removing their glasses. The manufacturers warn against opening them while riding. Shown is a Nolan modular with the front piece closed. *Cima International/Nolan Helmets*

A helmet will carry a sticker that lists the safety certifications it meets. The sticker on this Arai Profile states that it meets the Department of Transportation (DOT) standard, which is a requirement for every helmet sold in the United States, and also the Snell Memorial Foundation standard.

a rock-and-roll band or go to loud concerts or do something else where you want some auditory distinction, you can specify filters that reduce sound by 5 to 25 decibels.

The beauty of these filters is they reduce sound pressure equally across the frequency spectrum. This is referred to as "flat," and is much more pleasing, acoustically speaking. All the intricacies of the sound wave are retained; just the amplitude is reduced. Despite their high initial cost, most feel they're not only worth it, but a bargain. Besides, if you ride every day, and use a new set of foam plugs every, say, three days (they can get pretty foul), you'll come out ahead before the end of the first year. Unless you lose them.

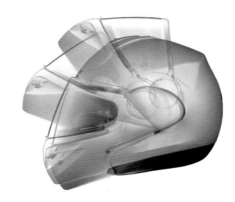

Price

Time was when you could look at a helmet on the shelf and easily tell the high-priced, full-face hat from the $50 unit—it was in their shape, paint, graphics, the look of the shield, and in the venting. Today, helmets are better than ever. Graphics and comfort liners on even the least expensive name-brand helmets are of very good quality. Quality differences between high-dollar and inexpensive helmets are now mostly in

the area of the fit and feel of the interior liner, the fit (but not necessarily the function) of the venting controls, and graphics and other fit and finish issues. My biggest complaint is that many helmets still do not have very good ventilation systems.

A major price factor is the helmet's place of manufacture. Most helmet production has moved overseas since the 1990s, and few if any helmets are still manufactured in the United States. Many of the less-expensive lids are now manufactured in Korea, Taiwan, and mainland China, while the high-priced spreads tend to come from Japan and Europe, where labor costs are higher.

TYPES OF HELMETS
Full-Face Helmets

This type of helmet is also called a "full coverage" because it completely covers the head and provides only an eyeport for an opening. It unquestionably provides the most protection of any style of helmet as it fully covers the face. Its flip-up face shield provides full protection from rain, insects, and flying debris.

The full-face helmet generally weighs from about 3.4 to 4.0 pounds, but is lighter than the modular-style helmet on which the front flips open. Because it fully covers the head, a full-face helmet should have effective controllable venting for comfort in warm weather, and to prevent fogging of the shield. Prices cover a wide range, from under $100 to over $500; the differences include graphics, the quality of the interior liner, standards met, and ventilation. Some full-face helmet manufacturers utilize high-tech, lightweight materials, such as carbon fiber and Kevlar, to strengthen the shell and reduce weight. The total weight saving will be about 10 to 15 percent.

Finally, for improved frontal protection, I suggest that any full-face helmet also have EPS foam in the chinbar.

Modular Helmets

A modular helmet is a full-face on which the front part, the faceplate (not the face shield,

A CLEAR VIEW

Nothing is more bothersome than having to peer through a scatter of bug carcasses on your helmet shield as you ride. Carry a wash cloth and a little spray bottle of cleaner for your windshield/helmet shield/goggles. Commercial shield cleaner is available in bike shops, or you can make your own shield cleaner by putting a 50/50 mix of ammonia and water in a spray bottle.

The chinbar vent's main function is to route the wind blast upward to de-fog the shield. Lifting the shield slightly will also send air up into the inside of the shield. *Shoei Safety Helmet Corporation*

By combining these controllable two-position intake vents with a three-position controllable exhaust vent, the Arai Profile helmet offers fine ventilation tuning. It brings in enough breeze to tousle the hair at highway speeds.

but the whole front of the helmet), has been fitted with a pivoting mechanism so it can be flipped up with the push of a button or lever. I use the terms *modular* and *flip-up* interchangeably. The flip-up feature allows one to enjoy a coffee without removing the helmet, cool off on a really hot day, shout to your buddy "I need gas," or walk into a store without scaring the bejeebers out of some poor clerk.

Flip-up helmets have some drawbacks, one of which is the weight added by the pivot, latch, and release mechanisms. When I tested 15 full-face helmets for Rider magazine in the April 2005 issue, they ranged in weight from 3.40 to 3.96 pounds. The eight modular helmets tested for the October 2005 issue ranged in weight from 3.64 to 4.14 pounds. In short, the average modular helmet weighed about the same as the heaviest full-face, and on average the modular was about 2 ounces heavier than the average full-face.

Granted, a 2-ounce difference is not much, but a companion consideration is that in order for them to clear the face and eyeglasses, the faceplate portion of modular helmets must protrude farther forward than on their single-function, full-face counterparts. Most flip-up helmets also have noticeably larger shells than full-face hats, and thus offer slightly more wind resistance, which translates to the rider's neck as weight and fatigue.

For maximum safety I suggest that you keep the faceplate closed while riding.

Because they're designed to open, there is the potential that under some foreseeable impact, the faceplate of a modular helmet could open and expose the wearer's face to injury. For this reason, inspect any modular helmet you may be considering to verify that it utilizes a metal-to-metal locking mechanism. To protect the rider in frontal impacts, it's a real plus when any helmet carries crushable expanded polystyrene (EPS) foam in the chinbar.

Leather clothing is traditional for motorcycle riders as it's very protective, classy, porous, and wears well. It requires some care and can be ruined if allowed to become wet. *Roadgear*

Textile clothing, such as these Xcaliber suits, has made real inroads for being less expensive, generally impervious to weather, loaded with features, and extremely versatile. *Roadgear*

The removable liner in this Rev'it Cayenne jacket features full sleeves. In addition to the obvious additional warmth to the arms, the liner also helps block the wind coming up the sleeves and thus seals better. The tradeoff is that it takes more time to remove and install a full-sleeve liner.

Many of today's motorcycle jackets have removable liners. All else being equal, a full-sleeve liner will keep the rider warmer than a vest liner. This jacket by Motophoria has an insulated vest-style liner that will keep the torso warm, but does not have sleeves.

Open-Face Helmets

An open-face (also called a "three-quarter") helmet comes down over the ears and the back of the head, but is open at the front, fully exposing the face. It's lighter and cooler than a full-face, and wearers will need eye protection in the form of a shield, goggles, or at the very least shatterproof sunglasses. As with the full-face, venting is a plus. The obvious disadvantage to open and half helmets is that your face is exposed to potential contact with damaging objects such as rocks, branches, and, of course, the road.

Half Helmets

Very popular with cruiser riders, the half helmet covers only the top of the head, yet is fully legal in the United States so long as it passes the DOT minimum standard for impact absorption. It's the lightest and least expensive type of helmet, but also offers the least protection. Under impact or a tumbling fall it's possible for these helmets to roll off the head, exposing the rider to severe or fatal injuries. The rider will need eye protection, and in cold or rainy weather they'll be the least comfortable. Some come with a neck curtain that provides warmth, and is removable for warmer weather.

OTHER HELMET CONSIDERATIONS
Helmet Safety Standards

As for their protective abilities, for any helmet to be legally sold for motorcycle use in the United States it must pass the U.S. Department of Transportation (DOT) minimum standard. The DOT specifies that examples of these helmets must have been tested in a controlled drop on a flat surface and passed no more than 400 g's— 400 times the force of gravity—to an instrumented headform inside. That 400-g number was chosen as it was considered to be the maximum amount of force the human brain could withstand without suffering significant damage. With that figure as the maximum, it is very possible that specific helmets may have passed along much less energy.

In the interest of making more protective helmets, a number of other standards that allow even less energy transfer have been advanced. The best known to American riders is the Snell Memorial Foundation standard, and we're now seeing helmets sold here that meet the BSI (British standard) and ECE (European standard). All of these standards, including DOT, are accepted internationally by the governing bodies that regulate motorcycle racing. Still, no matter what other standard it may also meet, any helmet sold in the U.S. must also meet the DOT minimum standard.

Today, there is a good deal of controversy surrounding the applicability of the various standards. I will not attempt to dissect these standards to choose a "best" one, as there are simply too many variables involved. For

Some standards require helmets be smacked against flat anvils, some call for hemispherical anvils, and others for "kerbstone" anvils. It's apples, oranges, and kumquats.

example, the DOT standard allows for 400 g's of energy to reach the headform, and the Snell standard allows for 300 g's; therefore, one might conclude that the Snell was the superior standard. However, it's not that simple. The DOT standard specifies a dwell time for how long the helmet may pass along the higher g forces, while the Snell standard has no dwell time provision.

To pass the DOT standard with its single drop on a flat anvil, a helmet with lots of cushion designed into its EPS foam will perform better. To pass Snell with its two drops, one against a flat and another against a hemispherical anvil, a helmet with a stronger shell and stiffer foam will perform better. In fact, numerous helmet manufacturers have told me it is difficult to make a helmet that will meet both standards because DOT was designed for a minimal hit, while Snell was designed for a maximum hit.

When one begins reading about the various standards and their testing procedures, things become even murkier. Testing methods differ. Drop heights and the number of drops differ, as do energy inputs allowed, where the helmets were struck, and what they were dropped against. Some standards require they be smacked against

A bandana or commercial neck warmer can really seal the neck if the jacket can't. *Roadgear*

WHICH STANDARD SHOULD BE STANDARD?

What about the real world? As we ride along, we pass by many rigid items such as rocks, trees, and curbs (or, in Britain, "kerbs"). We also pass by other less rigid objects, such as cars, shrubbery, and mailboxes. We go by them at varying speeds. While one standard may result in a helmet that withstands rigid objects very well, it may not do as well against less rigid items. Another standard may result in a helmet that handles a single hit very well, but would not withstand a second hit on the same spot very well. The mind reels.

To get some clarification I called on Dave Thom, a helmet expert who was associated with Dr. Harry Hurt and the latter's famous accident study in the late 1970s. One of the conclusions of the Hurt study was that, despite what we may expect, in 90 percent of motorcycle accidents, the impact delivered to the head was less than the 400 g's allowed in the DOT test.

Thom now works for a company called Collision and Injury Dynamics in El Segundo, California. After more than a quarter-century of involvement in accident research and helmet safety, Thom told me, "Performance can only be measured by the situation. However, we

know from the Hurt report that 90 percent of the impacts are at, or below, DOT impact severity. Therefore, it makes sense to lean toward performance in the expected region—although you can't ignore the other 10 percent completely." For that reason, Thom believes that a helmet meeting only the DOT standard is perfectly adequate for most accident situations.

Some critics suggest helmets that pass Snell necessarily have to be heavier than those that pass ECE or BSI. I also interviewed Steve Johnson, general manager of the Snell Memorial Foundation in Sacramento, California. Johnson told me, "It depends. Some less-expensive helmets tend to be heavier, as they may not use state-of-the-art materials. Most are not excessively heavy. Some lightweight helmets cannot perform to our requirements, and their lightness may reduce their protective capabilities. We don't want helmets to be heavier or hotter for the wearer." In my own research for my helmet tests in Rider magazine in 2005, I found that of the four lightest helmets in the test, two met the ECE standard and two met Snell. All, of course, met DOT.

Don't touch that pork chop! But if you do, be assured that the belt or drawstrings on many jackets will help the jacket seal around your waist. Such adjustments are very helpful as the rider adds and removes layers underneath.

Why is this man smiling? Because he's wearing a high-tech motorcycle jacket that seals well at the neck and has numerous pockets. Also, its sleeves are plenty long enough to accommodate the riding position.

Controllable vents contribute greatly to a jacket's temperature versatility. Slit vents in the chest can close when the rider brings the arms forward, but these flat vents utilize snaps so they stay open.

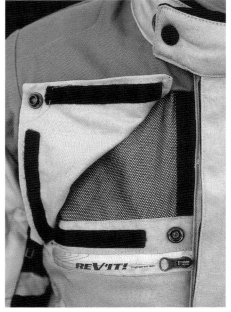

Fully perforated jackets with mesh are great for hot weather, as they will flow air constantly. When the weather changes, however, you'll want such a jacket only if it has a good liner or cover that can be added for warmth. Shown is the Marsee 3-Piece Full Flow jacket, which comes with a high-quality cover.

When it cools down, the Full Flow becomes a lot warmer when its cover-up is zipped on.

flat anvils, some call for hemispherical anvils, and others for "kerbstone" anvils. It's apples, oranges, and kumquats.

For those who wish to see the specifics of the major standards, Snell has published information about them on its website. Keep in mind that obviously Snell is going to favor its own standard over the others, but at least this site reveals how they differ. See www.smf.org/articles/mcomp2.html

I asked Snell Memorial Foundation General Manager Steve Johnson if it was true that more expensive helmets tended to pass fewer g's to the headform during Snell testing. Johnson answered, "Some less-expensive helmets perform very well. We have a pass/fail standard, so I cannot tell you who performs better. All helmets that pass Snell perform very well; 300 g's is fairly low, given what is accepted to be the threshold of brain injury or death. Some helmets perform better in flat-surface tests than in hemispherical—that's why we stay away from grading them. A thick, soft helmet performs well on a flat surface. Because they have to withstand impacts from two opposite anvil types, a flat and a hemispherical, they have to be built somewhere in the middle."

Was there any truth to the idea that heavier helmets lead to greater neck injuries?

"We know that weight is a factor, but we have no conclusive data or scientifically

collected physical evidence that this is occurring. Everyone's head is different, and everyone's neck is different, and every accident is different. We have seen a recommended maximum helmet weight of 1,800 grams [3.94 pounds] or less in one study, but we haven't seen any additional corroborating support for that data. It is logical that lighter is better, but we don't know how light that is."

Then Johnson took a swipe at any attempt to change the standards. "The push in the industry for less demanding standards would facilitate lighter helmets being produced, and it is our belief that many of these helmets will offer significantly less impact protection than the current products available. Some very light helmets do pass Snell."

Dave Thom offered the following opinion of the various standards. "No study, including the Hurt study, has ever showed a benefit for helmets meeting any standard. . . . There are benefits to coverage, etc., but not based on what standard they meet. I personally am completely comfortable wearing a DOT-only helmet—or a DOT/ECE—and slightly less comfortable with a DOT/Snell helmet." As for his conclusion, Thom recommends, "Wear a full-face helmet with lots of Styrofoam in the chinbar."

Regarding whether any standard is superior, I'll fall back upon a famous statement by a helmet manufacturer: "You tell me the impact you're going to have, and I'll build you a helmet that will protect you from it."

In conclusion, with the many variables of speed, what you may hit and at what angle, and how the various standards do or do not relate to the real world, I'll say this: Wear a good full-face helmet that passes at least DOT, and has foam in the chinbar. Wear one you can afford, one that's comfortable, and one that you'll want to wear every time you ride. That's the best helmet for you.

Ventilation

Most helmets have some form of controllable ventilation that allows for airflow in warm weather. Often it is in the form of controls in

the chinbar and above the eyeport that slide open to reveal an opening that passes through channels in the helmet's EPS foam; sometimes there is a controllable exhaust vent in the rear. Often this venting system is not very effective. Be certain that the vents have positive closure, and that they're easy to work while wearing gloves. Keep in mind that vents only work in airflow, and that if you ride behind a big windshield or fairing, these may disrupt that flow.

Some helmets have a chin curtain (a flexible nylon sheeting spread across the underside of the chin area) designed to prevent the noisy (and possibly cold) wind

Today your bike can be had in a true multitude of colors, as can your riding gear. Days and rides like this can be a whole lot more enjoyable with the right gear, and looking good makes it even that much better. American Honda Motor Co.

Did you ever have one of those days? If you're caught out in serious weather like Rider magazine's Ken Freund was at this bike intro, you'll be wishing for the very best possible riding gear. On days like this, it's best to turn around or just stay home. Triumph Motorcycles America

Reflective striping will help other motorists see us in their headlights. Here's how an Aerostich Darien jacket looks in bright sunlight when the sun hits it right. Headlights work a similar magic on it at night.

The European Community (CE) standard requires armor that consists of dense, closed-cell protective foam sandwiched between layers of plastic.

Look closely at the middle of this photo and you'll notice a zippered sleeve vent that puts the wind were it can do a lot of good.

blast from coming up from below. Some also have removable, washable liners in various sizes for easy cleaning and exact sizing.

While a particular helmet may be available in sizes XS, S, M, L, XL, and XXL, they may cover these various sizes with only two or three shell sizes. The rest of the sizing is done internally, by fitting different sizes of padding into those shells. If the helmet you like doesn't fit quite right, ask the salesperson if there are additional sizes of pads available for custom sizing.

Keep the Lid On

While most helmets utilize conventional D-rings to secure the strap, some utilize seat-belt-style or other types of buckles or latches. These may be easier to latch and release (often with the push of a button), but the potential drawback is that when locking them to the bike via a helmet holder, their mechanism is bulkier, and may be harder to stuff under the motorcycle's seat. Or the helmet may be easier to steal if the buckle unlatches with the push of a button.

MOTORCYCLE CLOTHING

Motorcycling is an exercise in versatility, both in terms of weather and in the types of roads we ride. You start out on a spring morning in the city and it's 45 degrees. Stop for lunch a few hours later in the flatlands and it's 75 degrees. By midafternoon you're in the mountains where the temperature has dropped to 60, then late in the day you're pulling into a motel at 6,500 feet and it's 40 degrees. Perhaps it's raining. How do you cope with all these extremes? By choosing the right riding gear.

Most apparel for motorcycle riders today is made of leather (usually cowhide and occasionally kangaroo or deerskin), textiles (usually some form of basket-weave ballistic nylon), or a combination of both. Both hides and textiles have their advantages and disadvantages.

Leather Clothing

Cowhide leather makes for an excellent motorcycling garment as it's a natural, fibrous, porous material. This porosity allows it to breathe, and its fibers help it hold together for abrasion resistance. Leather is classy, has the heft and feel of quality, it wears well, and I love the way it creaks when you move. Its pleasant aroma ranks right up there with chocolate-chip cookies or a good steak. It's repairable, and if well cared for, it may be possible to pass your leather garments on to your children.

Because leather is not inherently warm, most leatherwear is lined and often insulated. Its only major drawback is that, if you're caught in the rain, leather will lose its natural oils and (unless it's been specially treated) will turn stiff and discolor. Carry a rain suit.

Deerskin is softer and more supple than cowhide, has greater abrasion resistance, and is not nearly as susceptible to damage by rain. It has also been my experience that deerskin garments retain heat better in the cold, yet also breathe better, and are cooler in hot weather. The tradeoff is that deerskin is more expensive.

Kangaroo leather is said to be the most abrasion resistant. Whole suits are available, but they're quite expensive. Gloves that have kangaroo-leather palms, on the other hand, are a wonderful indulgence.

How Motorcycle Leather Is Different from Fashion Leather

You may be tempted to use a leather fashion jacket for motorcycling, but it's not likely to work nearly as well as true, purpose-built motorcycle clothing. Fashion leather is thinner and more supple, and not of sufficient thickness for serious abrasion protection. The open design of fashion wear will allow the wind to rush up the sleeves and waist, and come in at the relatively open neck. Collars will flap in the wind, shoulders will bind, and the sleeves will ride up as the rider reaches for the grips.

Jackets designed for motorcycling have lengthened sleeves that have been rotated forward to accommodate the riding posi-

tion. Often the back has been cut lower ("dropped") to protect the kidneys, and the extra pleat of material behind the shoulders that allows for greater movement is called the "action back."

Also, as the temperature changes during a ride, riders will be adding and subtracting clothing. To allow for expansion, many jackets have waist adjusters in the form of elastic, snaps, lacing, or hook-and-loop that fashion jackets do not offer.

Textile Clothing

It's every rider's dream to have such a great riding suit that, no matter what happens to the weather—whether it turns hot, cold, or wet—he would not need to stop to change clothing, but could just keep riding. That's where textile fabrics come in. They're made of synthetic materials such as nylon, often with trade names such as Cordura, Taslan, or Dynax, and are available in several weave thicknesses expressed as "denier." Nylon is made from petroleum—oil—and therefore resists absorbing moisture. A water-resistant coating bonded to these nylon fabrics renders them essentially impervious to weather, but stitch holes passing through the fabric can let in water. These must be taped, treated with seam sealer, or protected with flaps.

Often the jacket's back has been cut lower, or "dropped," so that it better protects the kidneys when the rider leans forward for the bars. If you look closely, you'll notice a unique feature of the Rev'it Cayenne jacket. That zipper to the left allows the wearer to zip off the entire lower, rear section and wear it independently as a fanny pack.

Motorcycling is an exercise in versatility, both in terms of weather and in the types of roads we ride.

That extra pleat of material behind the shoulders of a motorcycle jacket that allows for greater movement is called the "action back." It allows the rider to reach forward for the controls without the jacket binding.

To allow for the addition and subtraction of full-sleeve liners and sweaters, some jackets have sleeve adjusters in the form of elastic, snaps, or hook-and-loop that fashion jackets do not offer. This Rev'it jacket offers snap adjusters.

Regardless of how they're built, everyone looks best in apparel that's styled and sized specifically for them. This women's leather jacket by Triumph is designed to complement several of their bike models. *Triumph Motorcycles America*

To keep the heat in, it's very important that a jacket seals well at the neck. Not only that, but the neck seal must also be adjustable to accommodate the variety of clothing that can be worn underneath.

If properly made, sealed, and insulated, a textile riding suit can allow one to just continue riding in a light rain or cold weather, but they will eventually soak through. Add a waterproof, breathable membrane such as Gore-Tex, Hipora, Reissa, or others, and you've got not only a pretty secure outfit but also one that can breathe and offer a wider range of comfort. It is possible that the outer shell can become soaked while the liner keeps the inside—and the rider—dry. This means that while the rider may be physically dry, he'll be encased in a cold, sodden envelope. The shell material does not breathe that well, and without proper venting, a textile garment may become stuffy in hot weather.

Melting Point

As a petroleum product, nylon will melt if exposed to heat. Should your textile jacket slide off your bike's seat and onto its hot exhaust pipe, it may soon be sporting a nasty melted spot. It can likewise deposit an unsightly, smoking blob of molten nylon on your pristine pipes. Should you get thrown from your bike and go road surfing, the heat of friction could likewise melt a section of a textile jacket.

WHAT MAKES A GOOD RIDING JACKET

If you do a lot of riding, including touring, versatility is the key to a good jacket. It must

> **TIP**
>
> Layer clothing (a sweater over a shirt over a T-shirt) rather than wearing one heavy, bulky garment. You'll be warmer, and your gear will be more versatile. If the weather's going to be cold, wear a long-sleeved t-shirt and turtleneck. In an emergency, if you've got to keep riding and it's just too cold, stuff newspapers down the front of your jacket.

be livable on a 90-degree, humid Midwest summer's day, yet remain comfortable atop an 8,000-foot pass when it's 40 degrees and spitting snow. It must seal up like a bank vault to keep out the wind, and may offer controllable venting for hot days. For maximum versatility, the liner will zip or snap out for warm weather. Some liners are vest-style, but full-sleeve liners have the potential to be warmer. If you expect you may be removing the liner, be sure you have some place to store it during the ride, such as in a tank bag or tail bag. Whether they're leather or textile, here's a quick look at some desirable jacket features.

Staying warm on a motorcycle is all about sealing out the wind blast, and it's very important that any jacket have a good neck seal. If it doesn't, bring a scarf or a product such as the Aerostich Wind Triangle. It includes a layer of Gore-Tex sandwiched by two layers of nylon, with a soft backing.

On the sleeves, look for adjustable cuffs, sealed by zippers or hook-and-loop fastener, that are compact enough to fit inside long gauntlet gloves. Air stealing up from the bottom of a jacket can be chilling, so many jackets have adjustable belts or drawstrings to seal them around the waist. It's a real plus if a jacket and pants zip together.

Pockets

Motorcycle jackets are known for their pockets, as riders need to carry many small items. Check that pockets are covered by storm flaps, as exposed zippers will take in rain. Pockets are usually secured with zippers or hook-and-loop fastener. (By the way, hook-and-loop fastener is a generic term for the peel-apart fastener that is commonly known by the trade name "Velcro." By saying "hook-and-loop fastener," we avoid receiving nasty letters from the lawyers at Velcro.)

For walking around on cold days, hand-warmer pockets are a plus. Most riders will carry their wallet in an inner pocket secured by a zipper or button. Other pockets are handy for carrying earplugs, spare change, keys, a wind scarf, shield cleaner and rag, a candy bar (well wrapped), and summer gloves. Pockets are both practical and a styling feature. Remember, if you keep your wallet in your jacket, don't leave it on the back of a chair in the restaurant and go wandering off.

Temperature Control

Controllable vents contribute greatly to a jacket's temperature versatility, so long as they're properly designed. When opened, vents must have a mesh backing to keep out the insects, and they must remain open. Many jackets have zippered slit vents in the chest, but as soon as the rider reaches forward for the grips on some sporty bikes these vents naturally close again. A few

For sealing the neck and head, a balaclava is one of those silk items that pulls completely over the head, leaving only an eye port. We see a lot of these worn by night fighters in war movies, but they're quite comfy for riders.

Gauntlet gloves that fit over the cuffs are a great way of preventing the wind from stealing up into the sleeves. These are from Triumph. *Triumph Motorcycles America*

CELL PHONE

You can't find the motel. Can't find gas. Your bike has broken down. You're separated from your group. You need to check your messages. Need I go on? Many motorcycle jackets now include a cell phone pocket, and companies such as J&M and AutoCom offer equipment that allows hands-free cell-phone operation with helmet headsets.

In case of accident, paramedics will search an injured person's cell phone for identity and contact information. Create a file called "ICE" (In Case of Emergency) that includes the names and phone numbers of anyone who should be contacted, should you have a problem.

"Conspicuity" means making yourself as conspicuous as possible. In motorcycling it relates to being easily seen so other motorists notice you, and, as a result, don't pull out in front of you and put you in danger. This gentleman wears a brightly colored reflective vest that makes him more visible both in daylight and at night.

Chaps are a versatile, flat garment that fasten around the hips and back, fit loosely, and are simple to get into and out of. This is the Wanderer by Roadgear. *Roadgear*

I do not recommend suede

leathers for motorcycle use.

Leather pants have been a traditional motorcycle garment for a century. They're comfortable, have a pleasant aroma, break in well, and provide real protection in a spill. *Triumph Motorcycles America*

jackets also have mesh panels on the fore-arms. Back vents allow the wind to flow through, but their zippers are often hard to reach while wearing the jacket. When shopping, ask if you can step outside and try jackets you're considering while sitting on your bike. You need to determine if the sleeves are long enough to allow you to reach the grips, and if the cuffs can open wide enough to scoop some breeze up the arms in hot weather. Check that the front vents are easy to open while you're riding, and that they will remain open.

Some companies offer fully perforated jackets through which the wind will flow constantly. These are fine for those who live in warm-weather climates, but where the weather is changeable they may not be the best solution.

Care

If your helmet shield gets dirty and needs to be cleaned several times a day, what will your jacket look like after a season of riding? Wipe down smooth leather with a damp cloth, or clean it with saddle soap that has restorers built in. An alternative is a

> **TIP**
>
> If the jacket's zipper pull tabs are hard to grasp, extend them by looping leather lacing through them, or use key-chain pulls.

commercial leather cleaner. Test any cleaner or leather treatment product on an unexposed part of the garment to be sure it does not remove the color. Once the leather garment has been cleaned, apply a commercial leather-care product.

I do not recommend suede leathers for motorcycle use, as bike jackets can become very dirty and suede is difficult to clean. Leather garments should be treated periodically with cleaners and restorers.

Textile garments should be wiped down with a damp rag periodically to remove the most obvious bug carcasses. When gunk builds up, remove the armor pads and toss the garment in the washing machine, following the manufacturer's instructions. If the liner is removable, check it for any special washing instructions. Afterward, you may wish to treat them with a commercial waterproofing or protective spray.

Today, your bike can be had

in a true multitude of colors,

and so can many leather

and nonleather jackets.

Color

Cruiser riders seem to follow the words of Henry Ford by wearing every conceivable color of garment . . . so long as it's black. Attention purists: Bill Harley and the Davidsons were offering their machines in black or Renault Gray in 1906! Color *is* traditional. Today, your bike can be had in a true multitude of colors, and so can many leather and nonleather jackets. Lighten up already

TIP

In my many years of testing motorcycles and participating in photo shoots, one thing I've learned regarding color is that it's doubtful the shiny paint on a motorcycle and the more saturated color of a textile jacket will match. For example, the softer red of a textile jacket will rarely match the red on a motorcycle. Therefore, I suggest you bring your motorcycle along when you shop for colorful textile clothing, and match them at the store. Often, you'll find blue or blue/gray textile clothing will better complement a red motorcycle. Similarly, textile clothing with red, or red in combination with gray or black, will often better complement a blue bike. A helmet, because it also carries shiny paint, will often match or complement the bike. Many times we've done very satisfactory photo shoots in which the rider wore a red helmet on a red bike, while wearing a blue jacket.

Overpants are designed to be worn over street clothes for protection and comfort. They may be textile or leather, with lining and insulation or without. If you need to remove them as the day warms, be certain you have the room to carry them. *Roadgear*

One observation is that while very colorful textile riding suits look great in the store, once they become soiled it's difficult to ever get them as clean as new, and then they look grungy. Which brings us back to the reason why most motorcycle riding gear is black. Unless your bike has such good weather protection that you rarely get bug splat on your gear, you may wish to stick with those traditional dark colors.

Reflectivity

Most motorcycle jackets are black or brown so they won't show the dirt, but textile jackets come in a variety of colors. If other motorists already can't see us very well, even with our headlights on, how much more invisible are we while wearing dark colors? Some leather jackets have color accents, and some sport jackets are quite colorful. Reflective striping will help other motorists see us in their headlights. Consider it a plus.

Armor and Foam

Take a tumble, and any protruding parts of your body (hands, elbows, forearms, shoulders, hips, feet and knees) will potentially get banged up. It's common for motorcycle apparel to have a second layer of leather or textile material, along with some padding, sewn over these areas. Some just have comfort foam, the soft open-cell stuff that bottoms easily and is of minimal use in a get-off. Others will have a much denser, closed-cell protective foam, the best of which is sandwiched between layers of thin plastic and meets European Community (CE) standards. This CE-approved armor will absorb and disperse impact, and is also an insulator. A layer of foam, especially across the back, will add warmth.

Old-style armor is simply a molded plastic shell that covers the area it's designed to protect, such as an elbow or knee. The problem with a simple plastic shell, or even a plastic shell with a layer of foam inside it, is that it transfers the energy of a blow directly to the body part it's protecting; absorption is minimal. Granted, the ensuing bruise is much less severe than what would happen to an unprotected body part, but it still hurts. Modern armor designed to absorb an impact's energy is far superior and worth every penny. However, if it's a choice between old armor and no armor, well, the decision should be obvious.

WOMEN'S APPAREL

Because a large percentage of motorcycle riders are male, most companies cut their motorcycle garments specifically for men, then hide behind the "unisex" designation for women. Let's see, if men and women are built the same, why am I more interested in a Dallas Cowboys Cheerleaders calendar

With leather overpants, as with textile, look for a full-length leg zipper that makes them easy to put on and take off over boots. Because they're overpants, they'll be rather bulky and fit loosely. I recommend leather overpants rather than chaps for their greater protection and versatility. *Roadgear*

ON THE MOUNTAIN OR IN THE DESERT

Staying Warm

Staying warm means sealing out the wind, and the neck area is the most critical area to seal. Choose a jacket with particular attention to how well it seals the neck area. If you want extra warmth there, wear a dickie or turtleneck to hold in the warmth, and a wind scarf to seal out the wind. A primary problem with some jackets is that, while they seal well, they do not allow for the additional layers of clothing a rider may need in cold weather and thus don't allow for sufficient adjustment. If there's an adjustable tab at the neck, check that it is long enough to seal over cold-weather clothing.

For sealing the neck and head, balaclavas are great. They're those silk items with an eyeports that pull over your head,. You often see them in war movies being worn by commandos sneaking ashore or through the forest.

Gauntlet gloves that fit over the cuffs are a great way of preventing the wind from stealing up into the sleeves. For cold weather you'll need a lot of insulation on the outsides of the hands, but not in the palms, because they're curled around the grips. Motorcycle-specific gloves are a plus here, as most all-purpose winter gloves have too much insulation on the palms.

Staying Cool

Riding in the desert or in hot, humid weather makes additional demands on the rider. I still recall my first trip across the desert, in the summer of 1978, when I collapsed into an air-conditioned motel room in Needles, California, at 3 p.m., dangerously dehydrated. Here's how to stay cooler on the road in hot weather.

Rule One in the heat is to drink plenty of liquids, as this is how your body naturally cools itself. Without the evaporation of sweat, your body temperature can quickly rise to dangerous levels. Drink water and commercial thirst quenchers that replace the electrolytes your body loses. Do not drink alcohol; it will not only adversely affect your riding, but is a diuretic that will cause you to lose more fluid than you retain.

Drink liquids before you get out into the heat, because by the time you're thirsty you're already in danger. If you don't like carrying glass bottles commercial drinks come in, I suggest those plastic water bottles popular with bicyclists. They are light, inexpensive, come in a variety of sizes and colors, and have an easy-open spout.

Learn from desert dwellers that it's cooler in the shade. People who live in desert countries don't go out shirtless wearing shorts, but wear their shade in the form of loose-fitting, flowing clothing. Riding shirtless and in shorts not only exposes one to sunburn and serious road rash, but also speeds up the rate of dehydration from the wind's direct effects. In hot weather, wear your helmet and loose-fitting garments. A cotton shop jumpsuit can keep you from sunburn, and can be hosed down.

In most situations, wear sturdy footwear and ventilated gloves. In extremely hot weather, when the heat coming in exceeds body temperature, I've found it's more comfortable to wear nonventilated clothing and to keep my helmet shield closed.

Evaporation is the key to staying cool. Soak a bandana or other cloth and tie it around your neck. By being in the breeze and in close proximity to the arteries in your neck, it will cool you for hours. When it begins to dry out, pull over and use the water bottle in your tank bag to soak it again.

Another method which I've used, and highly recommend, is to soak a sweatshirt or other heavy riding shirt in water. You'll shiver when you put it on, and it will get your pants wet, but that won't last long. In the direct heat and airflow it will dry out relatively soon, so wear a nylon wind-breaker over it and it will keep you cool for hours. Some manufacturers offer cooling vests that have pockets that accept sodden sponges.

THE LOWER HALF

Chaps

Invented by cowboys in the Southwest, *chaparreras* were made of leather and designed to keep legs from being cut to red ribbons by thorns and cactus needles. Today's chaps are similar. A pair of chaps is essentially a flat garment that fastens around the hips and the backs of the legs, fits loosely, and is simple to get into and out of. Versatility is their reason for being, as many riders will wear chaps in the cool morning, and then stow them when the day warms.

Chaps will keep off the wind, but let the rain come around from behind. Their backless/crotchless design offers very little protection. In a get-off they'll likely rotate on the body and may even come off. Finally, they have a sort of, well, kinky look. But I'm not saying that's a bad thing . . . .

Pants Versus Overpants

Most riders tend to ride in denim jeans or a similar fabric pant, and suffer the cold consequences. Though you can't beat them for comfort and universal acceptability, jeans aren't warm or protective, nor will they keep you dry. But motorcycle pants can be heavy, and can become hot when the day warms up. One alternative is a protective overpant that you can wear all day if necessary over your jeans, or remove and store when the weather warms.

Overpants

Let's define an overpant as a motorcycle pant designed to be worn over other parts for the purposes of protection and comfort. Overpants take chaps that final step forward by offering full, wraparound protection. They C.Y.A.—if you know what I mean.

In order to cover the rider's jeans without putting on the big squeeze overpants are built a bit big and perhaps a little sloppy. It's the price we pay for that scosh more room. They're not going to look as svelte or show the curves for your

Overpants are built a bit big and perhaps a little sloppy. It's the price we pay for that scosh more room.

than a Dallas Cowboys calendar? More companies are now offering motorcycle clothing cut specifically for women, but the buyer must be careful to verify this fact. I'm all in favor of rewarding performance, and in the realm of motorcycle clothing that means buying from companies that offer specific products for your needs.

hindquarters to the best advantage for the opposite sex.

Another consideration is if you commute to an office job, or anywhere else you want to look your best, a jacket with overpants will protect your dress togs from bugs, dirt, and road grime. When you're giving that presentation on the 28th floor to the boys from Finance, no one has to prejudice his views by noticing the bug stains on your $1,000 suit.

When touring, the rationale behind overpants is you put them on when the weather is cool or questionable, and take them off when things warm up. If you didn't intend to remove them in fair weather, you may as well just go for full leather or textile pants. Therefore, it's a real convenience that overpants can go on and come off easily on the road without having to remove your boots. The tradeoff is that any dirt on your boots can become deposited on the overpant liner and then rub off on your pants. In any case, for convenience, overpants usually are supplied with a b-o-o-o-ong zipper up each leg.

A good overpant should allow access to the keys or change in your pants pockets, though none will likely offer access to your rear wallet pocket. Well, that's why jackets have wallet pockets.

The two main varieties are textile overpants that are often waterproof and sometimes armored, and leather overpants that are designed more with style and overall abrasion protection in mind.

Textile Overpants

These are often deluxe versions of rain suit bottoms and may offer such features as insulation, pockets, armor, and additional features. Some are actually the bottoms of two-piece suits so it's possible to purchase the jacket (sold separately) and have a coordinated outfit.

Keep in mind that textile pants and overpants, while wonderful in many ways, will likely make that dorky "whisk, whisk, whisk" sound when you walk.

The pockets and seams of some are sealed, but for those that are not it may be possible to spray them with a sealant (such as Scotchgard) and seam sealer to make them so. However, doing so may affect their breathability. Armor is a plus to protect knees and sometimes hips from impact.

Leather Overpants

It's cool, it's classy and comfortable, it looks like real motorcycle wear, and it won't melt on your exhaust pipes. Leather provides great abrasion resistance, won't flap as readily in the wind, and smells great.

FULL RIDING SUITS: ONE- OR TWO-PIECE?

A one-piece is a full suit that does not separate, so it will obviously seal well. Racing suits are most often one-piece, as they cannot ride up or separate, exposing the rider to road rash. The disadvantages are that it's usually necessary to find a place to sit down in order to don a one-piece suit, and it's rather bulky for walking around town. Pull into the restaurant and you'll need to find a chair to slip out of your one-piece suit, as the others in your group just

A one-piece suit seals well, but is not as convenient, since the jacket and pants cannot be worn separately. This textile Aerostich Roadcrafter one-piece suit is available in colors and with armor. It's ideal for commuting as it easily fits over street clothes but is not insulated. It is also available as a two-piece.

This two-piece leather riding suit offers the major convenience of being easier to put on and take off, and it allows the rider to throw on the jacket and walk to dinner. In general, a two-piece suit excels in convenience while a one-piece excels in safety and protection.

Rain suits should be large enough to fit over your standard riding gear, with longer arms and sleeves to give full coverage. Look for bright colors, reflective striping, and good closure at the neck and cuffs. *Triumph Motorcycles America*

Rainy weather is also dark weather. A brightly colored suit with reflective striping will make you more visible. This rider would really appreciate a full-face helmet right about now.

There was a time when a rain boot was made of, or coated with, nylon, and impervious to moisture. The problem was it did not breathe and soon became clammy. Triumph's answer is the leather Sympatex Explorer II, which is not only waterproof, breathable, and windproof, but also has reflective striping. *Triumph Motorcycles America*

I recommend rain gloves with breathable liners that will keep the hands dry, but won't become clammy. These Harley-Davidson FXRG gloves also feature a face shield wiper.

hang their jackets on the wall. If you left your keys in your pants pocket, it'll be tough to reach them while wearing a one-piece suit. It's simply not very versatile, which is why I favor the two-piece suit.

A two-piece suit is one that has separate jacket and pants that may zip together to form a relatively tight seal. The advantage to the zip-together feature is that it will prevent the jacket from riding up and letting wind through, or worse—riding up should you go sliding down the pavement.

The major practical advantage of a two-piece suit is that, when you arrive at your destination and wish to walk around in the cool evening, you may wear the jacket and leave the bulky pants behind. And obviously, a two-piece suit is much easier to put on.

RAIN SUITS
Rain Suits Versus Terrariums

Some summers ago, my wife and I were blasting across Germany on one of their excellent autobahns, heading for the Netherlands, making some serious, high-speed miles on this hazy, overcast day. We donned our coated-nylon rain suits when the salmon-strangling rains came, and were cozy and dry. However, when the welcome sun came out an hour later, the steam boiled off the pavement and our suits quickly became very hot and uncomfortable. We were stewing in our own juices; in their zeal to *keep* moisture out, the suit manufacturer had made no provisions to *let* moisture out. The rains came again, and the sun again, and each time we had to stop to change gear. We really regretted not buying rain suits made of breathable fabric, or at least with better ventilation.

There are two philosophies among rain suit manufacturers. The usually less expensive way is to wrap the rider in an impermeable coated-nylon shell through which moisture cannot pass in either direction; some add venting. The often more expensive way is to provide a breathable shell that fends off the rain, but allows humidity and the body's natural moisture to escape.

Being dry is easy—just encase yourself in a body-sized Baggie and seal up the openings where your appendages poke out. Staying dry, on the other hand, is tough. Dampness from the outside is bad enough on a rainy day, but when dampness from the inside permeates your clothing, you're stuck with that clammy, shivery feeling that just won't go away.

Like textile suits, nylon will also melt when it contacts a hot surface. For this reason, a few suits offer Nomex or other heat-stable fabric on the inner sides of the legs.

Sizing

Rain suits are sized to be worn over your riding gear. If you normally wear a size medium jacket, a medium riding or rain suit should be sized properly.

One-Piece Versus Two-Piece

Two-piece rain suits outsell the one-piece by a handy margin, mostly for reasons of convenience and versatility. Once you get your legs in, it's more difficult to squirm your shoulders up into a one-piece suit, especially when your leather is already wet. A mesh liner on the rain suit helps here, and also adds to comfort by providing a space for evaporation. Once it's on, however, a one-piece suit can potentially be dryer because it has no split.

The potential problem with one-piece suits is that, when the main zipper is long enough for easy entry, it usually dips past the crotch and may let rain through if not properly folded. Arrange the suit so that it will not allow water to pool in the crotch.

The two-piece rain suit is usually easier to get into because the jacket opens fully. And with no zipper in the pants above the knees, your crotch stays well protected. A well-placed drawstring will keep the rain out.

Rainwear Tips

Plan ahead. Because the riding suit's pockets will be difficult to access once you're all bundled up in a rain suit, transfer keys, wallet, and change to a convenient pocket in your outer jacket or rain suit.

Because wet weather is often cooler, I strongly recommend the use of electrically heated clothing in conjunction with rainwear. Electric gear plugs into your bike's battery, so a two-piece suit will be more convenient as the one-piece may not have a convenient opening for the plug to pass through.

Rainy weather is also dark weather. A brightly colored suit with reflective striping will make you more visible.

Rain suits block the wind very effectively. If you get cold, even on a dry day, donning your rain suit can keep you much warmer. Or if it has stopped raining but the road is still wet, wearing only the rain pants can protect your legs from road spray.

Once the suit becomes wet, allow it to dry overnight before packing it away to avoid mildew.

Hands and Feet

Many companies offer boots and gloves with breathable, rain-resistant membranes such as Gore-Tex, Hipora, or Reissa. Others offer nylon glove and boot covers, which are often slippery, and are yet another layer to get into. My main criticism of most rain suits is that they need greater adjustability in the cuffs for cinching around gloves.

Rain Suit or Textile Suit?

Textile suits are essentially high fashion, rain-repellent shells with insulation, venting, and armor, and some utilize a weatherproof, breathable membrane. Should you get a rain suit for $30 to $300, or a textile suit for $250 to $1,000?

The obvious benefit of a rain suit is price, and that it goes over your existing riding gear. If you think leather is cool and prefer wearing it, a rain suit will be your choice. The biggest argument in favor of water-resistant textile suits is that if you're already wearing waterproof boots and gloves, you don't even need to stop to get dressed when the rain begins—just keep riding. And perhaps that's the greatest benefit of all.

> **TIP**
>
> A rain suit can't protect you if you're not wearing it. The problem is, most riders delay putting on their suits until it's already raining in the (usually) silly belief that, somehow, they're going to be lucky this time. Most of the time you'll be climbing into a rain suit while parked beside the road, often in bad light and always in a hurry. For this reason, the legs must be wide enough for your boots to slide through easily.

An electric vest is less bulky than a full-sleeve garment, and by keeping your torso warm will make a real difference in cold weather. Look closely and you'll notice that this Widder vest features snap-on sleeves that can be added for cold weather. Widder also offers electric chaps and gloves.

An electric jacket liner, like this item by Gerbing's, offers full heat all the way down the sleeves and into the collar. Note the connectors at the cuffs for electric gloves. Get the optional thermostat ("Heat Controller") because electric garments may become too hot without it.

If you get cold, even on a dry day, donning your rain suit can keep you much warmer.

Gerbing's manufactures a fully electric jacket that features a full complement of heating wires. The company also offers electric pants and gloves.

How easy is it to attach the battery hookup for an electric garment to your bike? This easy: Expose the battery and remove the bolt to the negative post, then remove the bolt to the positive post. Put one bolt through the black lead and screw the bolt back into the negative post; put other bolt through the red lead and screw the bolt back into the positive post. Plug the garment into the exposed connector. Be warm.

I know you can't believe you could ever be too warm on a motorcycle on a cold day, but it will happen with a heated garment. For that reason, I suggest you get the optional thermostat so you can dial-in precisely the amount of heat you want. This one is by Gerbing's; one end plugs into the battery hookup, and the other plugs into the garment.

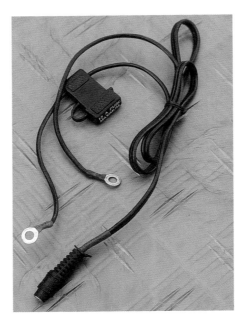

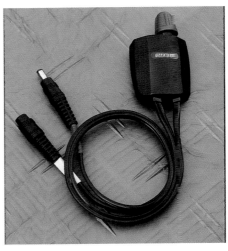

Touring boots, like the Expedition Boot, need to be overall riding and rain boots, comfortable enough for walking on hiking trails. They need a rainproof, breathable membrane to handle the vagaries of weather. *Triumph Motorcycles America*

The drawback to textile suits is that many of them wear their waterproofing on the inside, so the outer fabric layer will absorb water and become soaked. While the inner liner may not become physically wet, the rider is essentially wearing a wet bag and feels damp and chilly. If the suit does not dry out overnight (it rarely will if its shell is soaked), it's really unpleasant to have to slip back into it in the morning.

Some textile suits are made with a waterproof outer shell so they don't become wet, but if the day warms up the rider feels trapped in a mobile sauna. Either type of suit will also likely become filthy with road spray.

ELECTRIC CLOTHING
Baby, It's Cold Outside

What's the coldest you've ever been on a motorcycle? In my 40-plus years of riding I can recall riding my Vespa scooter in Michigan during a windy December day in 1965, grimacing and shuddering in a light jacket. And taking a Honda GL1000 Gold Wing to the South Rim of the Grand Canyon one March evening in 1979 with snow beside the road; I hadn't realized that the rim was at an altitude of more than 7,000 feet! And riding over a high pass in California during a snowstorm in 1983 on my BMW R100RS with my wife on the back, the snow packing

around the headlight and powdering my shoulders as little icicles formed off the fairing. If you don't have your own stories, you will someday.

Hooking Up

Wouldn't you love to pull the electric blanket off your bed and wear it on your motorcycle? That's essentially what you can do with electric clothing, starting with an electric vest or jacket liner. The difference is that the jacket liner has sleeves. I recommend a lightly insulated electric garment, as it will help hold in the heat without being too bulky.

Electric garments hook into your bike's battery via an easily installed wiring harness, and produce heat by passing a current through a series of wires of a specific resistance sewn into the garment. Installing a hookup for an electric garment is simplicity itself. The battery hookup has an eye at the end of each wire. Expose the battery connections and remove the negative battery screw first, then the positive. Place the screw through the eye and replace the positive cable first. The line with the fuse goes to the positive post. To prevent losing radio, clock, and other settings, keep the battery cables in contact with the posts as you add the harness hookup; it stays permanently attached to the bike.

Be very careful to not allow any tools touching the positive post to touch other metal, as that will cause a spark and could damage your bike electrically. Route the

TIP

To check if your bike can handle the added electrical draw, with the key off and garments unplugged, connect a voltmeter to the battery posts. It should give a reading of around 12.5 to 13 volts. Now start the engine, plug in a garment, and rev the bike to its usual rpm at highway speeds as you take a second reading. If this second reading is higher than the first, there should be no problem. Now plug in any additional garments, one by one. If at any time the reading goes lower than the original, indicating a discharge situation, end the experiment immediately and unplug the garments. Using all these products could blow the fuse or damage the electrical system. However, you should be able to use any garments up to that point when the battery began to discharge. Seek your dealer's advice.

garment hookup's wires carefully with zip-ties so they are not abraded by opening and closing the seat. Note the amperage of the fuse used, and carry spares. If you ride a BMW, utilize their handy accessory plug for the electric garment.

Modern motorcycles above 500cc offer charging outputs of 250–500 watts or more, and a bike with a well-maintained battery and no obvious charging problems should easily be able to handle the 50- to 100-watt draw of one electric torso garment, or perhaps two. Add electric gloves and pants when available, and the draw can exceed 160 watts. Too high a draw will likely blow the fuse on the garment's battery hookup, and could potentially damage the electrical system. However, the fuse should protect the system by blowing first.

Because these garments hook directly to the battery, they will draw electricity even with the ignition turned off. This means that when you're fueling up and standing beside the bike, you should be able to stay warm; just don't stay hooked up for more than a few minutes with the engine off, as this will soon

draw down the battery. When you're ready to ride again, turn off the electrical garments or unplug them before starting the bike, so as to not overload the battery. It's highly unlikely an electric garment will hurt you, as their inline fuse should blow if there is a problem.

How to Wear

Torso garments generate a lot of heat, are often insulated, and are designed to be worn over clothing. Their nylon interiors are not comfy against the skin, so wear them over a T-shirt and heavy shirt to even out and distribute the heat, with a sweater over them to hold in the heat. Get the optional thermostat because the day warms and cools, and electric garments can become uncomfortably hot.

The key to keeping warm is to wear windproof clothing and to seal the open-

ings. A heated garment will not be as effective if the wind is coming in around your collar or up your sleeves. The garment should fit snugly. When the torso is warm, the body circulates warmer blood to the extremities, which will also remain warmer. For this reason, a torso warmer is the basic garment, followed by gloves, because hand controls are so crucial to motorcycle operation. Heated pants or socks would be a distant third choice. While I love heated hand grips, I recommend heated gloves as

Summer gloves are usually perforated enough to let the breeze in, but not enough to allow the wearer to become sunburned. Still, safety must be uppermost, and these gloves should offer both padding and a wrist wrap to help them stay put in a get-off. *Triumph Motorcycles America*

A three-season glove is one with enough insulation to handle spring, summer, and fall use. This one, by Triumph, also offers sporty style and built-in protection. *Triumph Motorcycles America*

It's important that a winter glove have enough insulation and wind-stopping ability, yet not be so bulky as to bunch up under the palm or interfere with the controls. This is the Tour Master Winter Elite Glove. *Tour Master*

Here's an amusing alternative to buying rain gear. Gee, I wonder what the weather's like outside.

I have ridden with electric garments for more than 25 years, and have found that they are indispensable in cold weather.

BOOT COVERS

Sometimes a rain suit will come with nylon overboots that lace up at the top. Unfortunately, nylon is slippery, and I have not had good luck with these in the wet unless they had some additional type of rubberized sole material. My recommendation, if you don't go for all-out rain-proof boots, is the touring rider's favorite, Totes rubber overshoes, or something like them.

---

the best solution to hand comfort, because they cover the entire hand.

I have ridden with electric garments for more than 25 years, and have found that they are indispensable in cold weather. They can make the difference between a comfortable ride and a miserable one, and are also very handy for eliminating that damp chill of rainy weather.

While torso garments go on quickly and easily, getting into vest/pant/glove combinations takes some time. Heated pants will go on over jeans but are not intended as outer garments.

BOOTS

Styles of boots include touring, biker, cold/wet-weather, roadrace, and others in between. They may be made of leather, man-made fibers, or a combination of the two, but here are some suggestions. In my experience there are generally two types of street boots: those that are very heavy and protective, and those that are very light and aren't. Racing boots are the exception, as they're both very light and protective, but often so very high styled that you'll need to buy them to match your riding gear. If you care about such things.

Look for a shift pad atop the left boot so it won't wear through, and some protection on the ankles, such as an extra layer of material or perhaps even a gel pad, plus stiff shin and toe guards. Boots will be either side-opening or back-opening, and I've generally

found the former to be easier to enter. Look for a high-quality zipper with a flap that seals well, and they should be high enough that your pant legs will overlap them to keep out the breeze. It's important the boot grip the ankle snugly so the foot does not slop around inside and lead to blisters.

It's a plus if boots incorporate breathable liners, of Gore-Tex or similar material, that render them water and wind resistant. Reflective material on the backs and sides provide added visibility, and look for nonslip rubber soles that hold the road (and the pegs) well. Slip them off and take a good look at the soles. These are what are going to have to save you from going over on that wet day when you come to a stop and put your foot down in an oil spot on the road. Do they seem to have enough grip?

GLOVES

There was a time when gloves were gloves. The gloves you wore in the winter to shovel snow were the ones you wore on your motorcycle, or to drive your car in winter. They were just gloves.

Then bang, baseball players began wearing lightweight batting gloves. Sports car drivers wore ventilated gloves with leather palms. Bull riders wore gloves to help them grip the rope in rodeos. Today there are specialized gloves for snowboarding, skiing, kayaking. Heck, my kids even wear gloves to skateboard! Things were simpler when there were just gloves.

Simpler, but not better. Today, motorcycle gloves have become very specialized. Each attempts to address and balance several types of basic and specialized needs. The basic purpose of every pair of gloves is to protect hands from weather and bug hits, and from the road, should you go down. Along with that, they try to offer reasonable comfort, weather protection, and style.

Types of Gloves

Motorcycle street gloves generally fall into several categories, with some overlap. The well-dressed rider who travels a lot will

GLOVES ARE GOOD, GLOVES ARE GREAT

To protect, a glove must stay on your hand if you go down. That's why sportbike gloves usually incorporate a gauntlet and wrist strap that wraps around the wrist and secures with a hook-and-loop fastener. Many gloves add protection with an additional layer of leather or other protective material on the palms, the backs, and along the fingers. Some use closed-cell foam; others use high-tech materials (such as hard carbon fiber forms) over the knuckles.

need at least four styles, including summer, three-season, winter, and rain.

Summer: To dispel heat, summer gloves are often perforated. The trick is for the holes to be large enough to function, but small enough so that they do not overly compromise protection or allow the rider to suffer sunburn. I do not recommend the fingerless variety or those with large open, unprotected areas because of their lack of protection.

Three-Season: These are good, all-around gloves that offer dexterity, weather protection, and style. Because they're designed to be worn for long distances and for days at a time through a variety of weather conditions, they tend to offer a long gauntlet, some insulation, basic features, and additional protection.

Winter: They're the most heavily insulated, but on the backs rather than the palms. Insulation on the palms is largely useless and will bunch up on the grips, which is one reason we no longer wear our old snow-shoveling gloves for riding. Windproof fabric will keep them warmer. Look for long gauntlets and high-tech insulation that's not bulky, as thick fingers can interfere with operation of the controls.

Rain: As with outerwear, rain-proof gloves tend to offer either an impervious nylon shell that won't pass moisture in either direction and will become clammy, or they'll use a high-tech, breathable membrane that will make them quite expensive. If you can afford them, I suggest going with the latter. These membranes can wear out and tear, and their pores can clog, so to extend their life I suggest saving them for when it's actually raining.

Racing: The most protection for your dollar. There are racing gloves that literally have armor on their armor. While keeping your hands intact is their main function, they're surprisingly comfortable. This makes sense: the last thing a racer needs is a distraction, and gloves that interfere with use of clutch, throttle, brake, and other controls aren't just distracting, they're dangerous. As with racing boots, they tend to be highly stylized insofar as fashion is concerned.

Sport: Only one step (if at all) removed from racing gloves, they are often highly styled, colorful, and heavily armored. Protection comes in the form of closed-cell foam, carbon fiber, or other formed pieces, and high-tech fabrics such as Kevlar, Keprotec, and others. They focus on lightness, dexterity, and protection, rarely are insulated, and are often quite comfortable.

Cruiser: Cruiser pilots like things simple, basic, and with heritage. That means their gloves are often made of plain black cowhide or deerskin leather without any of the fancy features or additional protection, other than perhaps an extra layer of leather on the palm.

TIP

Nylon rain mitts are sometimes part of a standard glove, where they fold out of sight until needed, or are sold separately. These impervious mitts will keep you dry, but wet nylon will be slippery on the controls. Gloves with inner membranes will leave your hands encased in a cold, wet layer even if the liner remains dry. An alternative is extra-large, dish-washing gloves that will fit over your own gloves and will be less slippery on the controls. For footwear, the ever-popular Totes really can't be beat.

Sport gloves tend to be well padded, protective, and very colorful. Look for a wrist wrap that ensures they'll stay on your hand should you go sliding down the road, and some effective but unobtrusive armor. Tour Master

FIT

European gloves generally have a European fit, which to us Yanks usually means that they tend to run small for their listed size. I suggest that if you're trying on gloves made in Europe, go up one size from the standard American XS to XXL sizing. This is especially important when ordering gloves with hard carbon fiber or other protection, as it will not stretch or break in.

PERFORMANCE CONSIDERATIONS

Chapter 9

WHAT YOU WILL LEARN

- Basic ways to add power to your bike's engine

- How and why to adjust your bike's suspension

- How to lower a motorcycle safely

Modern motorcycles, especially sportbikes like this Kawasaki ZX-14, have so much stock performance that, from a purely functional standpoint, it's not usually necessary to upgrade them unless you're going racing. However, many riders enjoy personalizing and upgrading their bikes, and enhanced handling, power, and brakes can make a bike even more enjoyable and usable. *Kawasaki Motors Corp., USA*

Many riders regard their motorcycles as a personal statement, and no one wants that statement to read, "I'm dull!"

ADDING POWER

You can't get too much of a good thing, right? That certainly applies to power and performance, as motorcyclists are always trying to add more. "Power" generally refers to engine output, while "performance" is a broader term that takes into account such things as braking and suspension upgrades, tires, and chassis considerations.

While rebuilding an engine for greater displacement and compression goes well beyond the scope of this book, I will discuss the two most common ways to bolt on significant amounts of performance without having to open the engine to a major degree.

Exhaust Systems

The simplest and most direct way to add power is with an aftermarket exhaust system. This is probably why the aftermarket exhaust system is the most popular motorcycle accessory sold, especially for cruisers. Market research conducted in 2004 showed that 44.6 percent of the more than 6,000 new-bike buyers surveyed had purchased an aftermarket exhaust system within their first three months of ownership.

Stock exhaust systems are designed to develop a broad range of power for an "Everyman" rider within the sound and emissions limitations of the U.S. Department of Transportation and the Environmental Protection Agency. Why do so many riders tend to change them so frequently?

One reason, of course, is to personalize their bikes. Many riders regard their motorcycles as a personal statement, and no one wants that statement to read, "I'm dull!" We prefer to be perceived as a person with taste, stature, and power. A properly designed and set up exhaust system can indeed add significant power to a motorcycle, and also that "mellow" sound we all crave.

A properly designed aftermarket exhaust system will usually weigh less than stock, more stylish, allow the bike to develop more horsepower (usually higher in the rev range), and put out a more "throaty" sound than stock.

One way to extract more performance from your bike is to allow it to ingest and process mor air/fuel mixture. This Baron's Big Air Kit is designed to open up the breathing, and it also has a very custom look.

Because chrome tends to discolor and "blue" when it is heated and cooled, stock exhaust systems have a double-wall construction. The inner wall routes the exhaust gases, and the outer is designed essentially as a heat and cosmetic shield that not only minimizes the possibility of the riders being burned, but also hides that unsightly blue and presents an attractive, clean, chromed cover for the stock pipes. Stock systems are also well baffled, and in order to have sufficient volume to deal with the sound energy, they tend to have a bulky look.

A properly designed aftermarket exhaust system will usually be lighter than stock, it will allow the bike to develop more horsepower (usually higher in the rev range), and it will put out a more mellow sound (okay, it's louder) than stock. It may not meet emissions regulations, however. If you find a system labeled "for off-road use" or "for competition use only," it's the manufacturer's way of telling you that the pipe is not street legal.

Intake

While an aftermarket exhaust will often provide a slight power gain, it is important to be aware that an internal combustion engine is a system, and that installing aftermarket pipes alone may not deliver the sought-after power. In fact, it may negatively affect power. I have seen magazine dyno charts that indicate some aftermarket pipes actually produce less power than the stock units. At the very

least expect that the carburetor jets will need to be changed, as well as the air cleaner. Or, if your bike has fuel injection, you'll need to alter the fuel/air mixture map. Skilled technicians can work with the existing box, or you could get a piggyback electronic fuel-injection (EFI) module such as a Dynojet Power Commander. A piggyback EFI module plugs into the system between the stock EFI box and the injectors, and alters the signal sent by the stock EFI box. It comes with an array of preprogrammed maps that cover a range of engine/exhaust combinations, or you can use your PC to create your own map.

Small power gains are possible just by changing the exhaust system, but significant power gains are the result of five factors working in concert. These include: 1. a less restrictive air filter and/or larger air box; 2. new carburetors/injectors (or at least a jetting change or reprogrammed fuel/air mixture map); 3. higher-lift cams; 4. an ignition system that allows the engine to rev higher; and 5. a less restrictive exhaust system.

An electronic fuel-injection (EFI) system will adjust, to some degree, to the changing back pressure of an aftermarket exhaust, but not if it's a straight-through system. A product such as the Dynojet Power Commander is an electronic unit that allows the owner to richen the mixture by changing the EFI mapping, essentially fooling the injectors into modifying the fuel/air ratio.

Though the ramped collar is hidden beneath the chromed cover on this Harley shock, it works in the same manner as with any exposed shock. Put a drift through any of the holes at the base of the shock and turn it in the proper direction to adjust spring preload. On dual-shock systems, be certain that both shocks are placed on identical settings for spring preload and damping.

Other Modifications

The biggest immediate power gains come from changing the intake and exhaust systems. Modifying the ignition system enhances these changes. As you open the motor to start changing cams, valves, pistons, and cylinders, however, you begin to reach the point of diminishing returns in terms of dollars. Cams are a way of refining how the power is delivered, but you have to choose between low- and top-end power. Porting and polishing the heads can optimize flow patterns; done improperly, however, it can destroy them. Internal modifications involve complex issues. I suggest you do a lot of research and, unless you're a talented mechanic or willing to bear the cost (in time and money) of a lot of trial and error, have the work done by a professional. For some folk, wrenching is more fun than riding. The rest of us would rather feel the bike beneath us than sit with it in front of us.

SUSPENSION UPGRADES

There is a hierarchy in motorcycle suspension systems as to which style of motorcycle gets what quality suspension units. It's based upon the manufacturers' expectation of what the public wants, and how aggressively they'll be riding their bikes.

At the low end are cruisers and entry-level bikes, which get the base model suspension units. They usually have no adjustment other than spring preload. At the high end are sportbikes, which are sometimes used at track days and raced. Their suspension components are usually top-line, with adjustability in both spring preload and rebound and compression damping at both ends.

Adjusting Your Bike's Suspension System

Everything about riding, from how well a bike handles the bumps to how well it sticks to the racetrack, is largely influenced by the quality of your bike's suspension system and how well it's set up. In the days before swinging-arm frames and telescopic forks, motorcycles were like overgrown bicycles, in that they had rigid frames and the fronts had, at best, only a sprung fork.

Whenever the subject of suspension systems arises, most riders relate it to ride comfort. While comfort is a major reason for suspending a motorcycle, the far more important reasons are for traction and control. Think of an old balloon-tire bicycle being ridden down a bumpy street. The only suspension action is from tire flex and frame flex. As the bike bounces over bumps, its tires are sometimes not in contact with the pavement; at those times it is incapable of braking, accelerating, or turning. The suspension system keeps the tires in contact with the pavement, so you can control the motorcycle.

Depending upon the level of sophistication of your bike's system, the three primary suspension adjustments are spring preload, rebound damping, and compression damping. Only sporty bikes will offer all three at both ends, while more basic bikes will offer only spring preload on the shock absorber(s). Here's what these suspension components do, and how to adjust them intelligently.

Spring Preload

The length a spring assumes when not confined is called its free length. Place that

---

HAVE A PLAN

Consult a professional mechanic before starting your project, to learn which products work well in concert with others. For example, a friend of mine wanted to increase the power of his Harley-Davidson, so he installed larger cylinders and pistons with high-compression heads. Because of the higher compression, he now had to install a larger starter to turn over the engine. Because the starter was physically larger, it interfered with the dipstick, which had to be extended. Because of the higher compression, the studs that hold down the cylinders began to rip out of the cases; my friend was told that he needed to install aftermarket engine cases. What he thought would be a simple installation that would give him quick, trouble-free power turned into an expensive, long-term project. While the specifics on these types of changes are well beyond the scope of this book, the important consideration is to have a good overview of any project before you start.

spring in a motorcycle fork, or around a shock absorber, and it will be confined and compressed somewhat, even if the bike is on a stand with no weight on that component. Take the bike off its stand so it's sitting on its wheels, and the spring will now be compressed by the weight of the machine. This is called "static sag." Place the rider(s) and luggage aboard, and the spring is now loaded even more. This is "dynamic sag." But how much more or less should we adjust the "preload" of a spring for riding?

There is a long, involved ritual in setting up spring sag for racing, but we'll let the racing publications deal with that. For our purposes we want to know what effect dialing in more or less spring preload will have on the bike for street riding.

Types of Springs

Straight-rate (or constant-rate) springs are identified by the fact that the coils are the same size and distance apart all through the spring's length. The spring will compress at the same rate all the way through its length. If 100 pounds of force is required to compress the spring 1 inch, then another 100 pounds will compress it a second inch—and so on till the spring becomes coil bound. It has a constant spring rate throughout its travel.

A progressive-rate spring is wound in such a way that the coils have a different rate from one end to the other, and the spring rate gradually becomes stiffer as the spring is compressed. These are identified by the coils being closer together at one end than they are at the other. While only 50 pounds of force may be needed to compress a progressively wound spring its first inch, perhaps 80 pounds will be required to compress it a second inch and 130 pounds its third inch . . . and so forth.

Finally, a dual-rate spring involves having two springs (or occasionally three) with different rates stacked atop each other. The spring with the lightest rate will begin to compress first, then as the force increases

the heavier-rate spring will begin to compress. The use of both progressive or dual-rate springs are attempts to provide a suspension system that offers a softer ride under most circumstances, but one which offers greater resistance to bottoming as the suspension compresses further.

For our needs, the primary purpose in precompressing (or preloading) the springs will be to gain cornering clearance when the

---

FANCY SUSPENDERS ARE WORTH EVERY PENNY

How do you know your bike needs an upgraded suspension system? When it has no adjustments, but you wish it did so you could tune out the wallowing in turns, the way the bike feels like a pogo stick, the way the front end dives under braking or how, when you ride it over a series of bumps, it feels like it's constantly bouncing and does not settle down till the bumps are long past.

If you're going to buy aftermarket suspension components, choose ones that at least offer rebound damping adjustments along with spring preload. Compression damping adjustment is also desirable.

The spring preload and damping adjusters are located at the top of this fork tube. At the very top, turning the slotted screw head to any of its stops will affect damping. Just below it, turning the blue collar inward increases ride height and fork spring preload. Turning it out has the opposite effect. *Triumph Motorcycles America*

You can identify a progressively wound spring by the fact that its coils are tighter toward one end of the spring than at the other, such as the one on this shock absorber. The benefit of such a spring is that it offers an initially soft rate, then progressively increases the rate the more the spring is compressed. *Progressive Suspension*

This Ohlins shock absorber offers both spring preload adjustment and compression and rebound damping adjustment. The compression damping adjuster controls the rate at which the shock compresses, and is located on the remote reservoir to the right. How quickly the shock rebounds from impact is controlled by the black knob at the base of the shock, which is to the left. Spring preload is adjusted by turning the remote black knob at the bottom. *Ohlins*

TIP

Rake and steering will be affected by ride-height adjustments to a slight degree. Racers will adjust spring preload at both ends to subtly change rake and cause their bikes to steer more or less quickly. Whenever preloading the springs or adjusting the damping on dual shocks or on the fork, be certain that both shocks or fork legs are given the exact same settings; otherwise, the suspension will be imbalanced.

---

bike is leaned over. What is adequate spring preload under normal circumstances may become inadequate when luggage and/or a passenger are added. If parts of your bike drag in turns, increasing spring preload should raise it higher and help the situation.

Most bikes have a preload adjuster on the shock absorber springs. On bikes with dual rear shocks, it's usually a ramped collar that can be turned with a special tool from the tool kit. On bikes with a single shock, it may be a ramped collar, or an adjusting collar that threads on the shock body itself. These will have two threaded collars; one sets the adjustment, and the second is turned up against the first to lock it in place. Consult your owner's manual for the exact procedure in adjusting the suspension on your bike.

Most bikes do not have fork spring preload adjusters, but if they do it will usually be in the form of a large nut at the top of each fork tube that can be screwed into the tube to increase preload or out to lessen it. Adjusting fork preload will not only affect ride height, but also fork compression under braking.

Increasing spring preload will increase the bike's ride height, which will also raise seat height a corresponding amount. It will not, however, change spring rate unless the bike has progressive or dual-rate springs. In those situations, preloading will use up

more of the lighter part of the spring rate first, and leave the more firm part of the spring rate to deal with the load.

Damping

Imagine a motorcycle with only springs for suspension at each end. Each time it hit a bump the springs would compress, store the energy of the bump momentarily, then feed it back to the chassis as they rebounded. The result would be a very erratic ride as each end of the bike lurched up and down like a pogo stick. Instead, modern motorcycle suspensions have internal damping systems that are designed to control the ride as the system compresses and rebounds. Some are velocity sensitive, and will respond more aggressively to larger bumps at higher speeds.

These automatically damped systems work fine under most circumstances, but often those circumstances change. You will need more damping when you carry a passenger and luggage, or when you ride faster on a bumpy road. Also, as a suspension system ages, its damping characteristics begin to deteriorate. Under these circumstances, it would be handy to have the ability to fine-tune the system.

Damping Adjustment

Bikes with more sophisticated suspension systems often have fully adjustable suspension systems. If yours does, here's how to set it for street riding.

First, be mindful that what works for Rider A may not work for Rider B. It's very common for riders on the same racing team, who are similar in size and riding identical bikes, to set their bikes up quite differently for the same track. Some riders like a relatively plush suspension, and will push on through despite the suspension's movement. Others want a stiff ride and don't want the bike moving around on them a lot. It's a personal thing, so keep in mind that another rider's settings are not necessarily going to work ideally for you.

To get an idea of the limits of your bike's suspension system, set the preload according to the owner's manual and place all the damping settings on their minimal/lightest settings. Then take it out on the type of road you want to be able to ride well, at least for several miles. Ride through at your usual rate and feel the suspension working; note at what point it begins to slop around or move too much for your tastes.

When you reach the end of the section, place all damping settings at their stiffest/maximum, and then ride it again. Feel how differently it works. This will give you an idea of the range of adjustment.

For your third trip down the same road, place all adjusters at what you believe would be their ideal settings, which should deliver a nice compromise of ride comfort (plushness) with control. When further fine-tuning the adjustments, try to change settings one at a time; otherwise, you might not be able to discern which adjustment did what. Ultimately, you want suspension that feels well controlled without being harsh, and comfortable without feeling sloppy.

Air Suspension

You will sometimes notice a bike with a Schrader (air) valve atop each fork cap, or with rubber hoses leading to each shock and ending in a Schrader valve. An air suspension system utilizes air pressure as a spring, and often backs it up with a physical spring in case the system leaks. The problem with an air suspension system is that, as the air chamber is compressed, the pressure inside (and spring rate) increase dramatically. This is always a problem when air is kept in a confined area, such as a fork. Harley-Davidson got around this problem on some touring models by actually pressurizing the safety bars (some call them "crash bars") and utilizing them as reservoirs to increase air volume and even out the pressure rise.

Air pressure has such a dramatic affect on an enclosed container that a little goes a

If you intend to ride your bike at speed on the road or at a track day, you'll need to understand its suspension system and dial it in properly. Sportbikes such as this Honda RC51 have full suspension adjustment at both ends. *American Honda Motor Co.*

In an air suspension system, the air pressure acts as a spring; changing the air pressure serves as changing the spring preload. *Progressive Suspension*

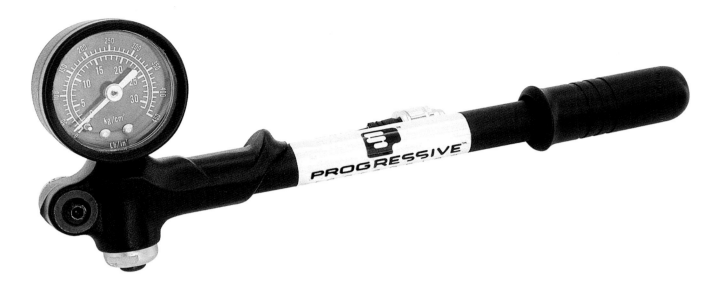

Because an air suspension system has such low volume, it should not be pressurized from a high-pressure air system. Progressive Suspension offers this hand-operated, gauge-mounted pump just for that purpose. *Progressive Suspension*

TIP

When removing shocks, you need to support the rear of the bike from above the shocks. This can be done by looping a tie-down over a rafter and hooking it to the rear subframe, or by placing a beam of some sort (like a 2x4) horizontally under the rear subframe and supporting each end from below. This method tends to encroach on your working space. Whichever method you use, be sure to brace the bike against lateral movement; if you don't, it will want to twist and fall down. Also, remember that the swingarm will drop when you pull that second-to-last shock bolt. It helps to have a friend support the swingarm as you work the bolts free, then set it down gently.

---

long way. Don't ever use a service station air hose on an air suspension system, as they can deliver such high pressure they'll likely blow the seals. Instead, obtain a little hand-operated pump (Progressive Suspension offers a selection of them at www.progressivesuspension.com). Air suspension systems hold such small volume that even checking the pressure can change the setting. I recommend a pump with a gauge mounted to it for precise readings.

LOWERING A MOTORCYCLE

Do you ever watch Supercross, or those X-Games contests, where riders launch over triple jumps or do those impossible stunts while flying 30 feet off the ground on their dirt bikes? If so, you're probably wondering how guys *do* jumps like that, and how their bikes take the abuse.

It helps that they ride very light dirt bikes with state-of-the-art forks and shock absorbers that may offer about 12 inches of suspension travel. Every inch of it is needed to disperse the huge amount of energy generated by launching one of those bad boys 20 or 30 feet into the air over a triple jump. With only 3.5 to 5.0 inches of suspension travel, a street bike could not disperse enough of the energy of such a major jump to prevent its suspension from

Because the fork controls your steering, ride, and braking, if you're not sure what you're doing, take it to a pro.

bottoming upon landing; the bike and rider would then absorb the excess. Ouch!

One of the reasons cruisers are hot is their low seat height. A low seat allows the rider to get both feet on the ground for a secure feel, and it also looks cool, but it usually doesn't improve the ride. **If low is cool, lower is even better, right?** Here's how to lower your bike the proper way.

Lowering the Fork

Lowering kits come with specific instructions, but here are the basics. To lower the front of the bike, support the motorcycle with the front tire off the ground. If the bike does not have a centerstand, use a lift or stand to support it.

There are three ways to lower a front suspension. The easiest is to simply loosen the bolts pinching the triple clamps around the fork tubes and slide the fork tubes a bit higher. Then tighten the bolts to their proper torque values and ride on. Of course, you need to make sure you slide each fork leg the exact same distance. Not only is this the easiest way, it also retains all of your fork travel.

The second way is to unscrew the fork caps and extract the fork springs. If they're not easy to reach, bend a stiff wire (like a clothes hanger) into a hook shape and use that to extract the springs. Cut about an inch out of each spring, and be certain they are of equal length when you're done. Reinstall the springs and check the fork oil level to make sure it's at the level prescribed in your owner's manual; you may have to add a little.

The third, and most difficult, way is to install a spacer under the damping rod in each fork leg. This effectively shortens the rod's stroke. A typical lowering kit will slice 1.0 to 1.5 inches off fork travel. Lowering a suspension unit more than 2.0 inches will seriously impact ride quality and ground clearance, and I don't recommend it.

You may have to disassemble the fork slider to remove the damping rod. Be sure to

However much the bike drags with just the rider aboard, it's going to drag that much more while carrying a passenger and luggage.

have a supply of the correct viscosity fork oil, since you'll have to drain the fork before you take it apart. Because the fork controls your steering, ride, and braking, if you're not sure what you're doing, take it to a pro.

Lowering the Shocks

The least expensive method of lowering a bike in the rear is to install hardware that relocates the bottom shock mounts farther rearward so the tire travels farther up into the fender. This allows the shocks the same amount of travel, but does change the

leverage, and ride quality may suffer slightly. On bikes with link-type single shocks, or those with their shocks mounted horizontally under the frame, lowering involves changing the length of the dog-bone arm that connects the swingarm to the link.

The other method is to replace the stock shock absorbers with shorter units. Of course, buying new shocks is much more expensive than buying a lowering kit, and with less stroke available to handle bumps, ride quality will likely suffer.

The Downsides of Going Down

If you've ridden with guys who have lowered bikes, you've probably seen and heard them

Braided-steel brake lines can offer more positive stopping, and they also give your bike a high-performance look.

Draining and flushing brake fluid requires special tools, and getting it wrong will result in spongy brakes. Because that's a safety factor, it's best to leave this job to experts if you don't know how to do it yourself. Shown is a vacuum-style brake bleeder by My-T-Vac, which allows for the full replenishment and replacement of the fluid. *My-T-Vac*

scraping their footboards and pipes while going around turns, and possibly have even seen them dragging their frames or engine components while going up inclines into driveways. Lowering the suspended portion of the bike drops the frame and everything attached to it, reducing ground and cornering clearance. However much the bike drags with just the rider aboard, it's going to drag that much more while carrying a passenger and luggage.

If your stock suspension kept the tires a few inches from the insides of the fenders and you lower the bike significantly, now the tires will rub the fenders on moderate bumps. It can also lead to clearance problems with the swingarm, drive chain, or belt, and brake calipers. A rear tire that contacts the inside of the fender can cause all kinds of

WHEN SPARKS FLY

While dragging footboards in turns may seem like cool, innocent fun, there is a serious side. Get too hot into a turn at 60 miles per hour, start dragging your footboards and exhaust system, and what are your options? Braking will drop the bike and limit cornering clearance even farther, and the bike will want to stand up and run even wider in the turn. Leaning it harder over onto its unyielding hard parts can lever the tires off the pavement, sending rider and passenger sliding to the outside of the turn—possibly into a rock wall or oncoming traffic. This is serious, life-threatening stuff!

TIP

To keep the bike riding level, raise or lower both the front and rear equally. Failure to do so will change the steering geometry and affect steering and handling.

Do not combine shorter shocks with a rear lowering kit.

Don't overtighten shock mounts. Remember, the shock needs to describe an arc as it compresses and extends. Use the proper washers and sleeves to prevent binding.

Finally, lowering a bike can gain you style points, but also can have serious consequences. Plan your moves before you do them.

problems, ranging from noise to wear on tires and fenders to ripping out taillight wiring to possible loss of control. If the front tire contacts the inside of the fender, it can also lead to steering and braking problems.

Then there's the comfort issue. When you subtract wheel travel, you subtract the suspension's ability to deal with bumps. Replace a 5-inch-travel shock with one having 4 inches of travel, and you've subtracted 20 percent (all else being equal) of that shock's ability to deal with bumps. The shorter shock will need a stiffer-rate spring to make up the difference.

The only way a shorter shock can be as comfortable is for it to be of much higher quality than the shock it replaced, or if you slow down. If you carry a passenger, and your passenger is already telling you the ride feels stiff or bumpy, perhaps you don't want to lower the bike.

BRAKES

Braided-Steel Brake Lines

In addition to their obvious custom looks, braided-steel brake lines also have a functional purpose. Under hard usage, rubber brake lines can swell slightly, so not all the force applied to the lever or pedal will reach the caliper. This results in a mushy feel. A braided-steel housing around the rubber brake line prevents it from swelling, so more of the braking force is utilized, making lever and pedal operation much firmer.

Braided-steel brake lines come in standard, -2, and -3 sizes. As the minus sign indicates, the latter two sizes are smaller diameters than standard. Smaller diameter means faster displacement of brake fluid when pressure is applied to the lever, due to the venturi effect. What this means in the real world is twofold: you don't need to pull the lever as hard to get really strong stopping power; and, it's much easier to modulate that stopping power. Gone are the days when you needed to close all four fingers

into a fist when clamping down on the brake lever—one or two fingers will now do just fine. The only problem with these smaller-diameter lines is that, as of this writing, they haven't been approved by the DOT for street use.

In addition to a variety of sizes, braided-steel brake lines are also available in a variety of colors. It used to be that if you wanted to customize your bike by adding colored brake lines you had to use lines made of Kevlar. However, Kevlar expands ever so slightly under pressure, and can crack if made to expand and contract too many times. So, although Kevlar brake lines are still made, they're no longer widely distributed. Luckily, the folk who make braided-steel lines took up the challenge and you can now get them with colored plastic sheaths. So, not only do they look good, they won't scratch painted and chromed surfaces.

Want to get a more integrated, high-tech look and improve your brakes' feel at the same time? Consider adding braided-steel brake lines that are color matched to your bike. *Goodridge (UK) Ltd*

BRAKE LINE INSTALLATION TIPS

Installation requires bleeding the brake system, so have a brake-bleeder kit and brake fluid from a sealed container handy. The reason the container must be sealed is that brake fluid is very hygroscopic, which means it's capable of easily absorbing water—ever present in the air. Brake fluid can become extremely hot, and when it does the moisture in it can boil, which is not good for delivering braking force to the caliper. Also, moisture promotes internal corrosion in the system.

MAINTENANCE

WHAT YOU WILL LEARN

- Why motorcycle oils are superior to automotive oils

- How to choose the right tires for your bike

- How to care for your battery

- How to pick up a fallen motorcycle

Sport riding is great fun, and to protect your bike when it's going this hard you'll need a high-quality motor oil. A motorcycle engine often generates two to three times the power of an automobile engine per displacement, and definitely requires special care. *Moto Guzzi USA*

The same oil reservoir must handle the cooling and lubricating needs for both the crankcase and the transmission—with only three quarts of oil!

OILS AND LUBRICANTS

What type of motor oil should you use in your bike? Here are some ways of thinking through the answer:

Dan commutes 40 miles each way to his job in the city. He goes mostly by car as weather and traffic are uncertain, and he worries that someone might rip off his sport-tourer. So he rides the bike mostly on weekends.

Friday night Dan drives home, his car idling in stop-and-go city traffic the first 20 miles, running at 35–45 miles per hour in heavy traffic for 10 miles, then traveling at 60–65 the final few miles, turning about 2,500 rpm. His car's engine rarely exceeds 3,000 rpm, and when traffic clears, it spends most of its time at steady-state cruising speeds. Not exciting.

Back home, Dan warms up his bike's engine so he can change its oil and filter. He has to make an important decision: does he use the $1.50-a-quart car stuff from the discount store, or the $3 to $8/quart motorcycle oil from his dealer? He figures, correctly, that bikes and cars have different oil needs, but wishes he knew more so he could justify spending $15 rather than $4.50 for a three-quart oil change.

At first light Saturday morning Dan is up and gone, his bike turning 3,800 rpm at 75 miles per hour on the highway. An hour later he meets a friend for breakfast, and they ride up into the mountains, where the real fun begins. They rev their engines to redline at 9,000 rpm, shift hard, and brake hard. His bike is liquid-cooled, with four valves per cylinder, and makes about 110 horses. Life is good!

Sunday night he returns home, weary from his 600-mile weekend ride. He puts the bike away, too tired to even clean it. There it will sit till next weekend—or longer if it rains. Life is still good.

This little scenario is meant to show part of the reason why a motorcycle's oil needs are different from, and more stringent than, a car's. Consider that the engine in Dan's sedan displaces 2,500cc, has two valves per cylinder, and generates 140 horsepower, which means that it takes 17.8cc of displacement to create one horsepower. A full oil-cooling system carries away the BTUs. The crankcase holds five quarts of oil, and there's a separate reservoir for the transmission.

His bike generates 110 horsepower from its 1,300cc engine; it extracts a horsepower from every 11.8cc, which means it has to work harder than his car's engine. And because of the recreational aspect of motorcycling, you can bet that Dan is riding more of those horses on his motorcycle more often than he is when driving his car. The cooling system on Dan's bike has much less capacity than his car's cooling system, despite the fact it has to dissipate the heat from 78.6 percent as much horsepower. And like so many bikes (except Harleys, most BMWs, and a few others), the same reservoir must handle the cooling and lubricating needs for both the crankcase *and* the transmission—with only three quarts of oil!

Oil Is Oil,
Except When It's Really Good Oil

What if you run your bike with integral transmission on inexpensive automotive oil? If you ride in a low-stress, steady-state manner, keep your bike tuned, and change oil frequently, it will probably suffer no damage. But if you run the bike hard, generating a lot of power and heat, your transmission is likely to suffer, which you may notice as a gradual increase in shifting effort. Also, accelerated valvetrain wear may cause more mechanical noise short-term, and in extreme cases eventual breakdown.

Generally, if you ride hard; travel two-up or haul a trailer; ride in hot, dusty or stop-and-go conditions; and intend to keep the bike for a number of years and many thousands of miles, it will likely survive in much better shape if you use high-quality, specialty motorcycle lubricants.

Finally, cars and bikes usually have plain-bearing engines, but on motorcycles with integrated gearboxes the oil has to also adequately deal with roller bearings, clutch plates, the gunk the clutch sloughs off, gear teeth, and much more power per cc. You bet motorcycles not only need a different oil, but they also need a superior type of oil.

The purpose of oil is to coat the hard parts of the engine and lubricate them, preventing them from rubbing together. It also carries heat away from hot spots. Let's see how it works.

Additive Packages:
What's in Oil

Here's a quick compendium of what's added to high-grade, four-stroke motorcycle engine oil.

Antiwear Agents: To protect the camshafts from the lifters, motorcycle oils carry zinc (an antiwear and antioxidant) in greater concentrations. Plain-bearing engines need phosphorus, an important antiwear ingredient.

Antifoam Agents: High revs, wet clutches, and gear teeth can churn oil into a froth. Silicone-based antifoam agents reduce surface tension so bubbles won't form. Bubbles are full of air and do not lubricate.

PJ1's Silverfire motorcycle oil is petroleum-based. The bottle shows that it's a 20W-50, which is a higher viscosity designed for warm weather use. *PJ1*

PJ1's Goldfire motorcycle oil is a synthetic blend, which means it has been specifically formulated for a bike's special needs. Its 10W-40 is a lower viscosity designed to remain thinner in cold weather for easier starting. *PJ1*

OIL IS OIL, PART II

The gear teeth in a motorcycle's integral transmission can slice standard polymers, reducing the oil's viscosity. The 20W–50 you put in your motorcycle's engine may have sheared down to a 10W–30 in just several hundred miles. The oil has lost some of its ability to thicken at higher temperatures, which results in some loss of protection. For this reason, specialty motorcycle oils use tougher shear-stable polymers that retain their viscosity over longer periods of time, and leave a more consistent oil film on metal parts.

Think you don't need a low-viscosity oil because you don't ride in the winter? This shot was taken in April in the mountains of Central California. When we left on our trip the previous day, it had been cloudy. The clouds turned to rain, which turned to snow in the mountains.

TIP

Motorcycles tend to be used infrequently, to sit idle for weeks or months, then to be used very hard for short periods. Quality motorcycle oils have extreme-pressure (EP) additives, rust and corrosion inhibitors, sulfur, zinc di-thiophosphate, and more. Some of these are also in quality automotive oils, but the concentrations of ingredients differ.

Your owner's manual may not make for exciting reading, but it's necessary stuff.

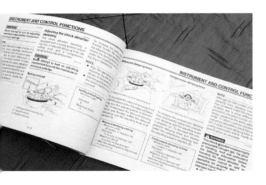

Antiacids: Acids are formed when condensed moisture reacts with combustion contaminants. They'll eat your engine alive from the inside out.

Detergents and Dispersants: If allowed to circulate, the bits of metal that flake off bearings, piston rings, clutch surfaces, etc., would eventually interfere with moving parts and clog oil lines. Detergents and dispersants help dissolve sludge and keep particles in suspension so they can be trapped by the filter.

The SJ Question

To increase fuel mileage, the oil industry has added more friction modifiers to certain oils and designated them SJ. Engine oils that are listed as "energy efficient" are designed to decrease friction by about 2.7 percent. These also carry about half the zinc and phosphorous antiwear agents of SH oils (which protect cam followers in motorcycles) as they supposedly clog catalytic converters. Energy-efficient SJ oils are fine for cars, but in a motorcycle with common gearbox and wet clutch, the friction modifiers can cause the wet clutch to slip and lead to valvetrain problems. SJ oils *formulated specifically for motorcycles* do not present these problems. Use JASO-MA (Japanese Automotive Standards Organization-Motorcycle/wet clutch) standard oils if your bike has a wet clutch with common gearbox.

Multi-Viscosity Oils

Many of today's quality oils are multi-grade, designed to change their apparent viscosities at different temperatures. For example, in cold weather a 10W–40 (the "W" means the oil meets viscosity specifications for low temperatures and is therefore suitable for winter use) flows like a 10-weight oil at zero degrees F, then performs like an SAE 40-weight at 212 degrees F. This viscosity shift is caused by chains of polymers that, like microscopic noodles, shrink when cold to allow the engine to turn over more easily for starting, then thicken at operating temperature to cling better to the surrounding oil molecules for better lubrication and protection. Use lighter weight oils for cool weather, and higher weight for the heat.

Synthetic and Petroleum Oils

Synthetic oils are those that have been synthesized, or formed from other components. They're made from either poly alpha olefins (PAO), which are petroleum based, or from esters, such as mineral oils, vegetable oils, or other natural sources. Both types are formulated in laboratories, molecule by molecule, from base stocks, a process that causes synthetic to be more heat stable. When an engine is used hard in hot weather, a low-quality, petroleum-based oil may overheat and begin turning to sludge.

When to Change Oil

Oil is worn out when it has used up a significant portion of its additive package and viscosity, and/or when it has become contaminated. Oil-change intervals specified by manufacturers are recommendations, but specifically how a bike is used determines when its oil should be changed. A person who rides a liquid-cooled touring bike solo

OIL IS OIL, PART III

Oils range from low-end, inexpensive, pure petroleum products adequate for most uses to high-end expensive synthetics with full additive packages able to handle racing stresses. In between are many petroleum/synthetic blends that keep costs down while increasing the performance value of the oil.

Hypoid gear oil is for driveshafts and hubs, and for bikes that have separate engine and transmission fluid reservoirs. Hypoid gear oil change intervals are much longer than those for engine oil. Consult your owner's manual.

on the highway at legal speeds, and runs a high-quality synthetic oil, may actually be able to extend oil drain intervals beyond factory recommendations. At the other end is the rider who runs on petroleum automotive oils in a high-powered, air-cooled bike, two-up in hot weather, at high speeds pulling a trailer, when he's not commuting through stop-and-go traffic. He had better drain and replace oil more often than recommended. Throw in a clogged air or oil filter, stuck choke and out-of-tune engine, and engine life may be shortened.

The bike manufacturer provides a warranty with each new bike, and its oil-change recommendations reflect what it believes to be a safe interval that will protect the bike under most conceivable conditions and minimize claims. Some riders have told me, "My bike manufacturer recommends that I change my motor oil and filter every 5,000 miles. Just to be safe, I change the oil every 2,500 miles. I figure I'm extending my bike's engine life." While this could be true to some minor extent, it would likely only apply if the rider were using his bike in an unusually aggressive manner. Otherwise, it's probably unnecessary. Over the course of 50,000 miles, this policy will cause the rider to pay for an additional 10 oil changes and dump 30 quarts of waste oil unnecessarily. When I started riding 40 years ago, I was told that changing oil more often was "cheap insurance." Now, with better oils, filters, and motorcycles, I'm not sure if that statement is still valid. It is unlikely that doubling up on oil

changes will extend engine life to any significant degree.

Mix It Up

What happens if your bike runs low on oil when you're traveling, but you can't find the particular synthetic brand you're running? Is it okay to mix a petroleum-based oil with a synthetic oil, so long as they're the same viscosity?

Yes. The two oils should be fully compatible in a chemical sense, but you're downgrading the overall quality of the

If you've been running automotive oil in your bike with integral crankcase and transmission, and it shifts rough, switching to a motorcycle-specific oil may improve shifting.

TIP

One of your two most important oil changes is in the fall before you store your motorcycle for the winter. If you store the bike with old oil, acids and other contaminants can chemically eat away at the inside of its engine over time. Instead, before storing the bike, run the engine long enough to warm the oil, then drain it completely. Replace the filter and put in fresh oil. Whether or not you should change that oil again in the spring is up for debate. For years, conventional wisdom said you should, because of naturally-occuring condensation during storage. Recently, however, a new school of thought has evolved which holds that the

condensation accumulation is so minimal that it evaporates the first time the engine gets back up to running temperature. If this is true, it eliminates the need to change the oil once more in the spring. Either way, the filter need not be replaced again.

The other most important oil change is the initial one during break-in on a new machine. Engines should be broken in with petroleum-based oil, which allows the slight metal-to-metal contact necessary for good seating of parts. Most manufacturers suggest that the initial oil and filter be changed at about 500–600 miles. Follow your manufacturer's recommendations.

A tire is a complex piece of high-tech equipment consisting of alternating layers of plies and much more, as this Dunlop cutaway illustration shows. How those plies are arranged determines if the tire is a radial or bias-ply. *Dunlop Tire*

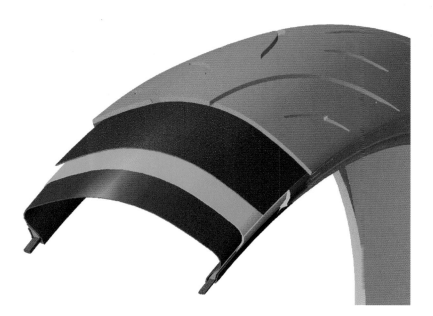

A tire's profile is a big factor in how the bike steers. Here is an Avon Venom R, a sporting tire with a profile designed for quick, precise steering. *Avon Tyres*

The ratio of solid rubber to channels (or "sipes") on a tire is referred to as the "land/sea ratio." More land makes for better grip (think of a racing slick), but in the real world the sipes are necessary to channel away water, such as on this Dunlop Elite 3 radial. *Dunlop Tire*

synthetic by mixing it. Of course, you understand that this would be an emergency situation. While the proper amount of mixed oils is much preferable to not enough oil, it's best to carry a spare quart or two of the good stuff.

Gear Oil

On motorcycles in which the transmission is separate from the engine, each component has a separate oil reservoir. Give each lubricant the sniff test and you'll note that engine oils tend to have a sweeter vegetable aroma, while motorcycle hypoid gear oils have the nasty smell of sulfur, an extreme-pressure additive that lays down a barrier to prevent metal-to-metal contact during the pushing/dragging action of the gears.

Motorcycle engine oils formulated for bikes with common engines and gearboxes include sulfur, but in much lower concentrations than in straight hypoid gear oils. Sulfur can get past piston rings and combine with condensation on cold engine walls to form metal-eating sulfuric acid. Automotive oils have less sulfur yet, which is why they offer less protection for motorcycle transmissions. If you've been running automotive oil in your bike with integral crankcase and transmission, and it shifts rough, switching to a motorcycle-specific oil may improve shifting.

TIRES

Just as a motorcycle is a tool for a job, so is a tire. Its job should reflect that of the motorcycle. Just as there are touring bikes, sportbikes, cruisers, dual-sports, and such, tires are as specifically designed as the bikes that carry them. Here are some basics about motorcycle tires to help you understand them so you can make informed choices when the time comes.

Every tire must balance several factors, including mileage (tread life), adhesion (grip), and ride/handling characteristics. In a perfect world, every tire would provide the perfect ride for every bike, would stick like a pit bull on a mailman's pants, and would wear like granite. But this isn't a perfect world. At one end of the spectrum are purebred racing tires, wide radial slicks with ultra grip and handling. However, they're not usable on the street because they need track speeds to reach operating temperature, and they lack tread grooves to channel away rain. At the other end of the spectrum are bias-ply touring tires that will carry two full-sized people and their belongings for in excess of 10,000 miles at highway speeds. While they wear well and carry a good deal of weight, they may not offer as comfortable a ride, and if you push them in a performance mode they'll turn gummy and slippery.

Radial Versus Bias Plies

In simplified terms, a motorcycle tire consists of the carcass and plies, the rubber compound and the tread pattern. The carcass is made up of layers of flexible belts, called plies, which tend to be arranged in either of two ways. When the plies run directly across the tire from edge to edge (bead to bead), 90 degrees to the direction of rotation, the tire is a true radial-ply. This construction will result in a very compliant, flexible sidewall that allows the tire to grip well and provides a comfortable ride, but it offers less relative load-carrying capability.

Now cut those plies at an angle (on a bias) of maybe 20 or 30 degrees and run them bead to bead. As several layers overlap, the tire becomes stiffer; this contributes to a higher load rating but

A rear tire is designed to get the power to the pavement, and as a result is much wider and heavier than a front tire. Compare this rear Avon Venom R with the front on the previous page. *Avon Tyres*

Because motorcycles don't carry spares, a tire patch kit is a necessity. This one by Progressive Suspension carries both plugs for tubeless tires and patches for tubes. Carry both because the flat may be on someone else's bike. *Progressive Suspension*

A battery charger is a must, especially if your bike undergoes long periods of idleness during winter storage. A "smart" charger is one that will bring the battery up to a full charge, then turn itself to "float" mode to maintain the battery at full charge without overcharging it. *Drag Specialties*

THE MIX

Making a tire is like making a cake. The manufacturer pours the ingredients into a mold, cooks them, and pops out a new tire. "Compounding" is the science of mixing the materials that give the tire its characteristics. It could result in a "soft" tire that wears like a pencil eraser but sticks like a federal indictment. Or it could create a "hard" tire that wears like a locomotive wheel on a steel rail—but slides about as easily, too.

Your home shop or garage should have a full complement of tools, but carry along a good selection for road emergencies. These may include open-end wrenches, an adjustable wrench, Allen wrenches, screwdrivers, pliers, a plug wrench, flashlight, tie wraps, and electrical tape. *CruzTools*

WHERE THE RUBBER MEETS THE ROAD

The ratio of rubber to sipes on tires is referred to as the "land/sea ratio." Until the 1980s, motorcycle tires tended to have a lot of sea, as the tread bristled upward from the carcass. With lots of sea, the tread begins to squirm under heavy cornering loads. From racing development, tire designers came to realize in the 1980s that a superior tire design utilized the solidity of the slick's solid block of rubber, with sipes cut into it. This came to be known as the "cut slick" design.

diminishes ride comfort. Those overlapping plies also rub against each other, generating heat, and they insulate the tire like a blanket. Bias-ply tires tend to run hotter than radials, and heat is the enemy of tires, as it softens the rubber and causes it to wear at an accelerated pace.

Another potential problem is that, at high speeds, centrifugal force can cause the tire to expand slightly (its diameter can grow as much as 3 percent), leading to clearance problems and accelerated wear. When a tire expands because of high speeds, its rubber becomes less dense at the very time the rate of flex and the resultant heat are placing more demands on it. To limit tire flex and growth, some manufacturers add a circumferential belt just below the tread surface.

Because a radial sidewall doesn't offer a great deal of load-carrying capacity, the tire manufacturers make them short, or low in profile. When designed for sportbikes, radial tires tend to be relatively wide in search of ultimate grip. By comparison, bias-ply tires tend to have high-profile sidewalls and are narrower.

Because of their different designs, if a bike came standard with bias-ply tires it is not advisable to switch to true 90-degree radials. The latter could tangle with the swingarm and fenders and may physically not fit. Even if they did fit, a low-profile radial in place of a bias-ply would lower the bike's ride height to such an extent that ground and cornering clearance would be affected, and parts would drag easily in turns. However, some tire manufacturers offer compromise radials with a slight bias cut and higher sidewalls with internal stiffeners that allow them to be used on a wide variety of motorcycles. For fitment information, see your dealer. Again, because radials and bias-ply tires are designed to flex in opposite directions, do not mix them on the same motorcycle.

Tread and Grip

The most visible part of the tire is the tread pattern, that series of squiggles and lines

that gives a tire its style. The proper term for these grooves is "sipes," which are channels designed to break the surface tension and push water away so the tire doesn't hydroplane. Racing tires, as we all know, have no sipes because maximum surface area equals maximum grip. The problem with slicks is that, without sipes, they aren't worth spit on sand or wet surfaces.

Because they are open areas, sipes are weak points, and allow street tires to be designed with a bit of "give" or squirm near their edges. When the rider is going hard and leaning way over, this bit of controlled squirm sends a message to the rider that it's time to slow down. A disadvantage of some racing tires is that they will provide maximum grip—right up to the point at which they slide away entirely.

While cutting-edge motorcycle tire design through the 1990s focused mostly on sportbikes (which spawned the radial revolution) and touring bikes (with high load-carrying capacity and good wear characteristics), manufacturers finally began to offer new tires for cruisers, too.

For sport riders, the job is to go fast for short distances, meaning they desire ultimate grip in a tire and are willing to sacrifice some degree of tread life to get it. Radial tires can be made very wide for traction, and with a low sidewall for comfort. Sportbikes are light and their riders generally ride solo, so their tires don't need great load-carrying capacity. Sporting riders don't often ride when it rains, so their tires don't need to be cutting edge in terms of wet-weather adhesion. Thick, heavy tread keeps in heat, so sport tires tend to have less tread depth—which is part of the reason they don't last long. Finally, high speeds dictate that sporting rubber should have a V or Z speed rating.

Now consider the two-up touring couple on their Honda Gold Wing. Their bike will spend hours rolling at the speed limit or above, loaded at or near capacity. They need a tire with a deep tread and great load-carrying capacity. They don't plan to go haring around in the corners, and as a result are willing to trade some sporting grip for longer tread life, higher load capacity, and wet-weather grip. Because their bike won't exceed 130 miles per hour (nor would they dream of attempting to do so), its tires require only an H speed rating.

A cruiser needs a tire that is somewhere in between. Its job is to handle a bike that may weigh from 400 to more than 700 pounds, and will often be ridden solo but sometimes will be taken on tour with a passenger. When the road starts winding, the cruiser's typical low cornering clearance limits its lean angle, so maximum performance grip usually isn't an issue. Cruiser riders are usually willing to sacrifice some cornering capabilities for longer tire life.

Since style is so important in a cruiser, the rider expects the tires to look as exciting as his bike. Cruiser riders like big, meaty rear tires that suggest horsepower, heroes, and hooliganism. The message many of these bikes present is that they're modified and need a flexed bicep of a tire to handle the power. As a result, cruisers tend to run bias-ply tires that are designed more for wear than ultimate grip, with a medium- to high-load rating and an H speed rating. For traditional bikes, white sidewalls are a plus.

Load Range

This refers to the weight a tire can support at its maximum inflation pressure. Some carry a code number such as 57H (230 kilograms, or 506 pounds; H speed rating), 62H (265 kilograms, or 583 pounds), or 68H (315 kilograms, or 693 pounds).

Inflation Pressures

How do you know what air pressures to run in your tires? Start with the listing in the owner's manual or under the seat, which gives a suggested pressure both solo and two-up. Also, the tire will have a maximum inflation pressure imprinted on the

Top Left: **Your pre-ride inspection should include checking tire pressure. The recommended inflation pressures should be listed on a plate either near the steering head or under the seat of your motorcycle.**

Top Right: **As my dad used to tell me, engine oil is the cheapest mechanic you can buy. By that he meant that keeping the proper amount of a high-quality engine oil in your vehicle would head off a lot of potential problems. Check your engine oil regularly.**

Periodically check the operation of your headlight on both high and low beams, brake light (actuate both the brake lever and brake pedal), and turn signals.

THE WRITING ON THE WALL
The information listed on the side of a tire makes for some interesting reading. Here is some of the information presented

Country of manufacture: Where the tire was made

DOT Compliance Symbol: Tire complies with U.S. Department of Transportation requirements.

Directional arrow: Mount the tire so that it rotates in this direction.

Tube or Tubeless designation: A tubeless tire can carry a tube if necessary.

Maximum pressure: This is the greatest amount of air pressure the tire can carry—it is not the recommended pressure.

A small lift that can raise both tires off the floor is a handy item for the home shop. It not only brings the bike up to a more convenient working level, but also makes changing tires and suspension units much more convenient. Most operate by air pressure, hydraulics, or hand cranking.

sidewall, but it is only for maximum speeds and loads and will not deliver a comfortable ride in most situations. Tires compensate for weight by adding pressure, but keep in mind that as you add pressure beyond optimal, the tire will suffer in ride compliance, handling, and possibly even grip.

Tube Versus Tubeless

A rubberized material along the inner surface of cast wheels helps create the seal that allows motorcycles to run tubeless tires. Wire spoke wheels cannot use this material, as it would gum up the spokes and interfere with the process of replacing them. Therefore, if you have wire-spoked wheels, you'll likely have to run tubes. A few wire wheels are sealed, and designed to run with tubeless tires.

The problem with tubes is that, if punctured, the tube will generally deflate in seconds. A tubeless tire will often capture a nail and hold it for a time, allowing the rider to limp to a dealer for repair or replacement. My advice is that if you have a choice between cast wheels with tubeless tires or wire wheels with tubes, go with the former. They may not look as trick, but one

flat will convince you that there's more to riding than style.

Sizes and Speed Ratings

A tire will fit on your bike only if it is the proper size. Here's a quick course in how to read metric tire sizing, which is by far the most common today. It is usually possible to mount a one-size-wider tire on a given stock motorcycle wheel, so long as no clearance problems develop. However, a wider tire will change the bike's steering and handling characteristics. Fitting tires wider than one additional size usually requires larger wheels and possibly a larger swingarm, frame, or both. That's a whole other story than what we're talking about here; see the discussion of wheels in Chapter Six.

If the tire is a size 140/90H-16, for example, this means that it measures 140 millimeters at its widest point when mounted on a rim and properly inflated. The 90 refers to its aspect ratio, which means it is 90 percent as tall as it is wide. The 16 refers to rim diameter in inches, and the H is its speed rating. An "R" or a "B" in the same space refers to a radial or a belted tire.

In Europe, the sustained high speeds possible on the autobahn can shred tires quickly. In response, the tire industry established speed ratings for automotive and motorcycle tires that alert consumers that properly inflated examples of these tires have been successfully tested at certain sustained speeds at certain loads. These tires now carry their speed ratings on their sidewalls as part of their sizing information. For example, on our 140/90H-16 tire, the "H" refers to the speed rating.

How to Patch a Tire

Because motorcycles are so hard on their tires, and they're so critical to your safety (after all, your bike only has two), repairing a tire or tube should only be considered as a last resort—a temporary emergency repair to get you home, or to last only until you can replace the tube or tire. And if the hole is in the sidewall, don't even consider patching it; call the tow truck.

Should you get a nail in the tread area of your tire, how it will be patched depends upon whether it is a tube-type or tubeless tire. In either case it usually is fixable to the extent that it can get you home if you have a proper repair kit. Place the motorcycle on its center-stand, or if it's not so equipped find some other means of taking the weight off the tire.

If you have tubeless tires, you do not need to remove the tire from the wheel. Locate the nail, remove it, and use the probe to roughen and enlarge the hole. Soak a tire plug with the appropriate rubber cement, and place it in the clip of the probe. Insert the plug in the hole and remove the probe, which should leave the plug securely in the hole. Inflate the tire with a pump, or those CO2 cartridges so popular in emergency repair kits.

Once the tire is inflated to the proper pressure, check the plug for leaks by soaking it in liquid and looking for bubbles (in a pinch, spit will do). If all is snug, cut away any excess plug material, wait a few minutes for the glue to set, and ride away. Again, remember that the tire is far from 100 percent competent; limit your speed to about 50 miles per hour until you can limp home and replace the tire.

BATTERIES

The Basics of Battery Care

If you have a savings account, you already have some understanding of your bike's

---

It is usually possible to mount a one-size-wider tire on a given stock motorcycle wheel

Many types of multitools are available, some with related kits. The Day Tripper by Wind Zone offers two multitools, an assortment of bits (including Torx), and a handy carrying case. *Wind Zone*

Get a good tire gauge and use it at least every few days of riding. If you notice tire pressure suddenly decreasing, carefully inspect the tire for a nail or other puncture. *Roadgear*

HUH?

What's that, warm weather is harder on a battery than cold? Then why do I usually only have starting problems on cold mornings?

Don't confuse starting problems with battery problems. The reason internal-combustion engines have starting problems in the cold is because fuel does not atomize as well and because oil thickens, which causes more resistance to turning the engine over.

battery. When utilizing the battery to start your bike, you're making a withdrawal from this account. When running at normal rpm, you are making a deposit and building it back up. Let either your bank account or your battery become overdrawn, however, and the results can be problematic.

A lead/acid battery requires only a little monthly maintenance. Charge it any time the starter sounds weak, the lights appear dim, or the battery hasn't been used for two weeks or more. At least every month do the following:

1. Check the electrolyte level on a conventional lead-acid battery: (If you have a maintenance-free sealed battery, you can skip this part.) Set the battery on a level surface and visually check that the electrolyte level is between the maximum and minimum lines. If any cells fall below the minimum level, the lead plates can be exposed to air, leading to sulfation and permanent damage. If any cells have a low electrolyte level, remove the filler plugs on those cells (first extinguish all fire and flames). Add distilled water to bring all cells to near the maximum level. Do not overfill, as this can cause leakage. Battery acid is corrosive, so be certain to not spill any. Wear eye protection, rubber gloves, and old clothes.

2. Keep the top of the battery clean: It's best to remove the battery from the bike for this step. If any electrolyte has spilled on the battery or bike, clean it and the terminals with a solution of baking soda and water. Leave the filler plugs in place so that no dirt enters the battery. Rinse with water and dry.

3. Check the cables, clamps, and case for damage: The most common cause of a sudden battery "failure" is a loose connection. Make certain the connectors on cables and clamps are snugged down, and that the rubber protective cap covers the positive terminal (+) when you're done. Be very careful that the tool you're using to snug the positive cable fitting does not contact any

metal, as a spark will result. Keep your hand fully around the tool to prevent this.

4. Clean the terminals and connectors if necessary: It's best to remove the battery cables before cleaning the terminals. If the terminals are corroded, clean them with a wire brush. For final cleaning, use fine sandpaper or emery cloth. You will lose any clock, radio, or other settings when the cables are removed.

5. Check the state of charge: A battery that's not in use will lose 0.5 to 1.0 percent of its charge per day, higher during warm weather and less in cool. An electric clock will drain the battery sooner. With a voltmeter hooked to the terminals, a fully charged battery should read 12.6 volts, or 12.8 volts for a sealed battery (the latter has a different electrolyte, which offers a slightly higher terminal voltage). If the battery is below this voltage, it needs a charge. I recommend using a trickle charger that charges at a rate of 1.5 amps, and switches to a float mode once the battery is fully charged. Some chargers come with connectors that can be permanently installed on the battery terminals to simplify access.

6. Check for excessive sediment or sulfation on the plates: This gunk on the plates can lead to early failure. If you see much of it, replace the battery soon, before it fails and lets you down. Skip this step on sealed batteries.

7. Check that the vent tube is open and free of kinks: Batteries build up pressure, and a hose blocked by a kink can potentially explode.

Battery Winter Storage

If you live in a cold-weather area where your bike is put away for the winter, remove the battery from the bike, perform the steps listed above, and fully charge it. Store it in a cool, dry area away from kids and pets. Mark on your calendar every three to four weeks to charge the battery, or simply place it on a smart charger that goes to a float charge once the battery is fully charged.

Follow this religiously, and in the spring it should only be necessary to place the battery back in your bike and start it up.

PICKING UP A FALLEN BIKE

Thirty years ago, when most of us were riding bikes up to 500 or 650cc (and we were 30 years younger), picking up a fallen bike was not that difficult. Today, with dressers weighing 800 to 900 pounds or more, it can be a real problem. I recall the time I rode a Honda GL1200 Gold Wing out into a field of flowers to photograph it . . . then had to hike back out to the road and flag down a guy to ask him to help me pick it up. That's before I learned the key.

The key is to remember that legs are stronger than arms, and that it all starts with a wedge. If you drop your bike, remove any dense items that can come off easily such as the camping gear on the seat, the case of wine in the saddlebags, and the anvil in the trunk. There's no big rush unless it's leaking gas or battery acid.

If possible, put the bike in gear so it won't roll. Get on the low side and turn the handlebar toward you. Now, lifting as much as possible with your arms, try to wedge your knee under some part of the engine that isn't hot. This could be a footpeg, floorboard, or frame member. Yes, it will probably get your pant leg dirty, but the alternative is to hang around and wait for help. Be sure you'll be able to deploy the sidestand if the bike has fallen on its left side; deploy the stand if it's fallen to the right. Then, through a process of lifting with your arms and legs and wedging your leg deeper into the bike, work it up high enough so that you can deploy the stand.

PRE-RIDE INSPECTION

Every motorcycle owner's manual comes with a pre-ride checklist. Use it as the basis for your riding. However, humans tend to be creatures of habit, and we may begin to neglect this important task. Consult your bike's owner's manual for its specifics, but if the manual is lost, here's a sample of what to check on your bike before every ride:

Tires: If you don't have a manual, the recommended tire pressures should be listed on a sticker under your bike's seat. These are cold tire pressures, and should be taken before the bike is ridden (when the tires are still cold). As air is heated, its pressure increases, so once the bike is ridden its tires will gain about 2 to 3 psi. Check tires periodically for cuts, damage, and tread depth.

Engine oil: This is quite simple to check if your bike has an oil sight glass and a centerstand. If not, pull and wipe the dipstick, center the bike, and insert and pull the dipstick again. The level should be between the lines.

Fuel supply: Check that you have enough, and estimate your range to the next fill-up. Occasionally check the condition of fuel lines. If you see cracks, replace them.

Coolant level: If your bike is liquid cooled, eyeball the coolant level before each ride. Note that coolant hoses should be replaced periodically.

Clutch: Check for adjustment. If it's a hydraulically actuated clutch, check fluid level in the reservoir and condition of hoses. If it's cable actuated, check for play and lubricate if necessary.

Brakes: Check for operation, and check hydraulic reservoirs for fluid level and for condition of hoses. If hydraulic brakes feel spongy, have your dealer bleed the system. Periodically check brake pads and shoes for wear.

Control cables: Check for smooth operation and lubricate if necessary.

Lights: Check for headlight operation on both high and low beams, brake light (as actuated by both the brake lever and brake pedal), and turn signal operation.

Drive chain: If your bike has chain final drive, check for slack and adjust if necessary, and be sure it's properly lubricated.

> ### TIP
> An alternative method of picking up a fallen bike is to stand with your back to the bike, bend at your knees, keep your back straight and grab any solid part of the bike you can. Then lean into the bike and push up with your legs. Just be careful you don't go over the other way.

Chapter 11

LET'S RIDE!

Up in the northern part of Oregon is this road near the Columbia River Gorge. No matter what type or brand of bike you ride, it's a wonderful experience on a sunny day. *Photo by Tom Riles and Brian J. Nelson. Yamaha Motor Corp., USA*

If you have a street-legal motorcycle, the world is your oyster.

WHAT YOU WILL LEARN

- Basic riding strategies

- What passengers need to know

- Rides, rallies and other fun bike events

- Why you should take a track school

WHERE TO RIDE

If you have a street-legal motorcycle, the world is your oyster. You can ride it on virtually any public road, anywhere. As for deciding where to go, here are a few suggestions.

The motorcycle magazines often carry stories about destinations and roads. *Rider* magazine (for which I have worked since 1990) not only carries frequent tour features, but also a section on Favorite Rides and another on Rallies & Clubs.

A second consideration is friends. Staying a couple days with friends allows one to have a nice time visiting, get some rest (maybe), sleep in a bed (or on a couch), do the laundry, get a home-cooked meal (sometimes), and see the local sights.

My third consideration is events. These include the national events like Daytona, Sturgis, Laconia, the Laughlin River Run, and other local and club events.

Depending upon your interests and what brand or type of bike you ride, I suggest you join a club that caters to those interests. There are major brand clubs (The Harley Owners Group, or H.O.G., for Harley riders; the BMW Motorcycle Owners Association for Beemer Riders; and many more), and clubs for particular kinds of motorcycles, including the Gold Wing Road Riders Association for those who ride Honda's big touring bikes, Star Touring and Riding for owners of Yamaha cruisers, and the Concours Owners Group (COG) for fans of the Kawasaki Concours. And many more.

ROAD STRATEGIES

Ride your own ride: It happens. Ted and Mary go to a rally and meet Jim and Alice, who are locals. They hit it off, and Jim and Alice offer to show them the local sights. Jim

Left: There's nothing like being out on the open road, going places, and having fun. Here's a solo rider in back-road California.

Right: The eastern United States is a wonderful place to ride in early summer. Here, a group of riders enjoy a scenic road in upstate New York.

Groups of riders stop for cappuccinos and espressos on the Passo Giau in the Alps. Motorcycling made it possible for them to enjoy such a day as this even more.
Beach's Motorcycle Adventures

MAPS

I love maps! If I have a few weeks with nothing to do and need to go somewhere, my first consideration is to spread out a map and make plans. I prefer maps with national and state parks marked in green, and plan my rides around these.

Set out a map and mark the locations of several friends around the country you'd like to see, several national parks, and several roads you've heard about and always wanted to ride. Check the events calendar of clubs of which you're a member or would like to join, and mark the locations. There's your general area to be covered and your general time frame. I'll leave the rest in your capable hands. Call your friends, set some dates, port and polish your credit card, and get your bike tuned. You're in business!

THE AMERICAN MOTORCYCLIST ASSOCIATION

Founded in 1924, the American Motorcyclist Association (AMA) is a nonprofit organization that not only sanctions motorcycle competition in the United States, but also serves as a watchdog for motorcyclists' rights. Antirider discrimination comes in the form of mandatory helmet laws, land closures, and discriminatory insurance practices, each of which the AMA opposes vigorously. Also, its monthly American Motorcyclist magazine is highly informative and entertaining. While the AMA is on our side, it also takes a reasonable approach by advocating that motorcyclists ride safely and responsibly, use land with care, and stay aware that "Noise Annoys."

I have been an AMA member for more than 25 years, and wish that everyone who rides were a member. For more information visit the AMA website at www.AMADirectlink.com, or call (800) AMA-JOIN.

Even if you don't own a motorcycle yourself, the world's still a prettier place from the back of one. Just get the right gear, the right trip, and the right friends to ride with.

The fun doesn't stop just because the sun goes down. Many motorcycling events such as Daytona, Sturgis, Laconia, and others have a major street scene in which checking out the bikes and watching the riders go by is part of the fun. At Americade, the sundown fun often includes going for ice cream.

likes to impress people with his riding skill and he knows the roads well, so he takes off hard, leaving Ted struggling to stay up. The result is usually only a strained early friendship, but sometimes it can be tragic.

Before the ride, make it clear "We just want to cruise and enjoy the sights." If they ride faster than you want to go, hang back. Don't feel obligated to ride with the pack. Ride your own ride. If Jim sincerely wants you to ride with him, he'll notice you're no longer in his mirror and slow down to wait for you. If he doesn't, well, maybe it wasn't meant to be.

Sharpen your skills: Take a Motorcycle Safety Foundation RiderCourse. Your dealer should have details. There is the Basic RiderCourse for beginners and the Experienced RiderCourse.

Tank up the night before: You awake before the sun to get an early start, then waste an hour running around town looking for an open gas station. Prepare your bike the night before by tanking up late.

No matter when you get up, check tire pressure when the tires are still cold, and check the oil supply. The oil usually won't vary much, but I once was alerted to a nail in my tire by the fact it was a few psi low every morning.

You need those stinkin' papers: If you get stopped by the law, you're going to have to produce your driver's license, registration, and possibly insurance papers. Make it easy on yourself by bringing them along, and by being polite to the officer. Attitude counts, and if you get belligerent—trust me—they've dealt with your kind before. In matters in which the officer has discretion as to whether or not to issue a ticket, did I mention attitude counts? And don't forget to bring your owner's manual. A shop manual can come in handy, too.

Contact information: Didja ever take a trip and become separated from others in your group? Before the trip, agree upon a contact phone number if anyone has trouble or becomes separated. The best number is that of anyone's cell phone in the group. Or, make it the number of someone who is always home and can relay messages, or an answering machine you can access from a push-button phone.

Also, I don't want to jinx anyone, but riding fiends should share contact numbers for family members in case someone has an accident or medical problem. In some cases, a next-of-kin must give permission for medical treatment if the individual is not conscious, and in situations like those, time is critical.

Learning to Ride: The MSF

Riding a motorcycle is an acquired skill. It takes time to become proficient and there is a definite learning curve. To really speed up the process of becoming a safer street rider, the Motorcycle Safety Foundation offers Basic and Experienced RiderCourses. These are available in every state, and Canada has its own version.

The MSF Basic RiderCourse is designed as a 15-hour curriculum that takes place over a few days or consecutive weekends. However, some locations add additional modules of instruction/discussion that lengthen the class. Most locations issue an MSF RiderCourse Completion Card, and upon successful completion some states (but not all) will waive the on-bike riding skills test and/or the written test required to obtain a motorcycle operator's license or endorsement.

The Basic RiderCourse begins with classroom instruction and progresses outdoors to a parking lot. There, students can suit up in safety gear and receive instruction on small (usually 125cc) bikes provided by the MSF. Students learn the basics by pushing the motorcycle around with the engine off, then riding it at very low speeds. They advance to braking drills, turning, braking in a turn, and all the useful riding skills that will soon become second nature. Once they have completed the basic RiderCourse, new riders can move out onto

the public roads with a confidence born of an actual level of skill.

The MSF also conducts three versions of its Experienced RiderCourse that teaches experienced riders the advanced skills that will make them better riders. Here, riders use their own motorcycles. To learn more about the Motorcycle Safety Foundation and its RiderCourses, call (800) 446-9227 or go to www.msf-usa.org.

The MSF also offers dirt-bike training that it bills as a fun, one-day, hands-on training session available to all riders six years of age and older in a low-pressure environment. It teaches basic riding skills, responsible riding practices, risk management, and environmental awareness. Call (877) 288-7093, or go to www.dirtbikeschool.com.

Canadian riders are directed to the Canadian Safety Council at (613) 739-1535 or go to www.safety-council.org.

MECHANICAL

Service Early: Stretching might be good exercise for you, but it's hell on your bike. Stretching that last tune-up, oil change, drive-belt adjustment, or tank of gas is just asking for it. Get your bike serviced early to handle delays or to work out the bugs. If

A touring bike is one on which you tour. It does not need to be a 900-pound dresser with integral saddlebags and trunk. Here, with the addition of luggage, a couple tours on a BMW K1200S sportbike. *BMW of North America*

In 1978 Hazel Kolb (who called herself "The Motorcycling Grandma") rode her 80-cubic-inch Harley-Davidson Electra Glide around the perimeter of the United States—alone. She spent her "80 Days on an 80" when she was nearly 60, partly as a tribute to her late husband, and partly because she wanted to prove something to herself. During the course of her "Perimeter Ride," her story was picked up by the national news media, and she appeared on *The Tonight Show with Johnny Carson.*

Want to party with a few thousand of your closest friends? Americade draws about 40,000 riders each June to Lake George, New York. In addition to all the typical rally events, it also offers cruises on Lake George.

As this shot shows, it doesn't matter what you ride when you head down to Knoxville, Tennessee, and hook into a nice curve at the Honda Hoot. *American Honda Motor Co.*

there's something wrong with your bike at the start of the trip, I can guarantee it won't get any better by the end.

PASSENGERS

Whether you call them passengers, pillions, or co-riders (a much more active term), the person on the back of the bike really adds to the ride—especially when you've reached your destination. Here are a few words for the person on the back about getting there, the riding part of the experience.

Get the okay: Don't mount the bike until the rider says it's okay. Ask "Ready?" and wait for the affirming nod. It's really disconcerting for the rider to be pulling on a glove or strapping on a helmet when the passenger suddenly begins to mount, and the bike lurches to the side.

Mount from the left: Always mount a motorcycle from the left side, meaning your left when sitting astride the bike. That's the direction in which the bike leans on its side-stand, and that's where the rider expects you to be coming from.

Keep in balance: Disrupt the bike as little as possible when mounting. If you're tall enough, stand on the ground, throw your right leg over the seat and slide on over. If you're not tall enough, allow the rider to straighten the bike, wait for his nod, and step up onto the left footpeg, then throw your leg over. When mounting this

way, place your hand on the rider's shoulder to steady yourself as you mount.

How to hold: If there's a backrest, lean against it. If there is no backrest, you'll have to lean forward and maintain muscle tension. Use the handholds (if any) on the sides of the bike if you must, but it's far better to wrap your arms around the rider's torso and clasp your hands in front of his belly. If that's too personal, you can grab the sides of his jacket. How chummy you get depends upon how well you know—or want to know—the rider.

Also, several outfits manufacture belts with handles attached. The belt straps around the rider's waist and the handles stick out to the sides. It's all quite impersonal, if that's what you need. The problem with handles attached to the motorcycle itself is they're usually located behind the rider and are, therefore, useless to counter forces generated by acceleration. The rider is in front of you, and that's one reason it's best to hold on to him.

Go with the lean: This is the second reason why it's best to hang on to the rider. I once took my sister for a ride, and she screamed every time the bike leaned. Unfortunately, I had not sufficiently alerted her to the fact that a lean is how a motorcycle turns, and is not necessarily the first step to a fall. The message to the co-rider is to go with the lean, and to trust that the rider knows what he or she is doing. If you don't trust them, why did you get on the bike in the first place?

Become one with the bike: The best passenger is the one who's completely neutral, the one the rider completely forgets is even back there. Becoming one with the bike is the best way to ride. An easy rule to help do this is to keep your shoulders directly behind the rider's shoulders. That way, wherever he goes, you go. The weight transfer will be completely natural, and, best of all for the rider, predictable.

Keep your feet up: When the bike comes to a stop, keep your feet on the pegs. You don't need to "help" by putting a foot down. Not only is the rider perfectly capable of holding up the bike alone, but your major weight shift to get a foot down will severely unbalance the bike.

Anticipate: Do you find you sometimes click helmets with the rider? Learn to anticipate shifting and braking, a skill you'll develop with time. This situation will also be minimized if there's a backrest against which the passenger can lean. If you expect to be riding with this person often, it's perfectly reasonable to request that they install a backrest for your comfort.

No surprises: As you ride along, you will see things that surprise and delight you. However, if the rider is lost in reverie it's not a good idea to suddenly shout into his ear. This can startle the rider and take his attention away from the road. Instead, devise a signal (such as squeezing his arm) to signal that you want to talk. Better yet, suggest to the rider that he pick up a rider/passenger intercom system that fits in the helmet and allows you to talk as you ride. In any case, resist the temptation to surprise the rider with nonessential information. It can be frustrating and distracting to try to converse on a motorcycle.

WOMEN WHO RIDE

The sight of women riding their own bikes is becoming increasingly common, and women have their own special situations. Because they're usually smaller of stature, women will usually feel more comfortable on lighter, smaller bikes. Cruisers are a good general choice, as they often have a low seat height. On the other hand, there are also standard, naked, and even sportbikes available that are quite manageable for inseam-challenged adrenaline junkies, no matter their sex.

To say much more is to buy into the old stereotypes about women: they don't know

The sight of women riding their own bikes is becoming increasingly common.

much about mechanical things, they're too weak to hold the bike up, they would be prey to unscrupulous men—you know the rest. I would rather just give women the same advice I give all riders. A motorcycle is a tool for a job. Define the job accurately and that will help you choose the right bike. And of course, with an increasing number of companies now offering women's apparel, it's pretty easy now to choose protective gear sized and cut for you.

Women are often leery of riding or traveling alone. However, as a means of encouragement I want to mention that I had the privilege of knowing Hazel Kolb, "The Motorcycling Grandma," who in 1978 rode her 80-cubic-inch Harley-Davidson Electra

Many of the major bike manufacturers offer free demo rides at the major rallies; here's the Kawasaki demo ride at Americade. All you need in order to participate is a valid motorcycle rider's license and appropriate riding gear. Of course, you'd better sign up early as demo rides tend to fill up fast.

It's always fun to walk through the parking lot at a rally, looking at all the bikes and noting how their riders have set them up and personalized them. At the Honda Hoot rally in Knoxville, Tennessee, you'll see everything from long-distance tourers to heavily customized bikes, from new machines to vintage bikes. *American Honda Motor Co.*

GO ALONG FOR THE RIDE

I've occasionally had passengers who actually gripped the bike with their legs and tried to stand it up as I gently leaned it into a turn . . . not a good practice! Remember, you want to allow the motorcycle to go where the rider wants it to go. To do otherwise is to invite disaster.

To help you go with the turn, look over the rider's shoulder in the direction of the turn. For example, if a left turn is coming up, look over the left shoulder. This will give you a better sense of what's happening on the bike, and the subtle weight shift will help the rider take the turn.

Many commuters utilize motorcycles for getting to work, because they use less gas than a car, slice through traffic jams, and are often easier to park.

Here's an example of why some people advise that you never volunteer. After viewing the Tommi Ahvala Stunt Show at Americade, not a single male spectator was able to walk away upright. No humans were hurt during the performance of this stunt.

Glide around the perimeter of the United States—alone. She spent her "80 Days on an 80" when she was in her late 50s, partly as a tribute to her late husband, and partly because she wanted to prove something to herself. During the course of her "Perimeter Ride" her story was picked up by the national news media, and she appeared on *The Tonight Show with Johnny Carson*, where she was interviewed by Carson himself.

I later helped Hazel write her autobiography, *On the Perimeter*, which is now out of print. Her attitude was "Other women talked about doing this sort of thing. I just went ahead and *did* it!" Good for her!

COMMUTING

Many commuters utilize motorcycles for getting to work, because they use less gas than a car, slice through traffic jams, and are

often easier to park. But there are drawbacks as well. A bike can't carry near as much, and you'd better have some good riding gear for inclement weather. Still, offsetting all of this is the enjoyment factor—riding a motorcycle is just a lot more fun than driving a car or taking a bus or train.

A full weatherproof suit that goes on over your work clothes, be it shop wear or three-piece suit, is a real plus. A briefcase will fit in most saddlebags, and lunch and other small items in a tank bag or the other saddlebag. I cover carrying a laptop in Chapter Six, but it can be carried in a saddlebag, so long as it's well padded.

Will a motorcycle reduce commuting costs?

With the high cost of gasoline some nonriders have asked about commuting to work by motorcycle to save money. I'm often asked how many miles a motorcycle can typically go on a gallon of gas, and if it would be a good idea to buy one for commuting.

To answer that first question, I have tested bikes from 250cc to over 2,000cc, and find that generally, under testing conditions (which means hard usage), new test bikes will usually average from about 37 to 50 miles or more per gallon. Fuel mileage varies, depending upon the size and orientation of the bike (heavier and more powerful bikes tend to be thirstier, and how it's used. I have found on rides that a rider on a smaller bike trying to stay with aggressive riders on larger bikes will sometimes get fewer miles per gallon, as he has to ride the smaller bike so hard.

Professional testers tend to be aggressive riders; it's fun to go fast and we're not paying for the gas, tune-ups, tires, or insurance. We probably use test bikes harder than the average person would use a personal bike. Therefore, I would estimate that a sane rider (that means someone *other* than a professional test rider) could probably improve my figures above by from 3 to 5 miles per gallon on the bigger bikes, and 5 to

WOMEN RIDERS
BY GENEVIEVE SCHMITT

One of the biggest shifts in the motorcycle industry in the last 30 years is the growth and impact of female motorcyclists. Women are taking up motorcycling in record numbers. According to the Motorcycle Industry Council's 2003 ownership survey, nearly 10 percent of all motorcycle owners are women. That's up 36 percent since 1998!

Why are so many women sliding onto the front of a motorcycle seat? Because they want to experience all the same excitement of riding one's own bike that men have enjoyed all these years. In society, more women are exercising their independence. They're asserting themselves and rising up corporate ladders and, as a result, have their own disposable income. Women are seeing other women on the road riding their own motorcycles, and are inspired by that. Old stereotypes of the loose biker babe are gone. There are no more societal barriers for a woman who wants to ride her own motorcycle, other than the ones she imposes on herself.

And that is one of the areas where men and women differ in the two-wheeled world. Many women are holding themselves back from motorcycling by what they perceive as barriers. Those barriers are confidence, product knowledge, skills, and life stage.

Confidence: Sometimes a woman is intimidated by the thought of handling such a big machine. "What if I can't handle it on my own?" and, "What if I drop the bike?" are some of the negative thoughts that run through her head. As with any sport or activity, there is a learning curve. As one gradually increases in skill level, confidence builds. There are many small women who can ride a motorcycle. One's size should not be a limitation.

In recent years, bike manufacturers have broadened their model lineups to include many different sizes of machines. The aftermarket industry has responded by offering plenty of parts to modify a motorcycle to fit riders better. There are ways to lower a motorcycle, bring the handlebars closer to the rider, lower the seat, or adjust the footpegs—nearly any part of a motorcycle can be changed to accommodate a particular rider. Size is no longer a limitation.

Product knowledge: If a woman has never been exposed to motorcycling, she may be intimidated by a lack of knowledge on how to operate a motorcycle or not knowing where the controls are located. Proper training takes students through every step of learning, starting with the basics.

Skills: For some, a barrier to pursuing the enjoyment of motorcycling is not knowing where to start. Fortunately, there are training classes in street and dirt riding in every state and in Canada. Most schools use a curriculum developed by the Motorcycle Safety Foundation, the industry standard in how-to-ride instruction. These classes are very popular among women, and one-third of all graduates are female. In some states, passing the riding test in the class satisfies the state motor vehicle licensing requirements. Taking the beginner class is also a good opportunity to see if motorcycling is something you might enjoy.

Motorcycling is like any other activity—the more you practice, the more proficient you become. No one can expect to be an expert rider right after graduating from the training class. Rather, some women and men will practice their newfound skills in a parking lot or in a quiet neighborhood before hitting the streets. Everyone learns at his or her own pace.

Life stage: Some women will use the excuse that they are too busy doing something else in their lives, so they don't have time to learn to ride a motorcycle. For example, "I just had a baby" or "I just started a new career." Women can always find an excuse not to ride. The question is how badly do you want to ride? So many female riders say they would have started riding earlier if they had only known how much joy it would bring to their lives.

For a woman, motorcycling is an expression of herself. Many say riding is very empowering, that the confidence she gets from riding her own motorcycle spills over into other areas of her life. It's that "you don't know what you're missing until you do it" kind of thinking.

So, if you've ever thought about donning a leather jacket, some cool black boots, and a pair of stylish shades and cruising along the open road in search of adventure, now's the time to do it. Motorcycle riding is the stuff dreams are made of, and so many women are living their dream right now. Isn't it time you did, too?

For more information on women riders, go to Genevieve Schmitt's website at www.womenridersnow.com.

The Americade parade is unique in that it makes a 180-degree turn and then turns back upon itself. In that way, riders can both participate in the parade and watch it at the same time. Sylvester and Tweety are worth watching, too.

TIP

I know a guy who bought a neat intercom system for himself and his wife, and decided to install the headsets the morning they left. It only took a few minutes to mount the headsets in the helmets, but when he tried to plug in the battery packs—oops, they were NiCads, and had to be charged for four hours. Be prepared.

Idyllic mornings and evening campfires make camping by motorcycle one of my favorite activities. Add in some good friends and it's one of the world's great pleasures.

Some smaller rallies are held at campgrounds, where riders of a like mind can congregate and kick tires. Here's a BMW club rally that took place in Southern California.

10 on the smaller. In general, 40 to 55 miles per gallon is well within reason for a street motorcycle. How much better mileage it will get than a car depends a lot upon the nature of the car, the bike, and the commute.

It's a complex question whether this mileage difference would convince someone who doesn't ride to buy a motor-cycle, learn to ride it, equip themselves for riding, and then insure and maintain the bike. I can't tell you the answer, but I can tell you how to go about thinking about it.

Let's say, for example, that your car gets 20 miles per gallon, and gas costs $3.00 per gallon. A motorcycle you might buy for commuting gets 45 miles per gallon. In every 1,000 miles, the car would require $150 in fuel costs, and the motorcycle would require $66.67. If you live 25 miles

from work, your daily commute would be 50 miles, so, assuming 20 work days per month, you'd commute 1,000 miles a month, or approximately 12,000 miles per year. Let's cut that figure by a third, though, because you'll take the car during inclement weather, on days on which you had to carry bulky items to or from work, when you need to give someone a ride, etc. Now you're commuting 8,000 miles per year on the motorcycle rather than taking the car. Your fuel costs for those 8,000 miles would be $533.33; had you taken the car you would have spent $1,200. Congratulations, you've have saved $666.67 in one year! Had you been diligent and taken the motorcycle *every single day*, your fuel saving over the 12 000-mile distance would have been $1,000!

However, for the first year at least, you've got to figure the minimal cost of outfitting yourself with a helmet ($100), jacket ($200), gloves ($50), boots ($100), and Motorcycle Safety Foundation course ($100). In 8,000 miles you will likely have gone through at least one set of tires (bike tires don't last nearly as long as car tires), and that may cost $200 or more. You have already spent $750, not including the orig-inal cost of buying the motorcycle, insuring it, and tune-ups. If you ride the bike five years, your total fuel savings will be $3,333.20 to $5,000, which may just approach what you paid for a used bike five years ago that now has an additional 40,000 miles on it. Only it still doesn't include five years of insurance costs, tune-ups, and maybe four more sets of tires. Discouraged? I have good news and bad news. The bad

> *Most of my closest friends are people I've met through riding, and they have enriched my life greatly.*

news is that all things considered, buying a motorcycle (in addition to keeping your car) for the sole purpose of saving money is not likely to work out. However, if you're doing it to save natural resources and energy, well, you've likely used at least 1,000 fewer gallons of gasoline, and possibly more than 1,600 gallons fewer. The other good news is that the great majority of people who ride motorcycles do so because they're wonderfully fun, and happily ride them even when they understand they're not saving any significant amount of money.

Personally, most of my closest friends are people I've met through riding, and they have enriched my life greatly. It has been said that motorcycling is the most fun a person can have fully clothed, and I cannot disagree with that statement.

MOTORCYCLE EVENTS, RIDES, AND RALLIES

There are many kinds of motorcycle rallies, and they're all fun. These gatherings run the gamut from highly organized to very loose affairs, and from family oriented to

SANE AND SOBER

We all know that drinking alcohol slows your reaction time, impairs your judgment, makes you more prone to take risks, and we know it's just plain stupid to drink and operate a motor vehicle. Be aware drinking can also make you sleepy, especially when combined with a late dinner. If you'd like to enjoy a nightcap, bring along a bottle and enjoy it once you've reached your destination and are in for the night. Pack a corkscrew and bottle opener—they may be on your multitool.

"biker" events complete with readily available alcohol and wet T-shirt contests. A rally is any kind of motorcycle event that tends to go on for a couple days or longer, while a ride is usually an event that starts at Point A and may end at the same place, or at a Point B. Rides are often among the major activities within a rally.

Motorcycle events, rides, and rallies come in all shapes and sizes. The largest events in the United States are Bike Week, held in Daytona Beach, Florida, every March, and the Sturgis Rally and Races, held in Sturgis, South Dakota, every August. More than 300,000 riders attend these events each year, and I've seen estimates of close to 400,000. They're huge!

Organized tours allow riders to experience places they could not normally reach without spending huge amounts of time and money researching and making arrangements. Tour companies handle such details on a daily basis. These riders are enjoying Switzerland's Klausen Pass. *Beach's Motorcycle Adventures*

How does one arrange for the use of a motorcycle in a foreign country? An organized tour company will rent you one so you can enjoy such experiences as the Alps' Susten Pass on such a day as this. *Beach's Motorcycle Adventures*

TIP

There are tours of the Canadian Rockies, California, China, the Alps, Australia, Mexico, South America, and many other places. Tour companies are often quite flexible. If you wish to bring your own motorcycle, for example, you probably can. If you wish to rent one of their motorcycles to go your own route, you probably can. Yes, some people tend to look down their noses at such tours as being for those who aren't sufficiently adventuresome, but when faced with all the paperwork and challenges involved in taking a motorcycle to a foreign country, well, I'd much rather take a tour than miss the trip of a lifetime.

Most rallies are much smaller and consist of anywhere from a few hundred riders to a few thousand. The largest touring rally in the United States is Americade in Lake George, New York, each June.

At rallies you will find a wealth of activities that can include races, field events (bike games), vendors, door prizes, bike shows (with judging and trophies), entertainment, seminars, and much more. The larger rallies will attract demo teams from some of the major manufacturers, and you can take free rides on new motorcycles.

There are three general types of rallies: brand, club, and open. Brand rallies are intended for riders of certain brands of bikes. These are often associated with Harley-Davidson and BMW clubs. If they're sponsored by a club, attendance may be restricted to members and guests only. Of course, if you show up at the gate and are not a member, there is usually someone who will cheerfully sign you up. Similar clubs are devoted to specific models like the Honda Gold Wing, Yamaha Star cruisers, or the Kawasaki Concours, to name a few. You will not necessarily have to ride that certain brand or model to the rally, but if you don't you're kind of missing the point.

Club rallies are usually restricted to members only, or members and guests, and they cover a wide area of motorcycling interests. While some are formed around brands or models as above, others may be centered on a certain area of interest such as touring, vintage, or performance riding.

Open rallies are those that welcome all comers. These include Sturgis, Daytona, the Laughlin River Run, Myrtle Beach, and many more. Membership is not required, but an entry fee may be, at least for certain rally events.

Parades and Rides

Many rallies include a parade as part of the program, in which case you'll be introduced to formation riding. The idea is to ride two bikes to a lane, but staggered so you're not riding right beside the bike in the other wheel track. This formation allows the riders more space should they need to meander from their wheel track to avoid an obstacle or pothole, or to take a better line in a turn. Increase following distance as speed increases, and if the parade heads out into the country where the roads are winding, break formation and ride single-file.

Group rides should follow the same format as parades: Formation riding applies in town as well as on freeways, with appropriate spacing depending upon speed. Rather than riding in huge groups, rides should be broken into smaller groups led by a ride leader. In this way, more compact groups can usually be led intact through stoplights. In the more organized rides, each group has a leader and a sweep rider, connected by radio. When a small group is broken by a stoplight the sweep rider will alert the lead rider by radio, who will pull the group over so that it can reunite. If this isn't practical, the sweep rider can ride to the head of the second-half group and conduct them till they join up with their front half.

CAMPING BY MOTORCYCLE

Motorcycle camping and backpacking have a lot in common. In both activities the main concerns are weight, and finding enough room to pack everything. At least motorcyclists have the upper hand—we don't have to carry the weight on our backs!

Camping styles are quite personal, and you'll learn a lot more about camping or backpacking in books about those specific activities than you will here, but let's cover the basics of motorcycle camping.

As you know, carrying a passenger by motorcycle not only nearly doubles your luggage needs, but also takes up that valuable bit of carrying room on the rear portion of the seat. For that reason, riding two-up makes camping more difficult. I have done it, but found that it really puts a strain on packing and luggage capacity. You'll still only need one tent if it's a two-person or larger, but what you have to carry in terms of sleeping bags, pads and clothing will double.

Camp cooking requires a lot of cubic space in terms of packing cooking gear and food, so to compensate for the additional luggage needs of a passenger I have found it necessary to simply do away with any attempt to cook meals in camp. We eat in restaurants when packing double.

If you're riding solo, I suggest using the rear portion of the seat for a large nylon bag that will accommodate the tent, sleeping bag, pad, and camp chair. If the bag is not waterproof, line it with a sturdy bag that is.

ORGANIZED TOURS

We all have our dream rides, and one of my dreams was to ride the Alps. However, such a trip was daunting in terms of shipping a bike over, dealing with several currencies and languages, and knowing where to stay and what to see. Thanks to organized motorcycle tours, I have not only ridden in the Alps, but also the Isle of Man several times.

Tours can set you up with a rental bike, accommodations, an itinerary, and a group of like-minded souls with whom to ride. They last from a few days to several weeks, and are often the best way to explore an area that you probably would never have visited on your own. Then, once you've taken a tour or two, you're much better able to make arrangements for returning on your own, if you wish. That is, unless you're too spoiled and just want to keep riding with tour groups.

On an organized tour, the day usually begins with the group meeting at breakfast. Members will need to have their luggage outside their rooms by a certain time. The luggage-van driver will haul their bags to the next location while the riders go out to play. There is usually a recommended route, with an alternate route or two, all of which the tour leader would have covered the previous evening at the dinner meeting.

For the day, riders are welcome to go with the tour leader, or simply ride on their

own. As the tour progresses, riders usually gravitate to their own smaller groups. A day's ride in the Alps is usually only going to cover 100 to 150 miles because of the slow, twisting nature of the roads, while a tour in the American West may cover 200 to 300 miles a day. While breakfasts and most dinners are usually included in the tour price, lunches are usually on your own. The only rule for the day is to be at the hotel in time for dinner, or call the tour leader so they'll know where you are.

THE TOURER'S PACKING LIST

Touring is travel by motorcycle, at least overnight or longer, and I've written several books on the subject that are now out of print. This book is actually an expansion of those, and much about touring is contained within it.

We looked at where to pack various types of items in Chapter Six, now let's cover what to pack. My method, which has worked for me for years, is to make a packing list on a legal pad for each trip I take; you may wish to keep your list on your computer. It is based on the list from an earlier trip that was similar. There are camping trips, motel trips, trips to rallies or races. There are trips on which I fly some-

The weather environment in the Alps is very changeable, so you'll need to wear good, versatile gear. Edelweiss Bike Travel, which provided this shot, also offers motorcycle tours in many other parts of the world.

Tours can set you up with a rental bike, accommodations, an itinerary, and a group of like-minded souls with whom to ride.

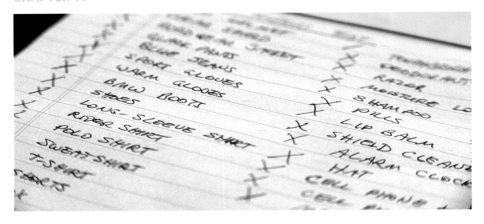

Make a list. Check it twice. After the trip, add anything to it you forgot, then file it away until your next ride, when you'll use it as a starting point.

where to pick up a bike and ride, and I even include lists from family vacation trips just to have a packing list for everything.

When it's time to plan the next trip, I pull out my most recent packing list from a similar trip, and use it as a base on which to start the new list. I label each trip with its date and destination, and when the trip is over add to the list anything I forgot to bring. In this way the list always stays current, and important things are not forgotten. Here's a sample packing list for a motorcycle camping rally at which I would not cook in camp. Your list *will* vary!

Outer Wear

Helmet	T-shirts
Jacket	Underwear
Boots	Bathing suit
Riding pants	Hat
Hot-weather gloves	Shorts
Cold-weather gloves	
Sport gloves	**Bike Items**
Rain gloves	Earplugs
Rain suit	Tinted helmet shield
Rain boots	Shield cleaner and rag
Socks	First-aid kit
Shoes	Jumper cables
	Owner's manual
Inner Wear	Multitool
Pants	Small tool kit
Short-sleeved shirt	Tire gauge
Long-sleeved shirt	Tire patch kit
Sweatshirt	Oil
Electric vest	Siphon hose
and thermostat	Map

Personal Items

Soap	Money
Shampoo	More money
Towel	Lots more money
Toothbrush and paste	
Deodorant	**Camping Items**
Shaving equipment	Tent
Moisture lotion	Sleeping bag
Lip balm	Air mattress
Other personal	Camp chair
hygiene items	Camera
Medications	Coffee cup
Toilet paper	Flashlight
Reading materials	Water
Legal pad and pens	Snacks

First-aid Kit

While a mere first-aid kit won't be of much use in a serious situation, a basic kit will help a rider get through minor mishaps. The most common injuries from riding involve burns and scrapes, so plan your first-aid kit accordingly. Cover a minor burn with antiseptic cream, then tape a loosely-wrapped gauze bandage over it.

Minor scrapes with the pavement (also known as "road rash") are a form of burn, and can be treated similarly. Wash the skin trauma immediately with soap and water and cover it with the antiseptic cream and gauze. Have it checked by a physician as soon as possible.

Handy items to pack also include a scissors, cleaning agents, aspirin, and a booklet of first-aid tips. More importantly, take a first-aid class; they're available through the American Red Cross.

Tools

I have it on good authority that the tool kits that come with most new motorcycles (assuming your bike even *has* a tool kit) are stamped out of taffy in a plant hidden in the wilds of mainland China. I have seen such substandard tools round the edges of bolts, round themselves on Phillips-head screws, and occasionally break while in use. The best thing to do with most standard tool kits is to make a list of the items they contain and replace them with high-quality versions of the same tools that won't likely let you down.

If your bike comes with a tool kit, fit the tools to all visible nuts and bolts to be certain the kit is adequate for your needs—include an adjustable wrench. It will deal with most odd sizes, and come in handy when, for example, you must turn a 12mm nut while holding a 12mm bolt at the other end.

The tool kit should allow the owner to remove or tighten any bolts on the motorcycle likely to need attention, change a fuse, adjust drive chain tension (on a bike with chain final drive), and deal with any standard road emergency, such as removing and replacing either wheel (if necessary) in case of a flat tire. A socket set can also come in handy, though is usually not necessary.

Once you have assembled your upgraded tool set, it will likely no longer fit within the bike's standard tool box. In that case you may wish to obtain a tool roll and store it elsewhere on the motorcycle.

Now that you have assembled your basic tools, consider some other handy carry-alongs:

Spark plug socket: While bikes hardly ever foul plugs these days, such things are still possible.

Multitool: Like a Swiss army knife, a multitool includes several knife blades, small screwdriver blades, little pliers, can opener, bottle opener, scissors, and other little tools.

Tire gauge: You really should check your tire pressure daily.

Tire changing tools: If your bike has tube-type tires, you'll need tire irons to patch the tubes.

Tire plugging and patching kit with CO2 air kit: The kit should consist of both plugs and glue for tubeless tires, and patches and glue for tube-type. Why? While your bike may carry only one type of tire, your buddy's bike may have the other.

Axle wrench: You'll need to remove a wheel to change a tire.

Flashlight: I don't need to explain this one.

Zip-ties: For routing wires and cable, and keeping things out of the way.

Duct and electrical tape: The all-purpose items. If you don't want to carry an entire roll of each, wrap a few feet of tape around a couple pencils.

Siphon hose: You'll need about 3 to 5 feet of the clear stuff.

Sewing kit: I grab those little kits from hotels, as they come in handy for stitching up snagged sleeves, torn trousers, gimped gloves, etc.

Pocket Pals

Some little gadgets are just indispensable. Carry a Swiss army knife or other multitool for their knife blades, bottle and can openers, scissors and miniscrewdrivers, minipliers, and miniwelders. Okay, I'm kidding about the welder part.

Other items to take along include a calculator watch with alarm.

Whenever you do a dirty job, like changing a tire or fooling with spark plugs or oil, you'll be a mess. For cleanup, bring along a rag and some dish detergent (it's formulated for getting grease off hands) in a film canister. An alternative is to pick up some Castrol Waterless/Towelless Hand Cleaner.

TRACK DAYS

While some riders envision racetrack days as being exclusively for those who plan to race, that's far from true for the great majority of riders who take them. I took my first track school (which included instruction) after I'd been riding for 20 years, and nothing I've ever done improved my riding to such a degree so quickly. In a single day I learned how to read the lines in a turn, how to brake properly at high speed, how to match engine rpm when downshifting, how to move my body on the bike to enhance steering, how

I have it on good authority that the tool kits that come with most new motorcycles are stamped out of taffy.

ROAD FOOD

Snackers: You ride, you get hungry, but a big, heavy meal (like a double bacon cheese fatburger) can make you sleepy. Some healthy, low-fat, easily packable snacks include raisins, trail mix, nuts, energy bars (check for the low-fat, low-calorie variety), apples, bananas, and many other fruits. Keep them handy in your tank bag. Wrap them in a plastic bag so they don't make a mess if they get smushed.

Eat first, ask questions later: It's late in the day, and you're tired, but you have a few hours to go yet. Stop. Rest. Get something light to eat, such as an energy bar. The break and food will likely give you the needed energy to continue, and will make your ride enjoyable rather than an ordeal. The short rest will make you a more awake and energetic rider.

Three-time World Gran Prix Champion Freddie Spencer offers a track school and provides bikes for his students to ride. Here Freddie takes a leisurely lap on a sportbike, showing his students how it's done.

What's the difference between a three-time world champion and a pupil? Freddie Spencer takes a tight right-hander hard, sharp, and fast with his knee on the deck. . .

far my bike could lean, what happened when things touched down, how far I could trust my tires, and much else. I was led through the entire process by trained instructors who, at times, worked individually with the students.

The track school was an eye opener, and it enhanced my riding abilities immensely. Previous to the school I had been a typical uneducated rider. When I wanted to stay with other riders who were

going fast I would wring the bike's neck to accelerate, brake in almost a panic mode for the next turn, then tiptoe through it and start the sorry scenario all over again. At the track school I learned, after 20 years, how to properly negotiate a turn at speed. That school, repeated periodically, did more for my riding ability than any mechanical device.

RACING

For those who want a little more intensity in their riding, roadracing is a good way to pursue the dream while improving your riding and mechanical skills. The American Motorcyclist Association (AMA) sanctions many types of motorcycle races in the United States including ATV, motocross, enduro, and roadracing. A good place to start is to contact the AMA in Pickerington, Ohio (800-AMA-JOIN, www.AMADirectink.com) for some basics about types of competition in your area. Attend a few races for some background and to pick up tips.

WERA Motorcycle Roadracing (770-720-5010, www.wera.com) is another nationwide organization that sanctions amateur roadraces. It's pretty big time, though. Lots of people spending lots of money. But, unless you go pro, it's the best way to run all the best tracks.

If you're more interested in having fun (not that WERA racing can't be fun; it's all in your attitude), there are literally hundreds of motorcycle roadracing clubs around the United States and Canada. Most stick to one or two tracks located in their geographic locale.

The best thing about club racing is the people. While the big-time organizations are populated by folk who'd rather sell their grannies than give out helpful advice (you might beat them if they do), club racers are genuinely nice people. Wherever you race, though, you'll probably notice that most everyone you meet is really smart. Some might not have a lot of book-larnin', but they're all really, really smart.

. . . and here a pupil takes that same turn at quite a less aggressive pace.

No matter what type of racing interests you, riding in the dirt is an excellent way to train, as it teaches a great deal about managing traction. There are several low-displacement amateur racing classes in which it's possible to buy a used bike, wrench on it, and come out with a competitive machine for local competition.

Finally, and most importantly, if you want to go roadracing, use track days to hone your skills—not the street. Whether or not you ever bring home a trophy, racing is an excellent way to improve your mechanical and riding skills. And, to meet a lot of good people.

THE MOST IMPORTANT PART OF YOUR BIKE IS THE NUT HOLDING ONTO THE HANDLEBARS

Some riders believe the money required of a track day would be better spent on a new go-fast part, such as a new pipe, shocks, brakes, or whatever. In my case, no matter how much better I made my bike perform, the choking point was always my lack of cornering ability. The faster I made the bike go, the harder I had to brake to bring it back down to a speed I could comfortably control for the next turn. By tuning up my riding ability with a track school, I was able to extract the performance already built into my bike, and that's what made me a better rider— and, eventually, a professional test rider.

The best thing about club racing is the people.

The closest you can get to motorcycle road racing is at the Isle of Man for the TT (Tourist Trophy) Races that have been held there on public roads for a hundred years. Here, spectators line the course at the Gooseneck, where the mountain climb begins. Unfortunately, this proximity and the dangerous nature of the course have put its future in jeopardy.

MOTORCYCLE TERMS

TECHNICAL DICTIONARY

While much of this information is presented throughout the book, here's a quick reference to some basic concepts and terms of motorcycling. This list is by no means complete, and of necessity repeats some topics listed elsewhere.

Words are defined as they apply to motorcycling specifically, and discussed briefly. Related words and concepts are grouped.

ELECTRICAL

Charging output, n: The amount of electrical power an engine's charging system is capable of producing

Modern bikes offer adequate charging output, but the addition of a couple of electric vests, auxiliary lights, and slow riding can strain some systems. Typical charging outputs will range from about 250 to 700 watts or more. Big dressers, those with anti-lock brakes and/or fuel injection, may have higher outputs. Note that maximum charging output is often achieved at rpm levels higher than normal cruising speeds. If your bike's charging output is barely able to handle the electrical draw, turn off unneeded items and/or shift to a lower gear so the engine will run at higher rpm.

ENGINE

Back torque limiter, n: A device placed on a clutch that allows it to slip in the reverse direction, thus limiting torque coming back through from the rear wheel

Have you ever downshifted, left the engine at too low an rpm, and let out the clutch abruptly? If so, engine compression may have caused the rear tire to break traction and slide. A back torque limiter allows the clutch to slip when "backward" torque is applied, minimizing or eliminating the slip.

Bore and stroke, n: An engine's bore is the diameter of any of its cylinders. Stroke is the distance any of its piston travels from top dead center (TDC) to bottom dead center (BDC). The total volume displaced by the piston(s) during their stroke(s) is the engine's displacement.

CV carburetor, n: A constant-velocity (sometimes called a constant-vacuum) carburetor

Long ago, before the Environmental Protection Agency became involved in emissions standards, the throttle cable was connected to the carburetor throttle plate. This resulted in a load of raw gas being dumped into the carb whenever the cable was yanked, which led to excessive hydrocarbon emissions. Today, the cable is attached to a slide, which changes the vacuum in the carburetor.

Displacement, n: The total cubic volume displaced by the movement of the piston(s) from top dead center to bottom dead center

Engine displacement may be expressed in cubic centimeters (cc) or cubic inches (ci). Greater displacement generally indicates a more powerful engine, but not always. Some 600cc sportbikes produce more than 100 rear-wheel horsepower, while a typical stock Harley Twin Cam engine with 1,450cc puts out about 65 horsepower. A thousand cubic centimeters equal 1 liter, or 61.02 cubic inches.

DOHC, n and adj: Double overhead camshafts

Back in the 1960s, it was common for the camshaft to be located down by the crankshaft, which required that overhead valve gear be actuated via pushrods. But pushrods induce rpm limitations that are unacceptable on high-revving performance engines, so manufacturers began using an overhead cam driven by a chain. Dual overhead cams offer more positive valve actuation, and allow for a more optimal combustion chamber shape and port location.

Larger, heavier rocker arms are required by a single overhead cam, but with DOHC the engineers are better able to put the valves where they need them. They can use bucket-and-shim actuators that offer less inertia, run lower valve-spring pressures for less wear and higher rpm, and require less frequent adjustment.

Engine type, adj: The arrangement and orientation of a motorcycle's cylinders, relative to the frame or each other

In addition to the number of cylinders, type also describes the manner in which those cylinders are configured. Examples: transverse, longitudinal, V, opposed, etc. In a transverse arrangement, the crankshaft is arranged across, or at a 90-degree angle, to the direction of the frame. On a longitudinal engine, the crankshaft runs parallel to the frame. A V engine has two or more cylinders arranged at less than a 180-degree angle to each other, joining a common crankshaft. The crankshaft of a V engine may run longitudinally (as with a Moto Guzzi), or transversely as with most cruisers. An opposed engine has its cylinders arranged in opposition to each other at 180 degrees, such as BMW flat twins and the Honda Gold Wing.

Engine as a stressed member, adj: A system in which the engine, along with the frame, supports part of the weight and stresses

This one got a lot of play with the introduction of BMW's new R1100 twins for 1994. Up until then, most motorcycles came with a tube-steel or perimeter frame within which the engine was bolted. The frame supported the engine; the engine lent rigidity to the frame. With a stressed-member engine, the frame relies on the engine to bear much of the stresses fed into the machine.

Some late-model BMW opposed twins have no conventional frame. Rather, the load is borne by the engine casting, while subframes support the fork and seat. The swingarm connects directly to the engine casting.

Four-valve head, n: A type of motorcycle head that utilizes two intake and two exhaust valves per cylinder

In motorcycling there are also two-, three-, and five-valve heads, the latter in the interest of freer breathing. Till the late 1970s, most motorcycle engines utilized the conventional single intake and exhaust valve per cylinder, but this arrangement reached its limits in terms of engine rpm. Multiple valves can be made smaller and lighter, reducing inertial stresses on the valvetrain and allowing the engine to flow more gases so it can be revved higher and more quickly.

Horsepower, n: A unit of power equal to 746 watts, and nearly equivalent to the English gravitational unit that equals 550 foot-pounds of work per second

Torque, n: A turning or twisting force

Horsepower and torque are different, but interrelated. Horsepower is a unit of work over time, but torque is instantaneous. In simple terms, torque is the twisting force that an engine generates, and horsepower is high-rpm maximum power. Horsepower equals torque (in pound-feet) times rpm, divided by 5,252. Because of this constant, the horsepower and torque curves on a dyno chart will always converge at 5,252 rpm.

Think of riding a bicycle. Torque is the twisting force you impart to the pedals that turns the crank at low speeds. At a certain point you're spinning the pedals so fast that the force diminishes; torque is dropping off. Beyond this point the only way to go faster is to shift to a higher gear or to extract more revs (which your body may not be able to provide). An engine can rev higher by utilizing more fuel. This carryover net effect of increased revs is more horsepower.

CHASSIS

Anti-lock braking system, n: A braking system that is engineered so that the brakes cannot lock and cause a skid

Pioneered on the BMW K100s in the late 1980s, ABS is now available on most BMWs and select models from various other manufacturers. The system includes a device for counting wheel revolution, and a computer that compares that figure with appropriate rpm. When wheel revs drop too suddenly, signaling imminent lockup, the computer signals the master cylinder to release braking force and reapply it immediately. This pulsing, which can happen 30 times per second or more and is constantly monitored by the computer, provides a safe, steady stop under most conditions. Note that ABS is not effective when the bike is leaned over.

Caliper, n: A device consisting of two plates, lined with a frictional material, that press against the rotating disc rotor on a brake system

Calipers commonly have one, two, three, four, or six pistons that push the frictional material outward against the rotor surface. Generally, additional pistons can result in improved braking force and "feel."

Cartridge fork, n: A fork design in which the damping apparatus is contained within a "cartridge" slipped into the fork legs rather than built into them. One benefit is that the cartridge can be immersed in fork oil, essentially eliminating foaming as a problem.

Damping, n: The degree to which the system of valves and orifices in a suspension system damp, or control and dispel, the energy fed into it

A suspension system works in two directions, compressing over bumps then rebounding, propelled upward again by the energy temporarily stored in the fork or shock springs. To control and dissipate that energy, suspension components utilize damping systems that force fluid through various orifices. Some suspension components have a series of damping controls that activate at various pressures. Some offer damping adjustment settings that allow the rider to select the amount of damping on the system. If a system has a single control, it will be for rebound damping. Some also offer a compression damping control.

Disc rotor, n: The round plate that rotates with the wheel, and which is gripped by the brake caliper when it is actuated

Rotors can be fixed or floating. A floating caliper is allowed some lateral movement, which allows it to slide between the caliper more freely when the brake is not in use.

Frame, n: The constructional system that gives shape and strength to a motorcycle

The frame is the structure (usually made of steel or aluminum tubing, or plates) that ties the motorcycle's various components together. It supports the engine (see "engine as a stressed member"), attaches to the swingarm, and its steering stem attaches to the fork via the triple clamps.

Gross Vehicle Weight Rating (GVWR), n: The maximum amount of weight that a vehicle can carry, including its own weight, luggage, and riders, and still meet certain design performance criteria

The GVWR figure is listed on a plate, usually affixed to the bike's steering head. Subtracting wet weight from GVWR results in the load capacity figure, which is the total weight of rider(s), luggage, and accessories the motorcycle can carry.

Linked brakes, n: A braking system in which applying either the hand lever or foot pedal actuates both front and rear brakes

On a conventional motorcycle, applying the hand lever on the bar actuates the front brake(s), and the rear foot lever actuates the rear brake. With linked brakes, applying either control may actuate both front and rear brakes. On the Honda Gold Wing system, the foot lever controls the rear disc, and one of the front discs. The hand lever controls the other front disc. Some systems are linked only on one brake control, but not both.

On some sophisticated systems, applying either brake control actuates various pistons on all three discs at varying pressures, depending upon how much force the rider uses on the control.

Male-slider fork, n: A fork on which the lower slider is smaller and slips up into the larger stanchion

With a conventional fork, the slider is the larger-diameter lower unit that slides up over the smaller fork tubes. On a male-slider fork, which has become common on sportbikes, the slider is the smaller-diameter unit that slips into the larger stanchion. The main advantage to a male-slider fork is that the stanchions can be much thicker and stronger, leading to a more rigid fork.

Rake, n: The angle at which the steering stem is inclined from the perpendicular

Generally, the steeper the rake the quicker the bike will steer. A less-steep rake gives the bike greater stability at speed.

Single-sided swingarm, n: A swinging arm that attaches to only one side of the rear wheel

Single-sided swingarms were originally developed for endurance racing applications, as they can be made quite rigid and allow for tire changes to be made more quickly. Today, they're also available on a number of high-tech streetbikes.

Spring preload, n: The amount a motorcycle's springs have been precompressed (preloaded); vt: The act of preloading a spring

If a motorcycle's suspension is sagging too much, or if it has inadequate cornering clearance and its hard bits are dragging in turns, preloading the springs can help raise it. This adjustment is accomplished by turning a ramped collar or a ring on the threaded shock body; some forks also have a preload adjuster at the top of the fork tubes. Precompressing (imparting a preload) on the spring(s) will raise the ride height, just as backing off the adjusters will lower it.

Spring rate, n: The resistance of a spring to being compressed

Common spring rates used on motorcycles are 80, 100, and 120 pounds of force required to compress the spring 1 inch.

Stiction, n: The amount of static friction, or drag, in fork operation

A combination of "static" and "friction," stiction refers to the relative amount of fork-seal drag as the sliders begin to slide up or down the fork tubes. In extreme cases, the fork seals will leave chatter marks on the tubes.

Swingarm, n: The swinging arm that supports the rear wheel and connects to the rear suspension

Until recent years, the swingarm was usually made of tube steel, like the frame, but higher-horsepower engines and modern cornering loads soon found the limits of contemporary frames and swingarms. On bigger, more powerful bikes, swingarms are now composed of welded-up steel or aluminum plates that form a much more rigid unit.

Tire: bias-ply, n: A tire on which the plies run at an angle (or bias) to the direction of travel

Tire: radial, n: A tire on which the plies run essentially bead to bead, at a 90-degree angle to the direction of travel

A tire is defined by the arrangement of its plies. Belts run circumferentially around the tire, but plies run bead to bead. If those plies are arranged substantially straight across the tire, 90 degrees to the direction of rotation, it's a radial tire. If they run on a bias, it's a bias-ply.

Because of their ply arrangement bias-ply tires (all else being equal) tend to have a more rigid sidewall that can support a greater amount of weight. A radial has a much more pliable, shorter sidewall. As a result, touring bikes and cruisers tend to run on bias-ply tires, while sportbikes benefit from the radial's wider footprint. Because radials and bias-ply tires are designed to flex in opposite directions, don't mix them on the same motorcycle.

Trail, n: The distance that an imaginary line drawn straight down from the front axle of a motorcycle would trail behind an imaginary line drawn from the steering stem

Rake and trail are separate entities, but interrelated in explaining steering characteristics. First, draw a line continuing the angle of the steering head down to the ground and place a mark there. Now draw a perpendicular line from the center of the front axle to the ground and place a second mark there. The distance between these two marks is trail.

Rake figures on big streetbikes range from about 23 to 36 degrees, and common trail figures are from 3 to 6 inches. Generally, the greater the rake (larger numerical) the greater the trail. Bikes with greater rake and trail tend to steer more slowly but can be more stable at speed, while bikes with lesser rake and trail figures tend to steer more quickly but offer less of an "on rails" feeling at higher speeds.

A big cruising bike, the Honda VTX1800 has lazy rake/trail figures of 32 degrees/6.5 inches. Honda's ST1300, a sport-tourer, offers medium figures of 26.0 degrees/4.0 inches. A sportbike needs to turn quickly, and Suzuki's GSX-R600 offers razor-sharp 24.0/3.7 figures.

Triple clamp, n: The upper and lower clamps (also called "triple trees") that connect the fork tubes to the steering head

They get their name from the fact that they clamp at three locations, two on the fork tubes and one on the steering head. The angle of these clamps also helps to determine the rake and trail.

Unified brakes, n: See linked brakes

Wheelbase, n: The distance between the front and rear axle centers of a vehicle

The wheelbase is the literal base upon which the motorcycle rests. All else being equal, bikes having a longer wheelbase tend to be more stable at speed, but are more reluctant to turn quickly. Bikes with shorter wheelbases will usually turn more quickly, but may tend to wander at higher speeds.

MISCELLANEOUS RIDING TERMINOLOGY

Apex, n: The tightest part of a turn; v: to ride across the apex of a turn

The apex is the tightest point of the turn. Before the apex, the turn is tightening; after the apex it's opening up. The preferred line through a turn is to enter it wide, tighten up and run in near the apex, then accelerate through and allow centrifugal force to bring you out wide.

Countersteering, n and v: The process of causing a single-track vehicle to go in one direction by turning its handlebar in the opposite direction

Huh? Probably the most misunderstood and indefinable concept in all of motorcycling, countersteering refers to the idea that when you lean left, the handlebar actually cocks slightly to the right. Which seems to make no sense at all. What happens is that as the rider cocks the bar away from the direction of the turn, the front wheel steers out from under the center of mass, changing the point on the tire that the motorcycle uses to steer. In essence, you steer counter to the direction in which you intend to go.

EPS foam, n: expanded polystyrene foam This is the type of closed-cell foam that absorbs impact in helmets. EPS foam will absorb a great deal of energy by crushing.

Face plant, n: What you may do with your face if you screw up a wheelie, stoppie, or any other riding maneuver

High side/low side, n: When a motorcycle is leaned over, the high side is higher and the low side is, well, you get the idea; **v:** To experience a high-side or low-side crash

Stay away from the verb tense. To high side is a scary accident in which the bike's tires lose traction in a turn, begin to slide to the outside, then catch traction and snap the bike back upright and over. This throws the rider forcefully over the high side, often resulting in spectacular cartwheels and broken bones.

A low-side accident starts the same way, with the tires sliding out, but instead of regaining traction the bike continues to slide until it eventually falls over onto its low side.

Hook and loop, n: 1. often used in articles about clothing or soft luggage, hook and loop refers to a fastening device composed of one half tiny hooks, and the other tiny loops that the hooks grip. 2. One type of such fastening device that goes under the trade name Velcro. 3. We get nasty letters from the people at Velcro if we don't call it "hook and loop."

Hygroscopic, adj: readily taking up and retaining water

If your owner's manual calls for using DOT 4 brake fluid in your bike, do not

think you're doing yourself a favor by using DOT 5 instead. DOT 5 is much more hygroscopic than DOT 4, and tends to pick up moisture from humidity and condensation over time, which contaminates the brake fluid.

Jacking action, v: Refers to the rising and falling of the rear end of a driveshaft-equipped motorcycle as the throttle is abruptly opened and closed

The condition can be controlled by installing shock absorbers with firmer damping characteristics. The cure is what BMW has done with its Paralever system, which is a driveshaft with a universal joint at each end. As one end of the shaft rises the other falls, canceling out these inputs.

Late apex, n and v: A riding strategy in which the rider enters a turn wide and stays wide longer, apexing much later than usual

Late apexing is a good strategy to use in situations when your line of sight is diminished, such as on a road with many blind turns. The rider stays wider longer so that he can see farther into the turn, rather than zapping across the apex.

OEM, n: original equipment manufacturers

Probably the most used and least understood abbreviation in all of road testing, it simply refers to the companies that originally built the bikes. You know, like Honda, BMW, Harley-Davidson, Kawasaki—those guys.

Range, n: A figure expressed in miles that is average miles per gallon multiplied by fuel capacity

Range depends upon fuel mileage, and will vary with each tank.

Stoppie, n and v: To stop a motorcycle so hard that the rear wheel lifts off the ground as the rider balances on the front

Wheelie, n and v: To accelerate so hard that the front wheel of the motorcycle lifts off the ground

On a horse, a wheelie-type maneuver is called a hoofie.

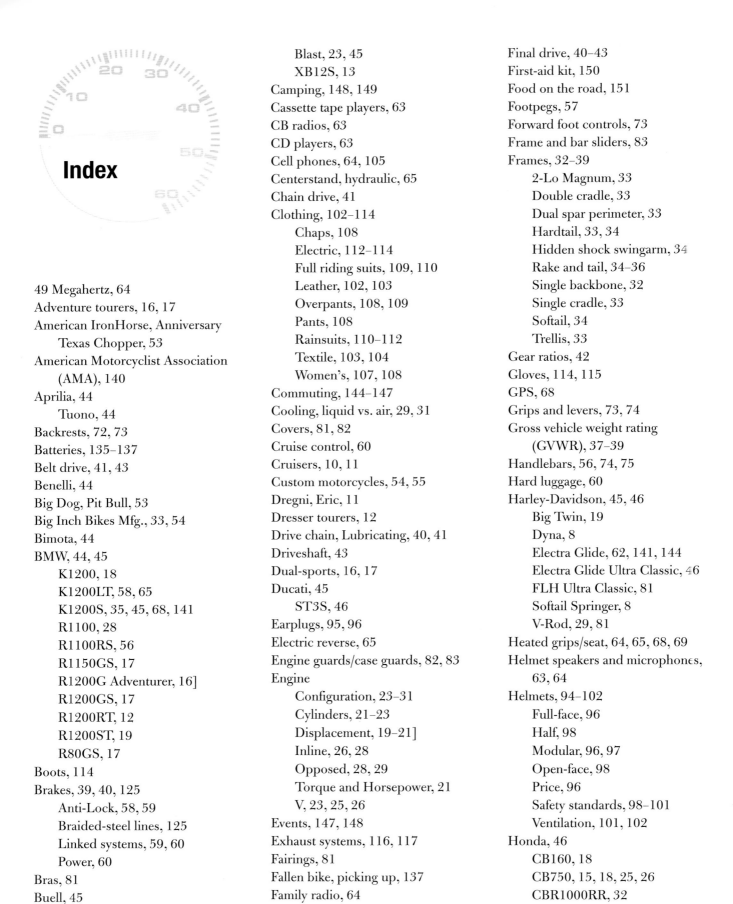

Index

49 Megahertz, 64
Adventure tourers, 16, 17
American IronHorse, Anniversary
    Texas Chopper, 53
American Motorcyclist Association
    (AMA), 140
Aprilia, 44
    Tuono, 44
Backrests, 72, 73
Batteries, 135–137
Belt drive, 41, 43
Benelli, 44
Big Dog, Pit Bull, 53
Big Inch Bikes Mfg., 33, 54
Bimota, 44
BMW, 44, 45
    K1200, 18
    K1200LT, 58, 65
    K1200S, 35, 45, 68, 141
    R1100, 28
    R1100RS, 56
    R1150GS, 17
    R1200G Adventurer, 16]
    R1200GS, 17
    R1200RT, 12
    R1200ST, 19
    R80GS, 17
Boots, 114
Brakes, 39, 40, 125
    Anti-Lock, 58, 59
    Braided-steel lines, 125
    Linked systems, 59, 60
    Power, 60
Bras, 81
Buell, 45

Blast, 23, 45
    XB12S, 13
Camping, 148, 149
Cassette tape players, 63
CB radios, 63
CD players, 63
Cell phones, 64, 105
Centerstand, hydraulic, 65
Chain drive, 41
Clothing, 102–114
    Chaps, 108
    Electric, 112–114
    Full riding suits, 109, 110
    Leather, 102, 103
    Overpants, 108, 109
    Pants, 108
    Rainsuits, 110–112
    Textile, 103, 104
    Women's, 107, 108
Commuting, 144–147
Cooling, liquid vs. air, 29, 31
Covers, 81, 82
Cruise control, 60
Cruisers, 10, 11
Custom motorcycles, 54, 55
Dregni, Eric, 11
Dresser tourers, 12
Drive chain, Lubricating, 40, 41
Driveshaft, 43
Dual-sports, 16, 17
Ducati, 45
    ST3S, 46
Earplugs, 95, 96
Electric reverse, 65
Engine guards/case guards, 82, 83
Engine
    Configuration, 23–31
    Cylinders, 21–23
    Displacement, 19–21]
    Inline, 26, 28
    Opposed, 28, 29
    Torque and Horsepower, 21
    V, 23, 25, 26
Events, 147, 148
Exhaust systems, 116, 117
Fairings, 81
Fallen bike, picking up, 137
Family radio, 64

Final drive, 40–43
First-aid kit, 150
Food on the road, 151
Footpegs, 57
Forward foot controls, 73
Frame and bar sliders, 83
Frames, 32–39
    2-Lo Magnum, 33
    Double cradle, 33
    Dual spar perimeter, 33
    Hardtail, 33, 34
    Hidden shock swingarm, 34
    Rake and tail, 34–36
    Single backbone, 32
    Single cradle, 33
    Softail, 34
    Trellis, 33
Gear ratios, 42
Gloves, 114, 115
GPS, 68
Grips and levers, 73, 74
Gross vehicle weight rating
    (GVWR), 37–39
Handlebars, 56, 74, 75
Hard luggage, 60
Harley-Davidson, 45, 46
    Big Twin, 19
    Dyna, 8
    Electra Glide, 62, 141, 144
    Electra Glide Ultra Classic, 46
    FLH Ultra Classic, 81
    Softail Springer, 8
    V-Rod, 29, 81
Heated grips/seat, 64, 65, 68, 69
Helmet speakers and microphones,
    63, 64
Helmets, 94–102
    Full-face, 96
    Half, 98
    Modular, 96, 97
    Open-face, 98
    Price, 96
    Safety standards, 98–101
    Ventilation, 101, 102
Honda, 46
    CB160, 18
    CB750, 15, 18, 25, 26
    CBR1000RR, 32

CL350, 18
GL1800 Gold Wing, 11, 34, 73
Gold Wing, 26, 31, 80
RC51, 121
ST1300, 9, 25, 47
VFR800, 9, 30, 61, 23
VTX, 9
VTX1800, 70
XL650, 16
XR650L, 27
Indian, 46
Chief, 48
Intake systems, 117
Intercoms, 64
Jackets, 104–107
Kawasaki, 46
KZ1300, 28
Vulcan 2000, 37
ZX1000, 39
ZX-10R, 48
ZX-14, 116, 25
KC Creations, 33, 54
KTM, 46
950 Supermoto, 48
Kymco 47
250 Venox, 49
Levers, 56, 57
Lighting
Auxiliary, 66
Halogen and xenon, 67, 68
Luggage
Hard, 75, 76
Soft, 76, 77
Maps, 139
Moto Guzzi, 47
Breva, 28, 49
Griso, 35
Moto Morini, 47
MP3 players, 63
MSF Basic RiderCourse, 141
MV Agusta, 47
MZ, 47
Naked bikes, 15, 16
Noise control, 94, 95
Norton, 47
Oil sight glass, 65
Oils and lubricants, 126–130

Packing, 78, 79
Parades, 148
Passengers, 142, 143
Power cruisers, 10
Pre-ride inspection, 137
Racing, 152
Radar detectors, 64
Radios, 62, 63
Rallies, 147, 148
Road strategies, 138–141
Royal Enfield, 47
Saddlebags
Fixed, 60, 61
Removable, 61, 62
Scooters, 11
Scooters: Everything You Need to Know, 11
Seats, 57
Aftermarket, 70–72
Security, 69, 70
Service, 141, 142
Shift lever, 57
Sidecars, 86
Sound systems, 62–64
Sport tourers, 12, 13
Sportbikes, 13–15
Standard bikes, 15, 16
Streetbike
Choosing, 8–10
Types, 10–17
Suspension systems, 118–125
Air suspension, 121, 122
Damping, 120, 121
Lowering, 122–125
Spring preload, 118, 119
Springs, 119, 120
Suzuki, 48
Bandit 1200, 14
C90T, 22
GSX-R1000, 25
Hayabusa, 51
SV650S, 20
Throttle lock, 60
Tires, 130–135
Patching, 135
Tools, 150, 151
Tours, 149
Packing list, 149–151

Track days, 151, 152
Trailers, 86–88
Brakes, 92, 93
Camping, 88
Cargo, 88
Electrical, 90
Enclosed, 91, 92
Fuel mileage, 90, 92
Hitches, 88, 89
Living quarters, 92
Maintenance, 90, 91
Motorcycle, 88, 91–93
Open, 91
Rider experience, 90
Safety chains, 89
Sway, 90
Tire inflation, 90
Tongue weight, 89, 90
Weather, 90
Wheels size, 90
Travel trunks, 62
Trikes, 93
Triumph, 48, 49
650, 18
650 Bonneville, 15
Daytona 675, 51
Daytona 955ci, 24
Rocket III, 57
Speed Triple, 14, 36
Thurston, 23
Tiger Adventure, 73
Victory, 49
Vegas, 51
Von Dutch Flying Dutchman, 54
WERA Motorcycle Racing, 152
Wheelbase, 20, 36, 37
Wheels, 83–85
Basics, 84, 85
Width, 83, 84
Where to ride, 138
Windshields, 58, 79–81
Women riders, 143–145
Yamaha, 50
Road Star Midnight Warrior, 10, 52
Roadliner, 38
Venture, 29, 60
Virago cruiser, 38

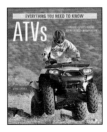

ATVs:
Everything You Need To Know
ISBN 0-7603-2042-X

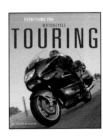

Motorcycle Touring:
Everything You Need To Know
ISBN 0-7603-2035-7

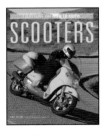

Scooters: Everything You
Need To Know
ISBN 0-7603-2217-1

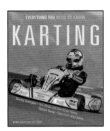

Karting:
Everything You Need To Know
ISBN 0-7603-2345-3

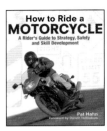

How to Ride a Motorcycle
ISBN 0-7603-2114-0

Sportbike
Performance Handbook
ISBN 0-7603-0229-4

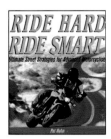

Ride Hard, Ride Smart
ISBN 0-7603-1760-7

Total Control
ISBN 0-7603-1403-9

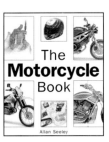

The Motorcycle Book
ISBN 0-7603-1745-3